THE EVERYTHING

ONE-POT COOKBOOK

Over 300 complete meals that
you can prepare in just one dish

Lisa Rogak

Adams Media Corporation
Holbrook, Massachusetts

An Everything Series Book.
The Everything Series is a trademark of Adams Media Corporation.

Published by Adams Media Corporation
260 Center Street, Holbrook, MA 02343

ISBN: 1-58062-186-4

Printed in the United States of America.

J I H G F E D C B A

Library of Congress Cataloging-in-Publication Data
The everything one-pot cookbook / by Lisa Rogak.
p.   cm.
ISBN 1-58062-186-4
1. Casserole cookery. I. Title.
TX693 .S55   1999
641.8'21—dc21   99-33168
CIP

This publication is designed to provide accurate and authoritative information with regard to the subject matter covered. It is sold with the understanding that the publisher is not engaged in rendering legal, accounting, or other professional advice. If legal advice or other expert assistance is required, the services of a competent professional person should be sought.
— From a *Declaration of Principles* jointly adopted by a Committee of the American Bar Association and a Committee of Publishers and Associations

Illustrations by Barry Littmann

This book is available at quantity discounts for bulk purchases.
For information, call 1-800-872-5627.

Visit our home page at http://www.adamsmedia.com

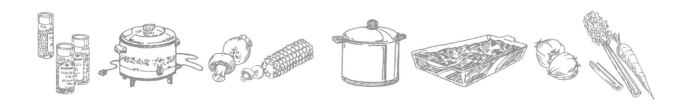

Introduction

In a time when microwave this and takeout that abound, why would anyone choose to cook? Why indeed? However, the truth is that in a world where you can have whatever you want yesterday, there are still many people who enjoy putting together a meal at the end of the day, and who like to control what goes into it, something that is not possible with even the healthiest takeout menus.

The Everything One-Pot Cookbook is a cookbook filled with recipes for tasty and nutritious dishes and you know what's going into the pot! But these recipes don't require you to spend hours in preparation time. In many cases, you can even adapt the recipes for use in a slow cooker or Crockpot; see the details later in the introduction for specifications.

As you leaf through the recipes in *The Everything One-Pot Cookbook*, keep in mind that just because the dishes are designed to be prepared with a minimum of fuss and muss, they're no less delicious. Feel free to personalize them as you see fit: If the recipe calls for two cloves of garlic and for you this amount is just getting started, by all means, add more.

After you've sampled how easy one-pot cooking can be, you will undoubtedly want to adapt your own more-than-one-pot recipes for one-dish preparation. Go ahead and experiment; adjust recipes here, and create your own.

Consider the recipes and tips in *The Everything One-Pot Cookbook* to be your road map to enjoying cooking more.

—Lisa Rogak

Making One-Pot Cooking Easy

Cooking in one pot is obviously easier than juggling a number of pots and pans on and off the stove. But to really get full enjoyment and satisfaction from the one-pot meals you prepare, you can take it to the next level so that every aspect of meal preparation is a relative breeze. Here are some hints:

Getting Ready

- Buy precleaned and chopped vegetables from the supermarket to save even more time in the kitchen. These bags come in a variety of sizes and are perfect for salads, stir-fries, stews, soups, and casseroles.
- Keep twins of utensils you use often, like wooden spoons, measuring cups, and measuring spoons. This will keep you from having to wash the equipment in the middle of preparing a dish, saving you even more time.
- Invest in a good menu-planning software program. It can help you to plan ahead, create detailed shopping lists, and avoid buying food items that you already have stocked in your cupboard.
- Many of the recipes in *The Everything One-Pot Cookbook* rely on staples that many people keep on hand, and require you only to purchase fresh meats and vegetables when necessary. You can save even more money and time by buying

fresh foods you frequently use in quantity, and freezing them for future use. This will save you time in the supermarket.

- Avoid extra trips to the grocery store by keeping an extra supply of staple ingredients on hand—flour, sugar, eggs, milk, etc.
- Keep an ongoing grocery list on your refrigerator door and write down items as they're used. Organize your list according to the layout of the grocery store. Be sure to identify how much you need, plus can and package sizes.
- Clean out your refrigerator before you go. Then you'll know what you need to buy, and it will be easier to put away the groceries when you get home.
- Before shopping, review grocery store newspaper ads. If possible, plan meals around weekly specials.
- Don't shop on an empty stomach!
- Plan to avoid after-work shoppers, paydays, days just before a holiday, and other times when you know the store will be busy.
- Do one bulk shopping spree a month. Buy staples that you always need like paper products, coffee, and sugar. This makes the other three weeks easier—fewer bags to carry in, fewer groceries to put away.
- Memorize the grocery store floor plan and get to know produce and meat department personnel. They can help you find what you need.
- Divide your shopping list into categories in the order they appear in the store. Be

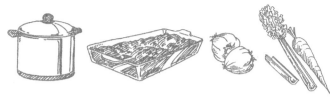

sure to list quantity and size of the needed items.

- Mark special items. Mark a "c" next to items for which you have a coupon and an "s" next to sale items.
- Stick to your shopping list. Avoid impulse purchases but be on the lookout for unadvertised specials.
- If it doesn't look good, don't buy it. Don't be tempted by a sale to buy something past its peak. It's no bargain if you have to throw it out before using it.
- Shop for refrigerated or frozen items last so they stay cold longer during the drive home. Or keep an inexpensive cooler in your car trunk and use it for frozen and/or cold foods if you have to travel a distance or plan on making another stop.
- Divide and rewrap such things as chops and chicken pieces. Make up hamburger patties and freeze in meal-size packages.

Prep Work

- Whenever you use the microwave, make sure to cover the dish with plastic wrap or a paper towel. Not only will this speed up the cooking time, but it will insure moist, even heat throughout the dish and also help to reduce spatters.
- You can cut ten to fifteen minutes off your total cooking time by buying skinned and boned chicken breast halves. Save even more money by buying large packages in bulk and freeze any extra breasts separately in order to have smaller servings with less preparation time.

Cleanup

- Streamline cleanup by loading dishes directly from the table into the dishwasher instead of resting them on the counter on their way to get washed.
- If you have a dishwasher, use it. Washing dishes by hand not only uses 43 percent more water than washing dishes in a standard-size dishwasher, but it also uses up a lot more of your time.

One-Pot Equipment

Buying a Crockpot

Popular sizes are $3\frac{1}{2}$-, 4-, and 5-quart models. Most have removable liners. The $3\frac{1}{2}$-quart models are fine for most dishes and needs, but the 5-quart models allow you to insert other dishes, such as soufflé, springform pans, or pudding molds, giving you a wider range of options. Manufacturers usually recommend filling the pot half to three-quarters full, so if you're cooking for two, this might be an important consideration.

- Make sure to get one with a removable liner. It is easier to clean.
- Buy one size bigger than you think you need. After you start using it on a regular

basis, you'll find yourself using it for more than you thought, and you'll wish it were bigger.

- With the traditional kind of Crockpot, the heat encloses the crockery insert all around, as opposed to the kind where the heat is just from the bottom (more commonly called a slow cooker). The traditional Crockpot provides more even, faster cooking and works best with most of the recipes in this book.

Using a Crockpot

- Most Crockpot recipes specify a cooking time of about 8 hours on low. If a recipe calls for less time or you will be out of the house for more than the maximum cooking time, use an automatic timer (the same kind of timer used to turn lights on and off when you're away) to start the Crockpot at the appropriate time.
- Try using your Crockpot for long-cooking dishes that you typically cook on the stove, such as beef stew, chili, etc. It cooks unattended, freeing you to do something else.
- Don't lift the lid while cooking, especially during the first three-quarters of the cooking period. The heat lost during a quick peek will add 30 minutes to the cooking time.
- Vegetables take longer to cook than meat, so place vegetables on the bottom of the pot.

- When purchasing large cuts of meat, make sure they will fit into your size Crockpot.
- The Crockpot is great for entertaining. You can use it to cook and serve appetizers at a party, such as hot dips or meatballs; hot soups at a buffet table; hot holiday beverages, such as Hot Spiced Cider, Wassail, or Mulled Wine.

Converting Traditional Recipes to the Crockpot Method

Many recipes can be adapted for use in a Crockpot. However, since Crockpots vary, you should consult your owner's manual for instructions.

- Crockpots vary, but generally, the low setting is about 200°F and the high setting is about 300°F. One hour on high is equal to approximately 2 to $2\frac{1}{2}$ hours on low. Most Crockpot recipes recommend cooking 8 to 10 hours on low. Some recipes recommend the high setting based on the nature and texture of the food. You will have to judge your recipe accordingly. For example, beef cuts will be better cooked on low for 8 to 10 hours to get a more tender texture, where chicken can be cooked on high $2\frac{1}{2}$ to 3 hours.
- It's a good idea to reduce the amount of liquid used in most oven recipes when using the low setting, since the Crockpot retains all moisture that usually evaporates when cooking in the oven. Add liquids for

sauces about an hour before done. You will normally end up with more liquid at the end of cooking times, not less. A general rule is to reduce liquids by half, unless rice or pasta is in the dish.

- You may need to reduce or increase the amount of spices in a one-pot recipe. Whole herbs and spices increase their flavoring power in Crockpot cooking while ground spices may lose some flavor. Add ground spices during the last hour of cooking. Whole leaves and herbs will probably need to be reduced by half.
- Rice, noodles, macaroni, seafood, Chinese vegetables, and milk do not hold up well when cooked 8 to 10 hours. Add these ingredients to sauces or liquid about 2 hours before serving when using the low setting (or 1 hour on high). If you want to use milk in an 8 to 10 hour recipe, use evaporated milk.
- For best results, use long-grain parboiled/converted raw rice in recipes, and use standard liquid amounts instead of reducing the liquid. For recipes with pasta, it's best to cook the pasta separately to al dente texture and add just before serving.
- Browning meats before cooking is a personal choice. It's not necessary, but it will reduce the fat content of some meats if you brown them before cooking.
- Sautéing vegetables like onions and garlic is not necessary beforehand; just add

them to the pot with everything else. Eggplant should be parboiled or sautéed first due to its strong flavor. You may wish to reduce quantities of stronger vegetables since they will permeate the other foods in the Crockpot with their full flavor.

- Dry beans can be cooked overnight on low as an alternative to soaking. Cover with water and add 1 teaspoon of baking soda. The next day, drain and combine with other ingredients. Be sure beans are softened before combining with any sugar or tomato mixture.
- For soups, add water only to cover ingredients. If thinner soup is desired, more liquid can be added at the end of the cooking time.
- Most uncooked meat and vegetable combinations will require at least 8 hours on low.

Using Slow Cookers Safely

To qualify as a safe slow cooker, the appliance must be able to cook slowly enough for unattended cooking, yet fast enough to keep food above the danger zone. To determine if a slow cooker will heat to a safe temperature:

- Fill cooker with 2 quarts of water.
- Heat on low for 8 hours or desired cooking time.
- Check the water temperature with an accurate thermometer (quickly, because the temperature drops 10 to 15 degrees when the lid is removed).

- The temperature of the water should be 185°F. Temperatures above this would indicate that a product cooked for 8 hours without stirring would be overdone. Temperatures below this may indicate the cooker does not heat food hot enough or fast enough to avoid potential food safety problems.

When preparing food in a slow cooker, follow these guidelines:

- Start with fresh or thawed meat, not frozen.
- Use chunks rather than large cuts or roasts. Use pieces of poultry—not a whole chicken.
- Cook meat on high for 1 hour and then turn cooker to low.
- Only use recipes that include a liquid.
- Check internal temperature to make sure food reaches 160°F.
- Do not delay starting time.
- Do not reheat foods in slow cooker.
- Keep the lid on.

Commonly Asked Slow Cooker Questions

Crockery cooker or slow cooker - what's the difference?

Most crockery cookers have a crockery pot insert and the heating elements are housed in the sides, so the heat actually surrounds the food. The two heat settings are low (200°F) and high (300°F).

The slow cooker, or "multi-cooker" usually cooks from the bottom and might have a thermostat allowing a wide range of temperatures. Even if your slow cooker has a crockery insert, you may need to stir some recipes occasionally to prevent scorching. Every time the lid is lifted, add 20 minutes to the overall cooking time.

The commonly used term Crock-Pot® is actually Rival Manufacturing Company's trademarked name. Most recipes designed for the Crockpot are with the two-setting Rival model in mind, so adjust accordingly if using another brand of cooker, and read the manufacturer's instructions.

What are some advantages of slow cooking?

- The extended cooking times allow better mingling of flavors in many recipes.
- The lower temperatures reduce the chance of scorching foods that tend to stick to the bottom of a pan and burn easily in an oven.
- Less expensive or tough meats are tenderized through the long cooking process. The slow cooker is a good choice for cooking many venison dishes.
- The slow cooker frees your oven and stove top for other uses, and should always be considered as an option for large gatherings or holiday meals.
- Convenience! A slow cooker can be left unattended all day for many recipes. You

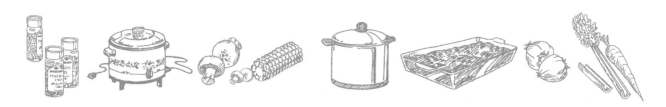

Oven to Crockpot Cooking Conversion Times

Oven	Crockpot
15 to 30 minutes	1½ to 2½ hours on high or 4 to 6 hours on low
35 to 45 minutes	2 to 3 hours on high or 6 to 8 hours on low
50 minutes to 3 hours	4 to 5 hours on high or 8 to 18 hours on low

General Cooking Times for Specific Foods

Artichoke	6 to 8 hours on low or 2½ to 4 hours on high (with water)
Beans, Dry	1 to 2 hours on high plus 8 to 9 hours on low
Brisket	10 to 12 hours on low
Casserole	4 to 9 hours on low or 2 to 4 hours on high (stirring occasionally)
Chicken	7 to 10 hours on low or 3 to 4 hours on high
Corned Beef & Cabbage	6 to 10 hours on low or 4 to 5 hours on high
Meat Loaf	8 to 9 hours on low
Peppers, Stuffed	6 to 8 hours on low or 3 to 4 hours on high
Potato, Baked	8 to 10 hours on low
Pot Roast	8 to 12 hours on low or 4 to 5 hours on high
Ribs	6 to 8 hours on low
Rice	5 to 9 hours on low or 2 to 3 hours on high
Soup	6 to 12 hours on low or 2 to 6 hours on high
Steak, Swiss	8 to 10 hours on low
Stew	10 to 12 hours on low or 4 to 5 hours on high
Vegetables	2 to 4 hours on low with liquid added

Remember to check the owner's manual for your particular Crockpot for full instructions on usage. The above cooking times are only very general guidelines.

can put recipe ingredients in it before going to work and come home to a meal.

Does a slow cooker get hot enough to cook foods safely?

Even at the low setting, internal temperatures of foods are raised well above 140°F, the minimum temperature at which bacteria are killed.

What foods are not suited to slow cooking?

- Natural cheeses should be avoided, as they tend to break down. Processed cheese can be used instead, or natural cheese can be added late in cooking.
- Milk will curdle over long cooking times, but you can substitute evaporated milk or stir in heavy cream or sour cream near the end of cooking.
- Fish and seafood are not usually good candidates for the slow cooker, and should be added late in any recipe for soup or chowder.

Do I have to brown meats before adding them?

Browning meat helps reduce the fat content and enhance the flavor and texture of dishes, but it is not necessary. Because of the condensation in a slow cooker, reduce the liquid if you are making a sauce or gravy from it.

Why are my potatoes still hard after hours of cooking?

Root vegetables, like potatoes, carrots, and turnips, should be cut in small pieces, about 1-inch, and layered on the bottom of the crock so they will start to cook as soon as the liquid heats.

Can I use an automatic timer on my slow cooker?

An automatic timer will allow you to cook a dish requiring 6 hours even if you will be away for 8 hours. Make sure all ingredients are chilled, and for safety, start the cooking no longer than 2 hours later. For poultry, start no longer than 1 hour later. The cooked food should not stand for longer than 2 hours after the cooking time ends.

Another alternative for a dish requiring a short cooking time is to cook it the night before, cool for no longer than 2 hours, and refrigerate. Heat it in the microwave the next day.

Cooking with a Clay Pot

Clay pot cooking is an ancient cooking method that works well for one-pot cooking today. Here's how it works:

Clay is a porous material. When the pot is saturated with water and put into the oven, there is a slow evaporation of steam from within the pores of the clay itself. During the cooking process, the food forms its own

juices. These juices cannot escape until the pot is completely dry. Then when the pot becomes dry, the food is cooked.

Because wet clay does not become as hot as metal, it is necessary to cook at a higher temperature than usual, that is, 450°F rather than the customary 350°F. However, in spite of this high temperature, the danger of burning is minimal and can only occur if the food is cooked for too long.

As a general rule, add 100°F and 30 minutes to the cooking time of any recipe to adapt it for use in a clay pot. For instance, if you normally cook a 3-pound chicken at 350°F for 1 hour, you will need to cook it in a clay pot at 450°F for 1½ hours.

The manufacturers of clay pots recommend that they always be placed in a cold oven. However, in an emergency, it's possible to put the pot into a preheated 350°F oven. It is also possible to reheat food in a clay pot. First soak the lid in cold water for 10 minutes, then cover the pot and pop it back into a 350°F oven for 30 minutes.

Cleaning a Clay Pot

As you use your clay pot more frequently, it will quickly lose its brand new appearance. Though the pot will initially start to look slightly mottled, it will eventually acquire a character of its own that will remain despite vigorous scrubbing.

The pot is, in fact, very easy to clean because food will not stick to the surface. To clean, let the pot cool thoroughly, then soak it in warm water for a few minutes. Sprinkle the pot with salt and scour it with a stiff brush. Rinse the pot and let it drain until it is dry. Since clay is porous, it is not wise to clean it with detergents or scouring powder.

To eliminate fishy odors or spices, soak the pot in hot water, adding three tablespoons of baking soda to each quart of water. This will clean it very thoroughly—even small black scorch dots can be coaxed from the clay with a minimum of effort.

Store the pot as you would any other utensil. It is less fragile than it appears, and unless you drop it on the floor, it will survive many accidental knocks and bumps. It's a good idea to take the precaution of storing the lid alongside, rather than on top of, the pot. This eliminates the risk of the development of mold inside the pot in case it was not completely dry.

Cooking with a Wok

- Make sure you have all the ingredients on hand before starting.
- Cut up the meat and vegetables and marinate any that require this process. If you are cooking several wok dishes at the same meal, do the prep work for all of the recipes before you start cooking.
- Place oil in wok, heat until oil just begins to smoke.

- Stir-fry the meat, onions, or garlic together. Then add other ingredients accordingly.
- If a gravy is desired, use a little cornstarch (about 1 tablespoon) dissolved in $\frac{1}{3}$ cup of cold water. Stir this mixture vigorously and pour into the wok on top of the cooked food. Mix thoroughly. If the gravy is too thick, add hot water a tablespoon at a time to thin gravy out. If the gravy is too thin, mix up more cornstarch solution and repeat the process.
- If you are cooking several wok dishes at the same meal, and are worried about keeping them all warm, heat your oven to 275°F and store cooked dishes in it until eating time. Maximum storage time is about one hour. Do not store cooked leafy green vegetables in this manner as they will turn yellow. Instead, leave those in an uncovered wok and reheat at mealtime. If you have an electric hot tray, it is excellent for keeping dishes warm.

Caring for a Wok

After cooking in the wok, it is best to run very hot water into it and clean the surface of the wok with a bamboo brush or plastic scourer. Dry the wok thoroughly with a paper towel and store for future use. Some gourmets will place a small amount of oil on their fingertips to recoat the wok to keep it in top cooking condition. A properly seasoned wok should not be scoured with abrasive material such as steel wool.

Eventually, through repeated usage, a dark brown film will develop in the wok. The wok is now truly seasoned. This film is essentially carbon and is not harmful. The bottom of the wok, the part that touches the cooking flame of the stove, should be scoured occasionally to free it of collected residue. If you accidentally burn food in the wok, it will be necessary to scour out the burnt material with steel wool and then season the wok once again. Each time you have to scour the wok with abrasive material, you should reseason it.

Omelettes and stir-fried meats sometimes stick in stainless steel woks. To overcome this problem, season the wok before use or spray a nonstick cooking spray on the surface of the wok.

Chapter 1

Vegetarian Dishes

Vegetables with Eggs or Cheese

If you consider only meat and potatoes dishes to be worthy of one-pot cooking and anything vegetarian as suitable for the rabbit population, then it's time to reconsider. As you can see by the following recipes, it's possible—and easy—to dine on vegetarian cuisine and still be satisfied.

Swiss Eggs

Serves: 4

> 1 tablespoon butter
> ¼ pound Gruyère cheese, sliced thin
> 4 eggs
> ¼ cup heavy cream
> 1 teaspoon salt
> ½ teaspoon black pepper
> ½ cup grated Parmesan cheese

Preheat oven to 350°F.

Melt butter in a shallow casserole dish. Line dish with thin cheese slices. Break the eggs neatly into the casserole dish, keeping them whole. Add salt and pepper to cream, and carefully pour over the eggs. Sprinkle with Parmesan cheese and bake for 10 minutes. Brown the cheese topping under the broiler for a few minutes, if necessary.

Eggs in Tomato Broth

Serves: 2

> 1 tablespoon olive oil
> 1 clove garlic
> 1 16-ounce can crushed tomatoes
> ½ cup water
> 1½ teaspoons chopped thyme
> 1½ teaspoons basil
> ¼ teaspoon salt
> ¼ teaspoon sugar
> 4 large eggs

Heat oil in a large skillet over medium heat. Add garlic and stir 3 to 4 minutes, until garlic is tender and golden. Discard garlic. Stir in remaining ingredients except for eggs. Bring slowly to a boil. Reduce heat and simmer uncovered for 7 minutes. Stir occasionally. Break eggs one at a time into a cup and gently slide them into the sauce. Cover and simmer for 5 to 6 minutes or until eggs are set.

California Rarebit

Serves: 4

3 tablespoons butter, divided
½ cup dry white wine
2½ cups cubed jack cheese, divided
1 large egg, lightly beaten
1 teaspoon Worcestershire sauce
½ teaspoon crushed basil
2 cups sliced mushrooms
½ teaspoon garlic powder
Toast points or triangles

Melt 1 tablespoon of butter in the top of a double boiler. Add the wine and heat, then stir in 2 cups of the cheese. Heat until melted. Add a little of the cheese mixture to the beaten egg and then add the egg mixture back into the cheese. Cook and stir about 1 minute. Add the Worcestershire sauce and basil; set aside, keeping the sauce warm. Sauté the mushrooms in the remaining butter until just tender, then sprinkle with the garlic powder. Remove from the heat.

Arrange toast points or triangles on individual heat-proof plates. Spoon the sauce over the toast then top with the sautéed mushrooms. Sprinkle with the remaining cheese and broil until bubbly.

Freezing Cheese

Placing a leftover hunk of cheese into the freezer not only conserves all those odd bits that are too small to use in another recipe, but also hardens up the soft cheeses enough for grating. Be sure to freeze soft cheeses when they have ripened; semisoft and harder cheeses can be frozen as is, or sliced or grated beforehand.

Cheese Rarebit

Serves: 6

2 tablespoons butter
1 pound sharp Cheddar cheese, shredded
1 cup beer
1 egg, beaten
1 teaspoon dry mustard
1 teaspoon paprika

(continued)

Melt butter in top of double boiler and add cheese. Stir until cheese begins to melt. Add beer gradually, stirring constantly until cheese is melted and mixture is smooth. Stir in egg, mustard, and paprika. Serve at once over hot buttered toast or toasted English muffins.

Cheesy Golden Apple Omelet

Serves: 2

  1 Golden Delicious apple, pared, cored, and sliced
  2 tablespoons butter, divided
  4 eggs
  1 tablespoon water
  $\frac{1}{4}$ teaspoon salt
  Dash pepper
  2 tablespoons crumbled blue cheese
  2 tablespoons grated Parmesan cheese

Sauté apple in 1 tablespoon butter until barely tender; remove from pan. Combine eggs, water, salt, and pepper until blended. Heat remaining butter in omelet pan; add egg mixture. Cook slowly, lifting edges to allow uncooked portion to flow under. Arrange apple slices on half of omelet. Sprinkle with cheeses; fold in half.

Easy Lentil Cheddar Casserole

Serves: 6

  1 12-ounce package lentils
  2 cups water
  1 bay leaf
  2 teaspoons salt
  $\frac{1}{4}$ teaspoon pepper
  $\frac{1}{4}$ teaspoon marjoram
  $\frac{1}{4}$ teaspoon sage
  $\frac{1}{4}$ teaspoon thyme leaves
  2 large onions, chopped
  2 cloves garlic, minced
  1 1-pound can tomatoes
  2 large carrots, thinly sliced
  $\frac{1}{2}$ cup thinly sliced celery
  1 green pepper, cut into thin strips
  2 tablespoons chopped parsley
  3 cups (about 12 ounces) shredded sharp Cheddar cheese

Preheat oven to 357°F.

Rinse lentils well under cold water and discard any foreign material. Pour lentils into a shallow 3-quart casserole or 9 x 13-inch baking dish along with water, bay leaf, salt, pepper, marjoram, sage, thyme, onions, garlic, and tomatoes (break up with a spoon) and their liquid.

Bake, covered, for 30 minutes. Stir in carrots and celery; return to oven, covered, for about 40 more minutes or until vegetables are tender. Stir in green pepper and parsley; sprinkle cheese on top. Return to oven,

4

uncovered, for 5 more minutes or until cheese is melted.

Baked Nordic Fondue

Serves: 8

⅔ cup softened butter, divided
1 small clove garlic, minced
1 teaspoon dry mustard, divided
1 loaf Italian bread
3 cups shredded Jarlsberg cheese
¼ cup sliced green onion (scallions)
1 teaspoon salt
½ teaspoon paprika
Generous dash pepper
⅓ cup all-purpose flour
3 cups milk
1 16-ounce can stewed tomatoes
1 cup coarsely chopped fresh tomato
3 eggs, beaten

In small bowl, blend ⅓ cup butter with garlic and ½ teaspoon mustard. Cut bread into ½-inch slices. Spread one side of each slice with butter mixture. Blend cheese, onion, salt, paprika, and pepper; set aside. In saucepan, melt remaining ⅓ cup butter. Add flour and cook, stirring, until bubbling. Remove from heat. Blend in milk and remaining mustard. Cook, stirring, until thickened and smooth. Add tomatoes. Blend ½ cup of the cheese/onion mixture into eggs. Add to sauce; blend well.

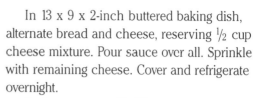

In 13 x 9 x 2-inch buttered baking dish, alternate bread and cheese, reserving ½ cup cheese mixture. Pour sauce over all. Sprinkle with remaining cheese. Cover and refrigerate overnight.

Preheat oven to 357°F. Bake, uncovered, for 45 minutes, or until golden and puffed.

Very Cheesy Casserole

Serves: 8

1 teaspoon peanut oil
1 cup chopped onion
3 cloves garlic, minced
1 cup chopped mushrooms
1 teaspoon dried basil
1 teaspoon thyme
1 teaspoon marjoram
1 teaspoon cumin
2 cups cooked or canned kidney beans
2 cups cooked brown rice
3 eggs, slightly beaten
2 cups low-fat ricotta cheese
¼ cup crumbled feta cheese
2 tablespoons soy sauce
Salt
Black pepper
Cayenne pepper to taste
2 medium tomatoes, sliced
½ cup grated Parmesan cheese
½ cup fine dry bread crumbs

(continued)

Preheat oven to 350°F. Heat oil in a large ovenproof skillet; sauté onion, garlic, and mushrooms until onion is nearly soft. Add the basil, thyme, marjoram, cumin, beans, rice, eggs, ricotta, feta, soy sauce, salt, pepper, and cayenne, and stir well.

Arrange the tomato slices over the top of the casserole. Sprinkle the Parmesan and crumbs over the tomatoes. Bake for 40 minutes.

Grated Cheese Secrets

To keep freshly grated cheese from sticking together, add a little cornstarch and toss cheese until mixed through.

Potato Gratin

Serves: 6

3 medium baking potatoes, thinly sliced
2 tablespoons all-purpose flour
1 medium onion, thinly sliced and
  separated into rings
1/8 teaspoon cayenne pepper
1 teaspoon paprika
1/2 teaspoon freshly ground pepper
1/4 cup grated Parmesan cheese
1 small zucchini, trimmed and thinly sliced
1/4 teaspoon nutmeg
1/4 teaspoon Spike seasoning
1 12-ounce can evaporated skim milk
2 teaspoons chopped fresh parsley for
  garnish

Preheat oven to 400°F.

Coat a circular baking dish, gratin dish or glass pie pan with nonstick cooking spray. Layer a third of the potatoes over the bottom of the pan, overlapping the slices in a spiral pattern. Over the potatoes, sprinkle 1 tablespoon of flour and arrange the onion rings. Dust with cayenne pepper and 1/2 teaspoon paprika. Layer another third of potatoes and add the remaining flour, black pepper, and 2 tablespoons of the parmesan cheese. Scatter the zucchini, and dust with nutmeg and Spike. Top with a spiral layer of the remaining potatoes. Pour the evaporated milk over the gratin and add the remaining paprika and Parmesan cheese.

Cover the gratin with aluminum foil and bake for 45 minutes. Remove the foil, reduce the oven temperature to 350°F and bake for about 15 minutes more, until the top is golden brown. Remove the gratin from the oven and allow to cool for 10 minutes. Garnish with chopped parsley.

Italian Potatoes and Swiss Chard

Serves: 8

> 2 pounds Swiss chard, stems trimmed
> 4 medium potatoes, peeled and cut into cubes
> 2 tablespoons olive oil
> 3 cloves garlic, minced
> 1/2 teaspoon crushed red pepper flakes
> 1 28-ounce jar pasta sauce
> 1 teaspoon basil
> 1/2 teaspoon oregano
> Salt and pepper to taste
> Grated Parmesan cheese for garnish

Coarsely chop Swiss chard. Place in a large pot of boiling water. Cook 8 minutes, uncovered; drain and set aside. Place potatoes in enough boiling water to cover; cook 15 to 20 minutes or until tender. Drain and set aside.

In a large skillet, heat olive oil. Add garlic and crushed red pepper; sauté lightly. Add pasta sauce, basil, and oregano; simmer 5 minutes or until heated through. Add Swiss chard and potatoes; stir to thoroughly combine. Cover and simmer 5 to 8 minutes. Season with salt and pepper. Garnish with Parmesan cheese.

Fettuccine Frittata a la Pesto

Serves: 4

> Water
> 1 3-ounce package dried tomato halves, halved or quartered
> 1 9-ounce package fresh spinach and/or egg fettuccine noodles or 8 ounces dried spinach or egg noodles
> 3 tablespoons prepared pesto
> 4 eggs, lightly beaten
> 1/4 cup milk
> Fresh basil leaves for garnish (optional)
> Grated Parmesan cheese (optional)

Bring large pot of water to boiling. Add the dried tomatoes and noodles and cook until al dente, about 8 to 10 minutes. Drain well. Return to the pot. Add pesto. Toss until noodles are evenly coated. In small bowl, beat together eggs and milk until blended. Pour over noodle mixture. Cook over medium heat, gently turning with a pancake turner, until eggs are thickened and no visible liquid egg remains. Garnish with basil leaves, if desired. Serve immediately with additional pesto and cheese, if desired.

Spinach Noodle Casserole

Serves: 8

8 ounces broad egg noodles
3 tablespoons butter
2 tablespoons flour
1 cup milk, scalded
½ teaspoon salt
½ teaspoon paprika
¼ teaspoon black pepper
⅛ teaspoon nutmeg
2 10-ounce packages frozen spinach,
   cooked and drained
½ pound Swiss cheese, shredded

Cook noodles according to package directions until just tender; drain and rinse. In saucepan, melt butter; stir in flour and cook, stirring, one minute. Gradually add milk and bring to a boil. Cook until thick, stirring constantly. Add seasonings and spinach. Stir and remove from heat.

Preheat oven to 400°F.

In greased baking dish, arrange half of noodles, and sprinkle with half of cheese; spoon all of the spinach mixture over cheese. Add another layer of noodles and sprinkle with rest of cheese. Cover, and bake for 15 minutes. Remove cover and bake 15 minutes more.

Easy Ways to Enhance Your Menu

"Grate" Cheese-Topped Veggies: Sauté or steam fresh vegetables, then top with butter and sprinkle with a freshly grated piquant cheese, such as Parmesan, Romano, or Asiago.

Hot Cheese Tomatoes: Top sliced tomatoes with a slice of cheese— Cheddar, mozzarella, or brick, and broil.

Veggie Melt Sandwich: Sauté mushrooms, onions, green peppers, tomato slices, broccoli, and other seasonal veggies. Place on a thick slice of grilled honey-oatmeal bread, and top with Cheddar, Muenster, or provolone cheese; broil and serve.

Creamy Cheesy Broccoli Topping: Blend cream cheese with shredded provolone as a topping for broccoli or asparagus.

Gouda & Beans: Add cubes of mellow Gouda to a calico bean blend; serve hot or cold.

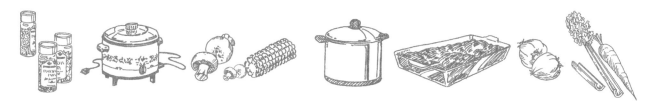

Vegetables, Vegetables, Vegetables

The wonderful thing about one-pot meals is their versatility; you can serve the dish in small portions and call it an appetizer, or dish it out in heaping spoonfuls and it's an entrée, supplemented with crusty bread and perhaps a salad.

The one-pot recipes in this section are a perfect example of this flexibility. Whether you choose the Cold Sesame Noodles or the Mediterranean Vegetable Couscous, one thing's for certain: nondairy vegetarian one-pot dishes won't leave you feeling stuffed.

Cold Sesame Noodles

Serves: 6

1 pound thin noodles
10 cloves garlic, minced
2-inch piece fresh ginger, minced
3 tablespoons water
⅓ cup tahini
3 tablespoons soy sauce
¼ cup cold strong brewed tea
2 tablespoons sesame oil
1 tablespoon vinegar
1 tablespoon sugar
½ teaspoon five-spice powder
6 scallions, minced

Cook the noodles al dente. Drain, rinse under cold water, and drain again. Transfer to a large bowl. Purée the garlic, ginger, and water in a food processor. In a medium bowl, combine the tahini, soy sauce, tea, sesame oil, vinegar, sugar, and five-spice powder. Add the garlic and ginger mixture and scallions and stir well. Add the noodles and toss well to coat.

Cold Szechuan Noodles

Serves: 4

3 tablespoons oil
3 tablespoons honey
1 tablespoon Oriental sesame oil
1 tablespoon rice vinegar
1 tablespoon soy sauce
1½ teaspoons grated gingerroot
1 teaspoon crushed red pepper flakes
4 ounces Oriental noodles or broken up
    spaghetti, cooked and drained
3 cups cooked and shredded chicken
1 cup finely chopped red cabbage
4 green onions, thinly sliced
2 shredded carrots

(continued)

1 red bell pepper, chopped
1/2 cup dry-roasted peanuts

In small bowl, combine oil, honey, sesame oil, vinegar, soy sauce, gingerroot, and red pepper flakes; blend well. Rinse cooked noodles in cold water to cool. In large bowl combine cooked noodles, chicken, cabbage, onions, carrots, and bell pepper. Pour dressing over salad; toss to mix. Sprinkle with peanuts.

Mediterranean Vegetable Couscous

Serves: 6

2 tablespoons olive oil, divided
2 teaspoons minced garlic
1 cup coarsely chopped onions
1 1/2 cups boiling water
1 fennel bulb, cut into 1/2-inch strips
(about 2 1/2 cups; chop and reserve fronds), or 2 large celery stalks cut into 1/2-inch slices, plus 1/2 teaspoon fennel seeds
1 large red bell pepper, thinly sliced
1 large carrot, cut on diagonal into 1/2-inch slices
1/4 pound mushrooms, halved
2 medium zucchini, cut into 1 1/2-inch chunks
1 1/2 cups coarsely chopped plum tomatoes
1/3 cup pitted oil-cured black olives

1 1/2 teaspoons dried basil leaves
1 1/2 teaspoons dried oregano leaves
1 teaspoon salt or to taste
1/4 teaspoon cinnamon
1/8 teaspoon freshly ground black pepper
1 to 3 tablespoons balsamic vinegar or lemon juice
1 1/2 cups whole wheat couscous
1/4 cup minced fresh basil or parsley

Heat 1 tablespoon oil in pressure cooker. Add garlic; cook over medium-high heat, stirring constantly, until just browned. Add onions and cook, stirring frequently, 1 minute. Add water, fennel bulb or celery and fennel seeds, bell pepper, carrot, mushrooms, zucchini, tomatoes, olives, basil, oregano, salt, cinnamon, and pepper.

Lock lid in place. Over high heat, bring to high pressure. Lower heat just enough to maintain high pressure and cook 2 minutes. Reduce pressure using quick-release method. Remove lid.

Stir in 1 tablespoon vinegar or lemon juice and couscous. Replace lid; allow to steam 5 minutes until couscous is tender. Add fennel fronds if using, basil, remaining 1 tablespoon oil, and additional vinegar or lemon juice to taste. Stir well.

Variation: Leftovers are terrific at room temperature when drizzled with olive oil and lemon juice, and garnished with olives.

Southwest Succotash

Serves: 6

1 tablespoon olive oil
³⁄₄ teaspoon cumin seeds
2 teaspoons finely minced garlic
1 cup coarsely chopped onion
1 medium red bell pepper, diced
1 to 2 jalapeño peppers,
    seeded and diced, or
    1 dried chipotle
pepper, seeded and snipped into bits,
    or generous pinch crushed
red pepper flakes
1 cup water
2 tablespoons tomato paste
1¹⁄₂ pounds butternut squash,
    peeled and cut into 1-inch pieces
2 cups fresh or frozen corn
Salt to taste
2 cups frozen baby lima beans,
    thawed
¹⁄₄ to ¹⁄₃ cup minced cilantro

Heat oil in pressure cooker. Add cumin seeds; sizzle 5 seconds. Add garlic; cook over medium-high heat, stirring frequently, until garlic turns light brown. Add onions, bell pepper, and jalapeño; continue cooking, stirring frequently, for 1 minute.

Add water, tomato paste, squash, corn, and salt. Lock lid in place. Over high heat, bring to high pressure. Reduce heat just enough to maintain high pressure; cook 2 minutes. Reduce pressure with quick-release method. Remove lid. If squash is not quite tender, replace but do not lock lid; allow squash to steam a few more minutes in residual heat.

Stir in lima beans; simmer, covered, until tender, 2 or 3 minutes. Stir in cilantro just before serving.

One Pots on the Move

You'll probably want to take many of the dishes in The Everything One-Pot Cookbook to potluck dinners and other community or social events. Most travel well; just be sure to keep the casserole level during the trip. A cardboard box lined with a dish towel or newspaper is useful to set the casserole dish in.

11

Vegetable Lover's Fried Rice

Serves: 4

5 beaten eggs
4 tablespoons soy sauce, *divided*
2 tablespoons oil, *divided*
1 small onion, chopped (⅓ cup)
1 clove garlic, minced
2 stalks celery, thinly bias sliced (1 cup)
4 ounces fresh mushrooms, sliced
    (1½ cups)
1 medium green pepper, chopped (1 cup)
4 cups cold cooked rice
1 8-ounce can bamboo shoots, *drained*
2 medium carrots, shredded (1 cup)
¾ cup frozen peas, *thawed*
3 green onions, sliced

Combine eggs and 1 tablespoon soy sauce in a small bowl. Set aside.

Heat half of the oil in a large skillet. Cook chopped onion and garlic in hot oil about 2 minutes or until onion is tender. Add egg mixture; stir gently to scramble. When set, remove egg mixture from the skillet. Cut up any large pieces of egg mixture. Let skillet cool.

Pour remaining cooking oil into the cooled skillet. (Add more oil as necessary during cooking.) Heat over medium-high heat. Cook and stir celery in hot oil for 1 minute. Add mushrooms and green pepper; cook for 1 to 2 minutes or until vegetables are crisp-tender.

Add cooked rice, bamboo shoots, carrots, and peas. Sprinkle with 3 tablespoons soy sauce. Cook and stir for 4 to 6 minutes or until heated through. Add cooked egg mixture and green onions; cook and stir about 1 minute more or until heated through.

Mixed Bean Salad

Serves: 12

2 pounds fresh green beans
1 pound fresh wax beans
1 1-pound can kidney beans, *drained*
1 cup chopped or thinly sliced onions
½ cup olive oil
½ cup cider vinegar
½ cup sugar
½ teaspoon salt
¼ teaspoon ground black pepper

Wash the fresh beans. Snap or cut, then cook the fresh beans together in about 2 cups of boiling water for 8 to 10 minutes. Drain. Mix with the drained kidney beans and onions. Combine the oil, vinegar, sugar, salt, and pepper in a jar or bottle and shake until well blended. Pour the dressing over the beans and toss.

Curried Bean and Rice Salad

Serves: 6

1 teaspoon curry powder
1 tablespoon butter or margarine

3/4 cup chicken broth
1/3 cup uncooked white rice
1/4 cup chopped celery
2 tablespoons chopped green onions
2 tablespoons chopped green bell peppers
1 tablespoon lime juice
1 16-ounce can kidney beans, drained
1/4 cup plain yogurt
2 tablespoons toasted slivered almonds
1/4 teaspoon salt
1 dash pepper
1 large tomato, cut in wedges, for garnish
1 sprig fresh parsley for garnish

Sauté curry powder in butter or margarine several seconds. Stir in chicken broth; bring to boil. Add rice; cover and simmer 20 minutes or until all liquid is absorbed.

Stir in celery, green onion, green pepper, and lime juice until smooth. Add the beans, yogurt, almonds, and seasonings. Garnish with tomato and parsley.

Black Beans with White Rice

Serves: 5

1 1/2 cups dry black beans
6 cups cold water
2 cups vegetable broth
2 large onions, chopped (2 cups)
1 medium green pepper, chopped
2 stalks celery, chopped
2 cloves garlic, minced
2 teaspoons crushed dried oregano

1 teaspoon salt
1/2 teaspoon crushed red pepper
2 bay leaves
1 16-ounce can tomatoes, chopped, with liquid
2 tablespoons lemon juice
2 1/2 cups hot cooked rice
Cooked green peas, sliced green onion, and/or sliced radishes (optional)

Rinse beans. Combine with the cold water in a 4-quart Dutch oven. Bring to boiling; reduce heat. Simmer, uncovered, for 2 minutes. Remove from the heat. Cover and let stand for 1 hour. Drain and rinse the beans.

Combine the soaked beans, broth, onions, green pepper, celery, garlic, oregano, salt, red pepper, and bay leaves in the Dutch oven. Bring to boiling; reduce heat. Simmer, covered, for 2 to 2 1/2 hours or until the beans are tender, stirring in the undrained tomatoes for the last 15 minutes of cooking. Discard bay leaves. Mash beans slightly.

Stir in lemon juice. Spoon beans into 5 soup bowls. Spoon rice on top of beans. Sprinkle each serving with peas green onion, and/or radishes, if desired.

Black Beans, Tomatoes, and Rice

Serves: 4

2 cloves garlic
1 medium onion
1 14.5-ounce can stewed tomatoes

(continued)

1 15-ounce can black beans, rinsed and
   drained
2/3 cup water
1/2 teaspoon oregano
1 1/2 cups instant brown rice

Sauté garlic and onion in a bit of water or oil. Stir in tomatoes, beans, water, and oregano. Bring to a boil. Add rice. Bring to boil again. Reduce heat. Cover and simmer 5 minutes. Let stand for another 5 minutes.

Soulful Black-Eyed Peas

Serves: 8

1 pound dried black-eyed peas
Water
1 tablespoon olive oil
1 cup chopped onion
2 cloves garlic, crushed
1 teaspoon salt
1 teaspoon crushed dried thyme
2 bay leaves
1/4 teaspoon freshly ground black pepper

Sort peas, then wash and drain. Soak 1 hour in water to cover. Drain and set aside.

Heat the olive oil in a large heavy saucepan. Add onion and sauté over medium heat until almost browned, about 5 minutes. Stir in garlic, 4 cups of water, salt, thyme, bay leaves, and pepper. Bring to boil. Add drained peas and return to boil. Reduce heat to low. Cover and cook 45 minutes to 1 hour, or until peas are tender. Remove bay leaves before serving.

Boston Baked Beans

Serves: 6

1 pound dry navy beans
1 teaspoon baking soda
1 medium onion, thinly sliced
1/2 pound bacon, cut into small pieces
1/3 cup molasses
1/4 cup sugar
1 teaspoon dry mustard
2 teaspoons salt
1 teaspoon pepper

Cover beans with plenty of cold water and soak overnight.

Pour off water. Cover with fresh water. Add baking soda and bring to a boil. Reduce heat and simmer, uncovered, 10 minutes, watching pot so it does not boil over. Drain and reserve liquid. Place sliced onions in bean pot. Add the bacon, then beans.

Combine the bean liquid with molasses, sugar, mustard, salt, and pepper. Mix well and pour over beans. Cover and bake at 300°F for 6 hours or use a Crockpot for 6 hours.

Note: Use any extra bean liquid to add to the pot to keep beans from drying out.

Grandma's Best Baked Beans

Serves: 20

1 medium onion, minced
1 gallon water
1/2 cup molasses

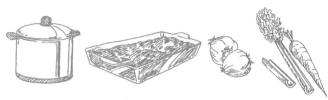

¹/₂ cup brown sugar
2 cups ketchup
2 tablespoons prepared mustard
1¹/₂ pounds navy beans, picked over,
*   rinsed, and soaked overnight in plenty*
*   of water to cover*
Salt and freshly ground pepper to taste

Sauté onion and cook until browned, about 4 minutes. Add water, molasses, brown sugar, ketchup, and mustard; bring to a boil. Drain beans and add to pot. Return to boiling, then reduce heat to a slow simmer. Cook 4 to 5 hours until beans are soft, adding water as necessary. Season with salt and pepper.

Orangey Sweet Potatoes

Serves: 6

3 large sweet potatoes
¹/₄ cup orange juice
1 tablespoon butter
¹/₈ teaspoon salt
¹/₄ teaspoon pepper
¹/₄ teaspoon ground ginger
3 oranges, peeled and cut into small
*   pieces*
Toasted almonds, slivered, optional

Preheat oven to 400°F.
Bake potatoes about one hour or until tender. Halve the potatoes lengthwise; scoop out pulp, being careful to keep the potato skins intact. Mash potato pulp with orange

juice, butter, salt, pepper, and ginger. Stir orange pieces into the potato mixture. Pile mixture into skins. Top with almonds if desired. Bake for 15 minutes or until heated through.

Variations: Add ¹/₂ cup raisins; use crushed pineapple and its juice in place of oranges and orange juice; mashed sweet potato can be put into a casserole dish instead of stuffed back into skins. Casserole can be prepared in advance and refrigerated until ready to be heated.

Potato Gratin

Serves: 6

3 medium baking potatoes, thinly sliced
2 tablespoons all-purpose flour, divided
1 medium onion, thinly sliced and
*   separated into rings*
¹/₈ teaspoon cayenne pepper
1 teaspoon paprika
¹/₂ teaspoon freshly ground pepper
¹/₄ cup grated Parmesan cheese
1 small zucchini, trimmed and thinly sliced
Nutmeg
¹/₄ teaspoon Spike seasoning
1 12-ounce can evaporated skim milk
2 teaspoons chopped fresh parsley for
*   garnish*

Preheat oven to 400°F.
Coat a circular gratin dish or glass pie plate with 3 sprays of nonstick cooking spray. Layer a third of the potatoes over the bottom

(continued)

of the dish, overlapping the slices in a spiral pattern. Over the potatoes, sprinkle 1 tablespoon of flour and arrange the onion rings. Dust with cayenne pepper and ½ teaspoon paprika. Layer another third of potatoes, adding the remaining flour, black pepper and 2 tablespoons of the Parmesan cheese. Scatter the zucchini; dust with the nutmeg and Spike seasoning. Top with a spiral layer of the remaining potatoes. Pour the evaporated milk over the gratin and add the remaining paprika and Parmesan cheese.

Cover the gratin with aluminum foil and bake for 45 minutes. Remove the foil, reduce the oven temperature to 350°F, and cook for about 15 minutes more, until the top is golden brown. Remove the gratin from the oven and allow to cool for 10 minutes. Garnish with chopped parsley.

Creamy Potato Sauce

Serves: 6

> 1 small potato, peeled and diced
> ½ cup water
> ½ cup skimmed evaporated milk
> 1 teaspoon butter-flavored granules
> 1 teaspoon onion powder
> 1 teaspoon chicken bouillon granules
> ⅛ teaspoon pepper (white or black)

In a small saucepan, combine potato and water. Bring to a boil, then cover and simmer until potato is tender, about 10 minutes. Using an electric hand mixer, blend potato until smooth.

Stir in the milk along with the remaining ingredients, blending until smooth. If needed, add more milk to reach a creamier consistency.

Oven Roasted Potatoes

Serves: 4

> 1 envelope onion mushroom soup mix
> 2 pounds potatoes, cut into chunks
> ⅓ cup vegetable oil
> 1 bunch fresh parsley for garnish
>   (optional)

Preheat oven to 450°F. In large plastic bag or bowl combine all ingredients. Close bag and shake, or toss in bowl, until potatoes are evenly coated. Empty potatoes into shallow baking or roasting pan; discard bag. Bake, stirring occasionally, 40 minutes or until potatoes are tender and golden brown. Garnish, if desired, with chopped fresh parsley.

Stovetop Corn Creole

Serves: 4

> 2 10-ounce packages frozen corn, thawed
> ½ cup frozen chopped onions
> ½ cup frozen diced green peppers
> 4 tablespoons butter
> 1½ cups drained canned tomatoes
> 1 teaspoon salt
> ¾ teaspoon pepper

In a large, heavy skillet or Dutch oven, sauté the corn, onions, and green peppers in

the butter, stirring constantly, until tender (about 5 minutes). Add the tomatoes and seasonings. Stir, then simmer until piping hot.

Corn Strada

Serves: 12

> 12 to 16 slices French bread, crusts removed
> Butter
> 1 16-ounce can cream-style corn
> 1 16-ounce can whole kernel corn, drained
> 1 7-ounce can diced green chilies
> 2 cups shredded Monterey Jack cheese
> 6 eggs, beaten
> 2 cups milk
> 1 teaspoon salt

Spread both sides of bread with butter. Line bottom of 13 x 9-inch baking dish with half of the buttered bread slices. Combine creamed corn and whole kernel corn. Spread half of corn mixture evenly over bread. Top with a layer of half of the green chilies and then 1 cup cheese. Repeat layers. Beat eggs with milk and salt. Pour over layers. Cover and refrigerate overnight.

Bake at 350°F for 1 hour.

John Barleycorn Casserole

Serves: 4

> 1 tablespoon olive oil
> 1 yellow onion, chopped

Freezing One-Pot Dishes, Part 1

It's a good idea to follow some time-tested hints when freezing one-pot dishes.

- Be sure to label all freezer containers with the date and contents. Use by the third month after freezing.
- When freezing stews, leave the potatoes out.
- Undercook the vegetables so they don't become mushy when reheated.

(continued)

2 cloves garlic, minced
1 cup grated carrots
1 cup uncooked pearl barley
3 cups vegetable broth
2 cups corn kernels, fresh or canned
1/4 cup chopped fresh parsley
Salt and pepper to taste

Preheat oven to 350°F.

In an ovenproof, flameproof casserole, heat the oil over medium-high heat. Add the onion, garlic, and carrots and cook for 5 to 7 minutes or until onion is translucent. Add the barley and broth. Cover and bake for 1 hour. Add the corn, parsley, and salt and pepper. Bake for 5 more minutes.

St. Tropez Vegetables

Serves: 6

6 pieces foil (about 15 x 15 inches each)
2 pounds summer squash, sliced 1/4-inch
    thick
2 pounds tomatoes, cut into wedges
1 onion, sliced very thin
2 teaspoons dried basil
1/4 teaspoon black pepper
4 cloves garlic, minced
3 tablespoons shelled and chopped
    pistachio nuts

Preheat oven to 400°F.

Spread out six squares of foil on counter. Divide squash, tomatoes, and onion evenly and stack on each square. Sprinkle with basil,

pepper, and garlic. To seal ingredients inside, bring together opposite sides of square; fold down tightly. Next, fold ends under to seal in juices. Place in a shallow pan and bake 40 minutes or until done. To check, peek into one bundle and check firmness and temperature. Be careful of steam. Sprinkle vegetables with pistachios before serving.

Caponata

Makes: 3 to 4 cups

2 tablespoons olive oil
1 small eggplant, peeled and cut into
    1-inch cubes
4 stalks celery, cut into half-inch slices
1/2 cup chopped pitted green olives
1 large onion, minced
1 clove garlic, crushed
1 tablespoon capers
1/4 cup tomato paste
1 cup water
1/4 cup vinegar
1 tablespoon sugar
1 teaspoon salt
Pita bread, cut into quarters

Heat oil in large skillet. Fry eggplant cubes until lightly browned. Add celery, olives, onion, and garlic. Cook until vegetables are tender.

Add the capers, tomato paste, water, vinegar, sugar, and salt. Stir lightly and simmer for one minute. Remove from heat. Serve warm and spread on pita bread.

Marinated Zucchini

Serves: 4

1 cup bottled chili sauce
2 teaspoons grated Parmesan cheese
2 tablespoons red wine vinegar
2 tablespoons olive oil
1 dash ground oregano
1 dash garlic powder
1/2 lemon, juiced
Salt and pepper to taste
4 8-inch zucchini

In an ovenproof casserole, combine chili sauce, cheese, vinegar, oil, oregano, garlic powder, and lemon juice, and beat with whisk. Season to taste with salt and pepper.

Wash zucchini and slice crosswise into 1/8-inch-thick slices. Add slices to dressing and chill 4 hours or longer, turning several times.

Cashew Vegetable Stir-Fry

Serves: 4

2 tablespoons sunflower oil
2 tablespoons sesame oil
1 inch fresh ginger, minced
4 cloves garlic, minced
1 small dried hot chili pepper
1 medium onion, cut into crescents
1 large carrot, peeled and sliced on the bias
2 stalks celery, sliced on the bias
1 red bell pepper, julienned

1 bunch green onions, cut in 1-inch lengths
10 mushrooms, sliced
2 cups shredded cabbage or bok choy
1 cup cashews, roasted
1 cup bean sprouts
1/4 cup soy sauce
Hot cooked rice

Heat oil in a large wok or skillet. When oil is very hot, add ginger, garlic, and chili. Stir-fry for 30 seconds; add onion, carrot, and celery. Cook over medium-high heat, stirring frequently, for 3 to 5 minutes until vegetables are barely tender.

Add peppers, green onions, mushrooms, cabbage, and cashews. Continue to stir-fry for another 3 minutes. Add sprouts and soy sauce; toss and stir-fry for 1 more minute. Remove from heat and serve immediately over rice.

Vegetable Stir-Fry

Serves: 6

1 tablespoon olive oil
1 tablespoon chopped garlic
1 tablespoon chopped fresh ginger
1 head broccoli, chopped
3 carrots, sliced
3 scallions, sliced
2 tablespoons vegetable broth
1 tablespoon soy sauce
1 teaspoon sesame oil
3 cups hot cooked rice

(continued)

In a wok, heat the oil briefly over a high flame. Add garlic and ginger and stir-fry for 30 seconds. Add the rest of the vegetables, tossing them to coat well. Add the broth, cover the pan, and cook the vegetables for several minutes over medium heat. Remove cover, turn the heat up to high, and cook the vegetables, stirring them, a few minutes longer until the vegetables are tender-crisp. Stir in the soy sauce. Remove the pan from heat, and sprinkle with sesame oil. Serve immediately with rice.

Stellar Stir-Fry

Serves: 4

> 1 tablespoon peanut oil
> 2 cups blanched broccoli florets
> 1 cup blanched diagonally sliced carrots, thin slices
> 1/2 cup thin onion wedges
> 6 ounces skinless chicken breasts, cut into thin strips
> 2 1/2 tablespoons red wine
> 1 tablespoon soy sauce
> 1/2 teaspoon cornstarch
> 1/4 teaspoon granulated sugar
> 1/8 teaspoon salt
> 2 cups hot cooked rice

In a wok heat oil; add broccoli, carrots, and onion. Cook, stirring quickly and frequently, until vegetables are tender-crisp and onions are browned. Stir in chicken.

In a small bowl combine next five ingredients, stirring to dissolve cornstarch. Add to chicken mixture and cook, stirring constantly, until sauce is thickened, 2 to 3 minutes. Serve each portion over 1/2 cup cooked rice.

Roasted Vegetables

Serves: 4

> 1 bunch asparagus, cut into 1-inch pieces on the bias
> 1 6-ounce bag baby carrots
> 1/2 pound green beans, trimmed, and cut into 1-inch pieces
> 2 whole ears of corn
> Any other kind of vegetable desired
> Olive oil
> Salt
> Freshly ground pepper

Preheat oven to 450°F. Trim the vegetables and place them in a shallow roasting pan in one layer.

Drizzle the vegetables with olive oil and sprinkle with salt and pepper. Roast in the oven for about 15 minutes, turning once or twice. (You may need to roast the vegetables in several stages until all are done.)

Italian Vegetable Bake

Serves: 8

1 28-ounce can whole tomatoes
1 onion, sliced
1/2 pound fresh green beans, sliced
1/2 pound fresh okra, cut into 1/2-inch
    lengths
3/4 cup finely chopped green bell peppers
2 tablespoons lemon juice
1 tablespoon chopped fresh basil
1 1/2 teaspoons chopped fresh oregano
3 7-inch long zucchinis, cut into
    1-inch cubes
1 eggplant, pared, cut into 1-inch chunks
2 tablespoons grated Parmesan cheese

Preheat oven to 325°F.

Drain and coarsely chop tomatoes. Reserve liquid. Mix together tomatoes and reserved liquid, onion, green beans, okra, green pepper, lemon juice, and herbs. Cover and bake for 15 minutes. Mix in zucchini and eggplant and continue baking, covered, 60 more minutes or until vegetables are tender. Stir occasionally. Sprinkle top with Parmesan cheese just before serving.

Lemony Asparagus and Carrots

Serves: 6

1/2 pound bag baby carrots
1 8-ounce package frozen asparagus spears

2 tablespoons lemon juice
1 teaspoon lemon pepper

Place the carrots in a steamer basket above boiling water. Cover and steam about 15 minutes or till crisp-tender. Rinse carrots in cold water; drain. Meanwhile, cook frozen asparagus spears according to package directions. Rinse asparagus in cold water; drain. Cover and chill drained carrots and asparagus.

To serve, arrange carrots and asparagus on a platter. Sprinkle with a little lemon juice and lemon pepper.

Turkish Tomato Pilaf

Serves: 8

1 tablespoon olive oil
1 1/2 cups uncooked long-grain rice
2 teaspoons salt
Boiling water
1/4 cup olive oil
4 tomatoes, chopped
2 1/2 cups hot water, in which 2 chicken
    bouillon cubes have been dissolved
1/2 teaspoon ground cumin
1/2 teaspoon salt
1/4 teaspoon pepper

In an ovenproof baking dish, heat the 1 tablespoon of olive oil for one minute. Add the rice and cook for 2 minutes, stirring to coat each grain. Stir in the salt and add boiling water to cover. Stir the liquid, allow it

(continued)

21

to cool, and drain the rice. Remove from the dish and set both aside.

In the same baking dish, heat ¼ cup of oil for one minute. Add the tomatoes, and cook, stirring, for 30 minutes, or until the mixture starts to resemble a paste.

Preheat oven to 350°F. Add the bouillon and seasonings to the tomatoes, stirring well to blend. Boil the sauce for 2 minutes. Add the rice, stirring once. Bake the rice, covered, for 15 minutes, or until it is tender and the liquid is absorbed.

Tomato Zucchini Casserole

Serves: 8

1½ teaspoons chili powder
1 tablespoon parsley flakes, divided
½ teaspoon garlic powder
½ teaspoon onion powder
⅛ teaspoon salt
⅛ teaspoon black pepper
3 cups thinly sliced fresh zucchini
1 pound fresh tomatoes, sliced
   (approximately 2 medium-size tomatoes)
¼ cup fresh white bread crumbs
1 tablespoon vegetable oil

Preheat oven to 375°F.
Combine chili powder, 1½ teaspoons parsley flakes, garlic and onion powders, salt, and pepper in a small bowl. Set aside.

Place half the zucchini in a lightly greased 1½-quart casserole. Layer with half the tomatoes. Sprinkle with half the seasoning mixture. Repeat the layers. Combine bread crumbs, oil, and remaining parsley flakes; sprinkle over vegetables. Bake, uncovered, until vegetables are tender, about 40 minutes.

A Year in Provence

Serves: 2

1 teaspoon olive oil
1 onion, chopped
1 teaspoon oregano
1 teaspoon basil
1 tablespoon water
¼ cup sliced ripe olives
2 tablespoons grated Parmesan cheese
7 fresh spinach leaves
2 French rolls
1 cup low-fat mozzarella cheese, sliced
2 plum tomatoes, sliced

Heat the oil in a large skillet. Add onion, oregano, and basil. Cook and stir 2 minutes. Add water. Reduce the heat, cover, and cook 5 minutes until onion is tender. Remove from heat; add the olives and Parmesan cheese.

Arrange 2 to 3 spinach leaves on bottom half of each French roll. Spoon half the onion mixture onto each; top with cheese slices and tomato slices. Top with spinach leaves and top half of roll.

Microwave Green Bean Casserole

Serves: 8

> 5 tablespoons butter, divided
> 2 cups cornflakes cereal, crushed to
>   ½ cup
> 2 tablespoons dry salad dressing mix,
>   divided
> 3 tablespoons all-purpose flour
> 1½ cups milk
> 1 cup shredded Cheddar cheese
> 2 10-ounce packages frozen French-style
>   green beans, cooked and drained
> 2 tablespoons slivered almonds, toasted

In small microwave-safe bowl, microwave 2 tablespoons butter on full power until melted. Combine with cornflakes and 1 teaspoon of the dry salad dressing mix. Set aside for topping.

Microwave remaining butter or margarine until melted. Stir in remaining dry salad dressing mix and flour. Gradually add milk, stirring until smooth. Microwave on full power for 4 to 5 minutes or until bubbly and thickened, stirring once during cooking time. Add cheese, stirring until melted. Place green beans in medium-size microwave-safe dish. Pour cheese sauce over beans.

Microwave on full power 5 to 6 minutes or until thoroughly heated and bubbly, rotating once during cooking. Sprinkle reserved topping and almonds evenly over top.

Microwave on full power 1 minute longer. Let stand 5 minutes before serving.

Fresh Vegetable Casserole

Serves: 8

> 2 cups broccoli florets
> 1½ cups sliced carrots
> 1 cup mayonnaise
> 1 cup shredded Cheddar cheese
>   (4 ounces)
> 3 to 4 drops hot pepper sauce
> ¼ teaspoon pepper
> ¼ cup dry white wine (optional)
> 1½ cups sliced zucchini
> 1 cup sliced celery
> ½ cup diced green pepper
> ½ cup diced onion
> 1 tablespoon minced fresh parsley
> 1 tablespoon minced fresh basil
> 3 tablespoons butter
> 12 soda crackers, crushed
> ⅓ cup grated Parmesan cheese

In a vegetable steamer over boiling water, steam broccoli and carrots until crisp-tender; drain and set aside. Preheat oven to 350°F. In a large bowl, mix together mayonnaise, Cheddar cheese, hot pepper sauce, pepper, and wine if desired. Add broccoli, carrots, remaining vegetables, parsley, and basil; stir gently to mix. Spoon into a greased 2-quart baking dish.

(continued)

Melt butter in a small saucepan. Add crushed crackers; stir until browned. Remove from heat and stir in Parmesan cheese; sprinkle over vegetables. Bake, uncovered, for 30 to 40 minutes.

Quick Onion & Vegetable Casserole

Serves: 4

¾ cup butter
1 pound mushrooms, sliced
¾ cup pearl barley
1 10¾-ounce can condensed cream of onion soup
2 cups water
2 10-ounce packages frozen mixed vegetables, thawed

Preheat oven to 350°F.

Melt butter in a shallow, ovenproof 3-quart casserole or 9 x 13-inch baking dish over medium heat. Add mushrooms and cook, stirring, until soft. Add barley and continue cooking and stirring until mushroom liquid is absorbed. Stir in soup and water; blend well.

Bake, covered, for about 1 hour. Stir in mixed vegetables; cover and return to oven for 20 more minutes or until barley is tender. Fluff with a fork before serving.

Freezing One-Pot Dishes, Part 2

Here are some more hints:

- When browning meat for a one-pot dish intended for the freezer, use little or no fat during the cooking process.
- Don't wrap tomato-based dishes in foil; the acid in the tomatoes will react with the aluminum.
- To keep from overcooking frozen one-pot dishes, partially thaw them first at room temperature.

Lentil Onion Casserole

Serves: 6

1 12-ounce package lentils
1 teaspoon salt
3 cups water
2 8-ounce cans tomato sauce
1 medium-size onion, finely chopped
¼ cup firmly packed brown sugar
2 tablespoons prepared mustard
⅓ cup molasses

Preheat oven to 350°F.

Rinse lentils; sort through and discard any foreign material. Drain well. Place lentils in a 3-quart casserole with a lid. Add salt, water, tomato sauce, onion, brown sugar, mustard, and molasses; stir well. Bake, covered, for about 2 hours, stirring gently every 30 minutes. Add a little more water if sauce becomes too thick. Lentils are cooked when they mash readily and when the liquid is bubbly and thickened.

Szechuan Tofu Stir-Fry

Serves: 6

⅓ cup teriyaki sauce
3 tablespoons Szechuan spicy stir-fry sauce
2 teaspoons cornstarch
1 red bell pepper
½ pound snow peas
1 14-ounce can baby corn
1 onion, chopped
3 cups chopped bok choy

2–3 tablespoons oil, divided
1 cup broccoli florets
1 pound tofu, cubed
1 7-ounce can straw mushrooms
3 cups cooked white rice

Combine teriyaki sauce, stir-fry sauce and cornstarch; set aside. Cut bell pepper into strips. Cut snow peas and baby corn in half. In wok, stir-fry onion and bok choy in 1 tablespoon oil for 2 minutes. Add broccoli and bell pepper; stir-fry 2 minutes. Remove from wok.

Stir-fry cubed tofu in 1 tablespoon oil for 2 minutes; add more oil if necessary. Stir sauce mixture and add to tofu; cook until bubbly. Add all vegetables; heat through. Serve over hot rice.

Sweet and Sour Tofu

Serves: 6

1 pound tofu
¼ cup lemon juice
¼ cup tamari sauce
6 tablespoons water
¼ cup tomato paste
2 tablespoons honey
1 teaspoon ginger
4 cloves garlic, minced
8 scallions, minced
1 green bell pepper, sliced in strips
1 red bell pepper, sliced in strips
1 pound mushrooms
2 teaspoons oil

(continued)

1 cup toasted cashews
3 cups hot cooked white rice

Cut tofu into small cubes; set aside. Combine lemon juice, tamari, water, tomato paste, honey, ginger, and garlic; mix until well blended. Add tofu to this marinade, stir gently, and let marinate for several hours (or overnight).

Stir-fry scallions, bell peppers, and mushrooms in 2 teaspoons of oil. After several minutes, add tofu with all the marinade. Reduce heat, and continue to stir-fry until everything is hot and bubbly. Remove from heat and stir in cashews. Serve over rice.

Crisp Fried Tofu and Greens

Serves: 8

2 firm cakes tofu, frozen overnight and
thawed
$\frac{1}{2}$ cup water or vegetable stock
1 teaspoon cornstarch
$\frac{1}{2}$ cup cornmeal or cornstarch
Oil

Marinade:

$\frac{1}{3}$ cup soy sauce
$\frac{1}{4}$ cup rice vinegar
1 tablespoon finely grated gingerroot
2 cloves garlic, minced or pressed
Dash cayenne pepper

Sauce:

3 tablespoons soy sauce
$\frac{1}{4}$ cup dry sherry
2 teaspoons rice vinegar
2 teaspoons honey or brown sugar

Vegetables:

3 tablespoons oil
3 cloves garlic, minced or pressed
1 cup thinly sliced onion
6 cups mix of coarsely chopped bok choy
*   and napa cabbage*

Gently squeeze as much liquid out of thawed tofu as possible. Cut tofu crosswise into $\frac{1}{2}$-inch thick slices, then cut each slice diagonally, to make 4 triangles. Combine marinade ingredients and mix well. Arrange tofu triangles in one layer in a dish and cover with marinade. Allow to sit for at least 10 minutes to absorb the flavors.

Prepare sauce mix by combining all ingredients in a small bowl. In a separate bowl mix the water or stock and the 1 teaspoon cornstarch. Set aside.

Dredge marinated tofu pieces in cornmeal or cornstarch and fry over medium heat in $\frac{1}{8}$ to $\frac{1}{4}$ inch of oil, for 3 to 4 minutes on each side. Drain and keep warm in 200°F oven.

Add leftover marinade to sauce mix. Heat 3 tablespoons oil in a wok. Stir-fry garlic and onion until onion is tender. Add greens and continue stir-frying until just wilted but not mushy. Add sauce mix and water-cornstarch

mix and stir-fry just until sauce is thickened. Add reserved fried tofu. Serve with rice.

Cashew Curry

Serves: 4

2 tablespoons olive oil
3/4 cup cashews
2 medium onions, minced
1 tablespoon curry powder
2 cloves garlic, minced
1 teaspoon salt
1 teaspoon fresh grated ginger
1/4 cup water
1 block firm tofu, cubed
2 red peppers, cut into strips
1 10-ounce package frozen peas

Heat the oil in a skillet. Add the cashews and onions and sauté over medium heat. Cook for 5 minutes. Reduce the heat and add the curry, garlic, salt, ginger, water, tofu, and peppers. Cover and cook for 5 minutes. Add the peas. Cook for 5 more minutes.

Tangy Greek Salad

Serves: 4

2 cups red wine vinegar
1/3 cup extra virgin olive oil
2 cups white wine
2 pounds button mushrooms, sliced
16 green olives
24 Greek olives
12 cloves garlic, chopped

12 small shallots, chopped
2 teaspoons fresh tarragon, finely chopped
1/2 teaspoon salt
8 large leaves butter lettuce
4 green onions, sliced and cut into
    2-inch pieces
2 carrots, julienned
4 parsley sprigs for garnish
2 lemons, cut into wedges, for garnish

In a large saucepan combine the red wine vinegar, olive oil, and white wine. Cook on medium-high heat for 4 to 6 minutes, or until the liquid is caramel colored and reduced by half.

Add the mushrooms, green olives, Greek olives, garlic, shallots, tarragon, and salt. Simmer for 4 to 6 minutes, or until the liquid is reduced by half. Let the mixture cool.

On each of 4 individual serving plates, place 2 of the lettuce leaves. Spoon on the cooked vegetables with the juice. Sprinkle on the onions and carrots. Garnish the dish with the parsley and the lemon wedges.

Basil Avocado Chutney

Makes: About 1 1/2 cups

2 cups packed basil leaves
1/3 cup blanched almonds
1 clove garlic
2 teaspoons fresh lemon juice,
    or to taste
1 avocado, peeled and cut into chunks
Salt to taste

(continued)

In a food processor blend together the basil, almonds, garlic, and lemon juice, pulsing the motor once or twice, until the almonds are ground fine. Add the avocado; add salt to taste and blend the mixture until it is combined well. Serve the chutney with grilled meats and fish.

Cranberry Chutney

Serves: 6

1 1/2 cups toasted walnut pieces
1 pound cranberries
1 cup golden raisins
1 small red onion, sliced
1/2 cup orange marmalade
1/2 cup orange juice
2 tablespoons orange zest
1/3 cup white wine vinegar
1 cup granulated sugar
1/2 cup firmly packed brown sugar
1/2 teaspoon salt
1/4 teaspoon red (cayenne) pepper
1/2 teaspoon ginger
1 cinnamon stick
1 bay leaf

In a pressure cooker, combine all ingredients. Stir well. Secure lid. Over high heat, develop steam to medium pressure. Reduce heat to maintain pressure and cook 5 minutes. Release pressure according to manufacturer's directions. Remove lid.

Remove cinnamon stick and bay leaf. Stir well. Pour hot chutney into a sterilized jar with lid. Store airtight in refrigerator up to 3 or 4 weeks.

Chinese Coleslaw

Serves: 6

4 cups shredded Chinese cabbage
1 8 1/4-ounce can crushed pineapple, drained
1 8-ounce can sliced water chestnuts
1 cup fresh, snipped parsley
1/4 cup sliced green onions
1/4 cup mayonnaise
1 tablespoon mustard
1 teaspoon grated gingerroot

Combine cabbage, pineapple, water chestnuts, parsley, and onion. Cover and chill.

For dressing, combine mayonnaise, mustard, and gingerroot. Cover and chill.

Spoon dressing over the cabbage mixture; toss to coat.

Chinese Sweet and Sour Sauce

Makes: 1 cup

3 tablespoons sugar
1/2 teaspoon ground ginger
3 tablespoons cornstarch
1 cup hot water in which 2 chicken bouillon cubes have been dissolved
1 20-ounce can pineapple chunks, with liquid
1/4 cup cider vinegar
3 tablespoons soy sauce

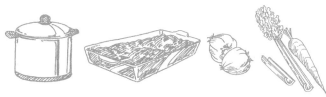

In a saucepan, mix the sugar, ginger, and cornstarch together. Mix in the bouillon, the pineapple and its liquid, vinegar, and soy sauce. Cook the mixture over high heat, stirring constantly, until it is thickened and smooth. Use as a sauce with meat, vegetables, poultry, or fish.

Guacamole

Serves: 6

2 ripe avocados, peeled and lightly mashed
1 medium-small ripe or canned tomato, diced
1 small onion, chopped (2 full tablespoons)
¼ to ½ teaspoon finely cut jalapeño or several dashes Tabasco sauce
2 tablespoons lemon or lime juice
¼ to 1 teaspoon cilantro
Dash salt
¼ cup salsa

In a medium bowl, combine the avocados, tomato, onion, jalapeño or Tabasco, lemon or lime juice, cilantro, salt, and salsa. Mix all ingredients well, keeping the guacamole lumpy.

Southwestern Apricot Salsa

Makes: 1 pint salsa

1 16-ounce can apricots in light syrup, drained, rinsed, and cut into chunks

2 tablespoons chopped red onions
½ tablespoon olive oil
1 tablespoon fresh cilantro
½ tablespoon lime juice
½ teaspoon white vinegar
½ teaspoon minced jalapeño peppers
¼ teaspoon grated lime peel
¼ teaspoon ground cumin
Salt, to taste
White pepper, to taste

Combine all ingredients in a medium bowl; stir gently. Cover and refrigerate for 2 hours until ready to serve.

Eggplant Caviar

Makes: 2 cups

1 cup finely chopped onion
1 cup finely chopped bell pepper
2 tablespoons olive oil
1 large eggplant, cooked and innards scooped out and mashed
1 tomato, finely chopped
Salt and pepper to taste

In a large skillet, brown the onion and green pepper in the olive oil. Add eggplant and tomato and stir often. Cook until the mixture is well done. Add more oil if it begins to stick. Add salt and pepper to taste. Transfer the mixture to a serving dish and chill.

Serve as a spread for crackers or vegetable dip.

Chapter 2

*Meat
Dishes*

Now *this* is the kind of one-pot dish most of us grew up with, except today you have the diversity to create a different meat-and-potatoes (or other starch) dish every day of the year.

Veal, ham, and good old beef are all represented in this chapter. They're all flavorful and will have you and your crew coming back for more. Now it's your turn to create meals for people to remember years down the road.

Beef

Most people think of tried-and-true beef stew when they think of a one-pot dish where the primary meat ingredient is beef. If you fall into this category and would like to break out of your rut, just try a few of the following recipes. You'll find that they're anything but run-of-the-mill and that a one-pot dish made with beef is much more than just stew.

Swedish Meatballs

Serves: 4

1 1/2 cups fresh bread crumbs
1 cup milk
1 1/2 pounds ground beef
1/2 pound lean ground pork
2 eggs
1 medium onion, chopped fine
1 3/4 teaspoons salt, divided
1/4 teaspoon allspice
1/8 teaspoon nutmeg
1/8 teaspoon cardamom
1 10 1/2-ounce can beef broth
1/8 teaspoon pepper
2 tablespoons butter, melted
2 tablespoons flour

Soak bread crumbs in milk for 5 minutes in a large mixing bowl. Preheat oven to 400°F.

Add beef, pork, eggs, onion, 1 1/2 teaspoons salt, allspice, nutmeg, and cardamom to bread crumbs. Mix well. Shape into 1-inch balls. Place on broiler pan and bake for 15 minutes.

Put browned meatballs in Crockpot. Add 1/2 can beef broth, pepper, and remaining salt. Cover and cook on low 4 to 6 hours, or high for 2 to 3 hours.

To thicken gravy, turn Crockpot to high. Combine butter and flour to make a smooth paste. Add paste to remaining 1/2 can beef broth and pour into Crockpot. Cook until thickened, about 45 minutes.

Italian Meatballs & Peas

Serves: 5

1 ½ pounds ground chuck
1 cup bread crumbs, soaked in ½ cup
    milk and wrung dry
2 onions, minced
½ cup seedless raisins
½ cup grated Parmesan cheese
½ cup chopped parsley
2 eggs, lightly beaten
1 teaspoon thyme
1 ½ teaspoons salt
1 teaspoon pepper
3 tablespoons olive oil
3 large onions, chopped
1 clove garlic, chopped
3 large tomatoes, peeled, seeded, and
    chopped
1 teaspoon oregano
1 10-ounce package frozen peas, fully
    thawed to room temperature

In a mixing bowl, combine and blend thoroughly ground chuck, bread crumbs, onions, raisins, cheese, parsley, eggs, thyme, salt, and pepper. Roll the mixture into 18 balls. Place the meatballs on a greased tray and place them under the broiler, turning them until they brown. Place in a layer in an ovenproof casserole and keep them warm.

In a saucepan, heat the oil. Add the onion and garlic and cook until translucent. Add the tomatoes and oregano. Simmer the mixture, covered, for 10 minutes.

One-Shot Sauce

Makes: About 1 cup

1 pound butter
½ cup finely chopped onion
2 cloves garlic, minced
½ cup whiskey
¼ cup Worcestershire sauce
1 tablespoon freshly ground pepper
1 ½ teaspoons dry mustard
1 teaspoon salt
¼ teaspoon Tabasco sauce

Melt butter in a saucepan; add onion and garlic and cook slowly until soft. Add remaining ingredients and beat to mix.

Use as a sauce to top beef, steak, or chicken.

(continued)

Preheat oven to 300°F. Add the peas and simmer them in the sauce, covered, for 5 minutes, until they are tender. Pour the sauce over the meatballs and bake, covered, for 30 minutes.

Hawaiian Meatballs with Rice

Serves: 4

> 1 20-ounce can pineapple chunks in juice
> ½ cup water
> ¼ cup cider vinegar
> 1 teaspoon soy sauce
> ¼ cup brown sugar
> 2 tablespoons cornstarch
> 1 small green pepper, cut into ½-inch squares
> 20 cooked meatballs
> 5 ounces sliced water chestnuts
> 2 cups cooked white rice

Drain the pineapple chunks, reserving ¾ cup of juice (if there is not enough, add water to make ¾ cup). Combine juice, additional ½ cup water, vinegar, soy sauce, brown sugar, and cornstarch in a medium saucepan and stir until sugar and cornstarch dissolve. Cook over low heat until thick and bubbling, stirring constantly. Add green peppers, meatballs, water chestnuts, and 1 cup of pineapple chunks (use the rest elsewhere). Heat until meatballs are hot, stirring frequently. Serve with white rice.

Chili & Corn Meatballs

Serves: 4

> 1 onion, chopped
> 1 small green pepper, chopped
> 1 16-ounce can tomatoes, cut up
> 1 16-ounce can kidney beans, drained
> 1 8-ounce can corn
> 1 8-ounce can tomato sauce
> 1 teaspoon salt
> 2 teaspoons chili powder
> 1 bay leaf
> 24 cooked meatballs (your own recipe, or if frozen, thawed)
> Cheddar cheese, grated
> Corn chips

In a saucepan, combine onion, pepper, tomatoes, kidney beans, undrained corn, tomato sauce, salt, chili powder, and bay leaf. Bring to a boil. Add meatballs; cover and simmer for 45 minutes, stirring occasionally. Remove bay leaf. Serve in individual bowls, topped with cheese and corn chips on the side.

Meatball & Vegetable Stir-Fry

Serves: 6

> 1½ pounds ground beef
> 2 eggs
> ½ teaspoon ground cumin
> 1 teaspoon salt

½ teaspoon pepper
3 tablespoons oil
6 or 8 scallions, sliced diagonally
2 cups chopped Chinese cabbage
    (bok choy)
1 10-ounce package frozen snow peas,
    fully thawed to room temperature
1 5-ounce can bamboo shoots, drained
3 tablespoons ginger, chopped
1½ cups hot water, in which 2 beef
    bouillon cubes have been dissolved
1 teaspoon sugar
2 tablespoons cornstarch
¼ cup soy sauce

Mix the ground beef, eggs, cumin, salt, and pepper together and shape into 36 small balls. Set aside.

In a wok or large deep-sided skillet or casserole, heat the oil; brown the meatballs for about five minutes. Place on paper towels and set aside. Reserve the meat drippings in the skillet.

Reheat the meat drippings; add the scallions and bok choy, and cook, stirring constantly, for 2 minutes. Add the remaining vegetables and cook, stirring constantly, for 2 minutes. Add the reserved meatballs. Add the bouillon and sugar, stirring constantly. Bring to a boil.

Mix the cornstarch and soy sauce in a small bowl, and add to the pan. Cook, stirring constantly, for 3 minutes, or until the sauce is thickened and smooth.

Stroganoff Meatballs

Serves: 4

1 cup sour cream
1 cup water
3 tablespoons flour
1 package beef bouillon granules
½ teaspoon dried dill weed
24 cooked meatballs (frozen or thawed)
1 9-ounce package egg noodles, cooked
    and kept warm

In a medium saucepan blend sour cream, water, flour, bouillon granules, and dill. Cook over medium heat until thick and bubbly, stirring occasionally. Add meatballs to sauce. Cook for 15 to 20 minutes or until meatballs are hot, stirring occasionally. Serve over hot egg noodles.

Quick Sloppy Joes

Serves: 16

2 pounds ground beef
1 large onion, minced
2 teaspoons salt
¼ teaspoon pepper
¼ cup flour
3 cups water
1 teaspoon Worcestershire sauce
1½ cups ketchup
1 teaspoon chili powder
16 hamburger buns

(continued)

Cook beef, onion, salt, and pepper in skillet. Drain the fat from the skillet. Stir in flour, water, Worcestershire sauce, ketchup, and chili powder. Simmer uncovered 20 minutes. Split and toast buns; spoon mixture over buns and serve.

Sloppy Joes

Serves: 8

> 3 pounds lean ground beef
> 1 cup chopped onion
> 2 cloves garlic, minced
> 1 1/2 cups tomato sauce
> 1 cup chopped green pepper
> 1/2 cup water
> 1/4 cup brown sugar
> 1/4 cup spicy mustard
> 1/4 cup vinegar
> 1 tablespoon chili powder
> 8 hamburger buns

In a large skillet, brown ground beef, onion, and garlic. Cook until meat is brown and onion is tender. Drain off fat. Combine remaining ingredients (except buns) in Crockpot. Stir in meat mixture. Cover and cook on low 6 to 8 hours or on high for 3 to 4 hours. Spoon onto hamburger buns.

Easy Ground Beef Stroganoff

Serves: 4

> 1 pound ground beef
> 2 tablespoons dried minced onion
> 1 package or cube beef bouillon
> 1/8 teaspoon garlic powder
> 1 tablespoon ketchup
> 1 teaspoon Kitchen Bouquet or Gravy Master
> 1 can condensed cream of mushroom soup
> 1 4-ounce can mushrooms, drained
> 1/2 cup sour cream
> 1 9-ounce package wide egg noodles,
>   cooked and kept warm

In a large skillet, brown beef. Drain. Stir in remaining ingredients, except sour cream and noodles, and heat to boiling. Cover and simmer 10 to 15 minutes. Remove from heat and stir in sour cream. Serve hot over egg noodles.

Easy Stuffed Cabbage Casserole

Serves: 6

> 4 slices bacon
> 1 pound ground beef
> Cabbage leaves, about 1/4 head
> 1 medium onion, chopped
> Salt and pepper to taste
> Garlic salt to taste
> 1/2 teaspoon oregano
> 2 cups cooked rice

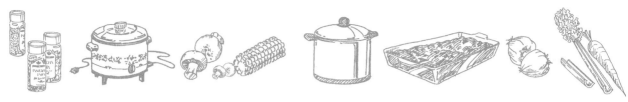

1 28-ounce can sauerkraut, well drained
1 32-ounce jar spaghetti sauce

Fry the bacon fairly crisp and reserve it. Cook the ground beef. Drain, set aside. Use the bacon fat to grease a 2-quart casserole. Preheat oven to 325°F. Tear cabbage leaves as necessary to line the bottom of the casserole, about 2 or 3 leaves thick. Break up the ground beef and crumble on top of the cabbage leaves. Crumble the bacon pieces on top of the beef. Add the chopped onion, and then add the salt, pepper, garlic salt, and oregano. Cover this with the cooked rice and then the sauerkraut. Cover with another layer of cabbage leaves, about 2 or 3 leaves thick. Finally, pour the spaghetti sauce on top, distributing it evenly. Bake, covered, for about an hour, until cabbage leaves are tender.

Cabbage, Beef & Barley Skillet

Serves: 6

2 pounds chopped beef
3 medium onions, sliced
1 clove garlic, chopped
4 cups packaged coleslaw mix (half of a 1-pound bag)
3 cups beef broth
1 teaspoon caraway seeds
1/4 teaspoon black pepper
1 1/2 cups instant barley

Spray a large skillet with nonstick cooking spray and place over medium-high heat. Add beef and garlic; cook 5 minutes, or until beef is browned, stirring constantly. Transfer beef to a plate and set aside.

Spray skillet again and add onion. Cook 1 minute, stirring constantly. Add coleslaw, broth, caraway seeds, and black pepper. Bring the mixture to a boil. Reduce heat to medium-low and stir in barley. Cover and simmer 10 to 12 minutes, or until barley is tender and liquid is absorbed. Serve immediately.

Hash

Some people feel that hash is best dished up on buttered toast or biscuits. If you don't have the meat a hash recipe calls for, don't worry; use leftover cooked meat from a previous meal as a substitute. It will still be delicious.

Clean Out the Refrigerator Hash

Serves: 8

4 tablespoons butter
4 onions, chopped
3 cups diced cooked beef, pork, or
  chicken
4 large potatoes, peeled and diced
1 10-ounce can condensed beef broth
1 tablespoon Worcestershire sauce
Salt and pepper to taste
Leftover gravy
Leftover cooked vegetables

In a large skillet, heat the butter until it browns. Cook the onion until translucent. Add the meat, potatoes, broth, Worcestershire sauce, and salt and pepper to taste. Bring the liquid to a boil, reduce the heat, and simmer the mixture, covered, for about an hour.

Uncover the hash and continue to cook it for about 30 minutes, or until most of the liquid is absorbed. Add the gravy and any vegetables to the hash. Heat the dish, covered, for 5 to 10 minutes more, or until warmed through.

Danish Hash with Fried Eggs

Serves: 4

1/2 cup butter, divided
2 large onions, finely chopped

2 cups peeled cooked potatoes, cut in
  1/2-inch cubes
3 cups cooked lean beef, cut in 1/2-inch cubes
1/4 cup beef broth
1 teaspoon Worcestershire sauce
1/2 teaspoon salt
1/8 teaspoon pepper
4 eggs
Butter lettuce and cherry tomatoes for
  garnish
Coarse (kosher-style) salt (optional)

In a wide frying pan over medium heat, melt 3 tablespoons of butter. Add onions and cook slowly, stirring occasionally, until they are limp and golden (about 15 minutes). When onions are cooked, transfer to another large container and keep warm.

Then, in the same frying pan over medium-high heat, melt 3 tablespoons more of the butter and cook potatoes, turning as needed to brown on all sides; add to onions and keep warm.

Add 1 tablespoon more butter to the pan and cook beef, stirring occasionally, until it is heated through. Add beef to container with onions and potatoes; keep warm.

Again using the same frying pan, combine broth, Worcestershire, salt, and pepper. Cook over high heat until reduced by about half, then pour over hash mixture. Mix lightly but thoroughly. Using the same pan, melt 1 to 2 tablespoons butter and fry eggs until done as desired. Spoon hash onto a warm platter and

arrange eggs on top. Garnish with the lettuce and tomatoes. Serve with coarse salt, if you wish.

Texas Hash

Serves: 6

> 1 pound ground beef
> 2 stalks celery, chopped fine
> 2 large onions, diced
> 2 green peppers, chopped fine
> 1 16-ounce can chopped tomatoes
> ½ cup uncooked white rice
> 1 tablespoon chili powder

Preheat oven to 350°F. In a large oven-proof skillet, brown meat; add celery, onion, and peppers and cook slightly, stirring with meat. Add tomatoes, rice, and chili powder; stir. Cover and bake for 45 minutes.

Confetti Casserole

Serves: 8

> 1 pound ground beef
> ¼ cup chopped onion
> 1 teaspoon salt
> ⅛ teaspoon pepper
> ¼ teaspoon dry mustard
> 1 tablespoon brown sugar
> 1 4-ounce package cream cheese
> 1 8-ounce can tomato sauce
> 1 10-ounce package frozen mixed
>   vegetables, thawed
> Crushed corn chips

Preheat oven to 375°F.

Brown meat in an ovenproof skillet; add onion and cook until tender. Add salt, pepper, dry mustard, brown sugar, and cream cheese; stir until cheese melts. Add tomato sauce and defrosted vegetables. Sprinkle with corn chips.

Cover and bake 40 minutes. Uncover and bake 10 minutes longer.

Stovetop Beef, Bean & Bacon Casserole

Serves: 8

> 1 pound bacon, diced
> 2¼ pounds lean ground beef
> 2 onions, chopped
> 1 41-ounce can pork and beans
> 1 29-ounce can tomato sauce
> ½ cup brown sugar
> ¾ cup ketchup
> salt and pepper to taste

In a large pot, brown bacon until cooked; remove and drain. Brown ground beef and onions in same pot until cooked. Mix in remaining ingredients and bacon and simmer about 7 minutes until warmed through.

Browning Ground Meat

To brown ground beef or turkey, add water to your skillet as the meat cooks. This way, the hot fat won't splatter out of the pan and the meat will stay very moist. Try it the same way the next time you're frying a burger.

Another way to keep hot fat from splattering is to sprinkle a little salt or flour in the pan before frying.

Hamburger Curry

Serves: 4

1 tablespoon olive oil
1 medium-size onion, chopped
1 pound lean ground beef
1 3- to 4-ounce package pine nuts
2 teaspoons curry powder
¼ teaspoon garlic salt

Salt and pepper to taste
1 8-ounce can tomato sauce
1 cup water
¼ cup finely chopped parsley
4 cups hot cooked rice
Assorted condiments: sliced green onions (including tops), crisp bacon (crumbled), raisins, salted cashews, chopped cucumber, shredded coconut

Heat oil in a wide frying pan over medium heat. Add onion and cook until soft. Add ground beef and cook until well browned and crumbly; stir in pine nuts, curry powder, garlic salt, salt and pepper to taste, tomato sauce, and water. Bring to a boil. Reduce heat and simmer until sauce begins to thicken slightly (about 5 minutes).

Just before serving, stir in parsley. Serve over rice and pass condiments at the table.

Beef Skillet Dinner

Serves: 8

2 tablespoons shortening
1 pound ground beef
1 29-ounce can tomatoes, cut up
1 teaspoon salt
1 teaspoon Worcestershire sauce
1½ cups chopped cabbage
2 tablespoons parsley
1 cup uncooked macaroni
½ cup Cheddar cheese, grated

Heat shortening in a large skillet, then add ground beef and cook until browned. Drain fat from skillet. Blend tomato, salt, and Worcestershire sauce with ground beef in skillet. Bring to a boil. Add cabbage, parsley, and macaroni. Cover, reduce heat, and simmer for 15 to 20 minutes. Sprinkle with cheese and serve hot.

Steak & Marinara Sauce

Makes: 4 cups

> Water
> 1 pound ground top round steak
> 2 cups canned plum tomatoes
> 1/2 cup chopped onion
> 2 cloves garlic, minced
> 2 teaspoons tomato paste
> 2 teaspoons dried oregano
> 2 teaspoons dried basil
> 1/2 teaspoon red pepper flakes
> Pinch sugar
> Freshly ground black pepper
>   to taste
> 2 teaspoons olive oil (optional)

Put about 1/2 inch of water in a frying pan. Add beef and sauté until it loses its pink color. Add tomatoes and juice, onion, garlic, and tomato paste; stir well, and simmer 5 minutes. Add oregano, basil, red pepper flakes, sugar, and pepper. Cover and simmer 10 to 15 minutes, until thickened slightly or to degree of thickness desired. Add olive oil if desired for flavor.

Serve over pasta or rice. Freeze or keep in refrigerator for up to five days.

Mozart Mozzarella

Serves: 6

> 2 pounds ground beef
> 1 onion, chopped
> 1 15-ounce can tomato sauce
> 1 3-ounce can mushroom pieces, drained
> 1 1/2 cups shredded mozzarella cheese
> 1 1/2 cups shredded Cheddar cheese
> 1 8-ounce tube crescent rolls
> 1 8-ounce carton sour cream
> Oregano
> Basil

In a large ovenproof skillet, brown the hamburger and onion until hamburger is brown. Drain. Add tomato sauce and mushrooms; mix thoroughly. Spread cheeses over hamburger mixture.

Preheat oven to 350°F.

Lay out the crescent rolls on a baking sheet and spread with sour cream. Sprinkle with oregano and basil. Roll them up and place on top of cheese. Bake for 35 minutes or until rolls are brown and done.

Pasticcio

Serves: 8

> 1 pound ground beef
> 2 onions, chopped
> 3 cloves garlic, chopped

(continued)

1 teaspoon oregano
1 teaspoon basil
1 teaspoon allspice
1 teaspoon cinnamon
1 teaspoon sugar or to taste
1 16-ounce can whole tomatoes, chopped
  and liquid drained
1 16-ounce package elbow macaroni;
  cooked al dente
4 tablespoons butter
4 tablespoons flour
2 cups milk
3 tablespoons grated Parmesan cheese
6 ounces feta cheese
2 to 3 eggs, beaten

Brown the meat with the chopped onions and garlic. Add the herbs and spices, sugar to taste, and the drained tomatoes. Let the sauce simmer 30 to 45 minutes.

Mix in the cooked pasta and put in a baking pan. Preheat oven to 375°F.

Melt the butter in a saucepan and mix in the flour to form a paste. Add the milk and heat over medium heat, stirring constantly until mixture thickens. When thick, add Parmesan and crumbled feta cheese, and stir until melted. Let the mixture cool completely, then add the beaten eggs. Pour this mixture over the meat and pasta. Bake about 45 minutes or until brown.

Moussaka

Serves 8 to 10

5 large eggplants, about 1 1/2 pounds each
Salt
10 tablespoons butter, divided
3 pounds ground beef
1 1/2 cups chopped onion
2 tablespoons tomato paste
1/4 cup chopped parsley
1/2 cup red wine
1/2 teaspoon salt
1/8 teaspoon pepper
1/2 cup water
1/8 teaspoon ground cinnamon
3/4 cup grated Parmesan cheese
1/2 cup bread crumbs, divided
1/2 cup all-purpose flour
4 cups hot milk
1/8 teaspoon grated nutmeg
3 eggs, slightly beaten
Vegetable oil for brushing
Pepper to taste

Remove 1/2-inch-wide strips of peel lengthwise from eggplants, leaving 1/2-inch of peel between strips. Cut into 1/2-inch rounds, sprinkle with salt, and let stand in a colander under a heavy or weighted plate for 1/2 hour.

Rinse and dry eggplant rounds. Melt 4 tablespoons butter in a saucepan and sauté meat and onion until brown. Add tomato paste, parsley, wine, salt, pepper, and water. Simmer until liquid has been absorbed. Cool.

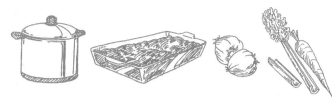

Stir in cinnamon, $\frac{1}{2}$ cup cheese, and half of the bread crumbs.

To prepare the sauce, melt 6 tablespoons butter in a saucepan over low heat. Add flour and stir until well blended. Remove from heat, and gradually stir in milk. Return to heat and cook, stirring, until sauce is thick and smooth. Add salt, pepper, and nutmeg. Combine eggs with a little of the hot sauce, then stir egg mixture into sauce and cook over low heat for 2 minutes, stirring constantly.

Preheat broiler. Lightly brush eggplant slices with oil on both sides. Place on an ungreased cookie sheet and broil until lightly browned. Set aside to cool.

Preheat oven to 350°F. Sprinkle bottom of a 10 x 16-inch pan with remaining bread crumbs. Place a layer of eggplant slices on the bread crumbs, then spread meat mixture over eggplant slices. Cover meat with remaining eggplant. Spoon sauce over eggplant; sprinkle with remaining $\frac{1}{4}$ cup grated cheese. Bake for 40 minutes, or until golden brown. Cool for 10 minutes before cutting. Serve warm.

Easy Stovetop Chili

Serves: 4

   1 pound ground beef
   1 cup chopped onion
   1 cup chopped celery
   1 $\frac{1}{2}$ teaspoons sugar
   $\frac{1}{2}$ teaspoon salt

   $\frac{3}{4}$ teaspoon garlic powder
   1 $\frac{1}{2}$ tablespoons chili powder
   $\frac{3}{4}$ teaspoon oregano leaves
   $\frac{1}{4}$ teaspoon pepper
   1 15-ounce can tomato sauce
   1 6-ounce can tomato paste
   2 $\frac{1}{2}$ cups water (may need more)
   1 15 $\frac{1}{2}$-ounce can kidney beans, drained

In a large heavy skillet, brown beef and onions. Drain juices. Add all remaining ingredients except kidney beans. Mix well. Bring mixture to a boil. Reduce heat and simmer, covered, for 30 minutes.

Add the beans and simmer, uncovered, for 10 minutes to heat beans. Add more water if needed.

Beef & Kidney Bean Chili

Serves: 10

   3 pounds lean ground beef
   1 onion, chopped
   1 28-ounce can tomato sauce
   3 cups water
   3 tablespoons chili powder
   1 $\frac{1}{2}$ tablespoons cumin
   $\frac{3}{4}$ teaspoon oregano
   1 $\frac{1}{2}$ teaspoons paprika
   $\frac{1}{4}$ teaspoon cayenne pepper
   1 tablespoon salt
   2 15-ounce cans kidney beans
   $\frac{1}{4}$ cup masa flour (or $\frac{1}{8}$ cup flour +
       $\frac{1}{8}$ cup cornmeal)

(continued)

Brown the meat and onions; drain. Add the remaining ingredients except masa. Simmer about 1 1/2 hours.

Mix the masa with enough water to make a thin paste. Add slowly to the simmering chili, stirring constantly. Cook 15 minutes more.

Meatless Chili

Serves: 4

1 tablespoon olive oil
2 Spanish onions, chopped
1 teaspoon cumin
1/2 teaspoon cinnamon
4 cloves garlic, minced
1 35-ounce can whole tomatoes with purée, drained, with liquid reserved
1/3 cup water
1 tablespoon Tabasco sauce
Salt to taste
1 cup bulgur wheat
1 19-ounce can red kidney beans, drained

Heat the oil in a skillet over medium heat for 20 seconds. Add the onions and cook until translucent. Add the cumin, cinnamon, and garlic. Stir, then add the reserved tomato liquid along with the water, Tabasco, and salt. Cook for five minutes. Add the bulgur, stir, and cook for 5 more minutes. Chop the canned tomatoes and add to the skillet with the kidney beans. Reduce the heat; cover and cook for 10 more minutes.

Wintertime Chili

Serves: 6

1 green pepper cut into 1-inch pieces, seeds reserved
1 red pepper cut into 1-inch pieces, seeds reserved
1 cup very coarsely chopped onion
3 cloves garlic, minced
1 teaspoon ground cumin
1 1/2 to 3 tablespoons chili powder
1/4 teaspoon finely chopped habanero pepper (very hot), jalapeño pepper (medium hot), or 2 tablespoons chopped ancho pepper (mild)
1/2 teaspoon cocoa powder
1/2 teaspoon brown sugar
1 8-ounce can tomato sauce
1 to 2 16-ounce cans dark kidney beans, drained
1 1/2 cups water
1 cup tomato juice
Salt (optional) and freshly ground pepper to taste

In a large nonstick saucepan, combine all the ingredients (plus seeds). Bring to a boil. Reduce the heat and simmer for 35 to 50 minutes, covered, stirring to loosen the bottom occasionally. Adjust seasoning; serve hot.

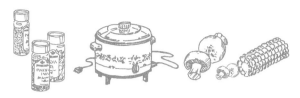

Black Bean Chili

Serves: 4

2 1/4 cups dried black beans
Water
1 cup tomato sauce
6 tablespoons tomato paste
2 tablespoons lime juice
2 tablespoons red wine vinegar
1 cup chopped onions
1 cup chopped celery
1 cup chopped green bell pepper
1 cup chopped tomatoes
1 medium jalapeño pepper, seeded and
    chopped
4 cloves garlic, finely chopped
1 tablespoon fresh cilantro, finely chopped
1 1/2 teaspoons ground coriander
1 1/2 teaspoons ground cumin
1 1/2 teaspoons chili powder
Salt and pepper to taste
Sour Cream (optional)

Wash beans and place them in a large bowl. Cover with plenty of water to allow for expansion. (Beans will double in size during soaking process). Soak beans overnight.

Drain beans and place in a large soup pot. Add about 7 1/2 cups water. Bring beans to a boil and simmer for 2 hours or until beans are almost cooked. Stir in tomato sauce, tomato paste, lime juice, vinegar, vegetables, and seasonings. Continue cooking until beans are soft, 45 minutes to 1 hour. Top each serving with a dollop of sour cream if desired. Note: When preparing hot peppers, wear rubber gloves for protection against oils that later cause burning sensation on skin.

Turkey Chili Casserole

Serves: 6

2 tablespoons margarine, melted
2 tablespoons unbleached flour
2 cups skim milk, at room temp
1 tablespoon fat-free grated Parmesan
    cheese
4 1/2 cups cooked egg noodles
2 cups skinless, cubed cooked light
    turkey meat
1 cup chopped onions
1 1/2 cups chopped bell peppers
1 tablespoon prepared mustard
2 tablespoons bread crumbs

Preheat oven to 375°F. Spray a 2-quart casserole dish with nonstick cooking spray; set aside.

In a saucepan, melt margarine over medium-high heat; sprinkle with flour. Cook, whisking quickly and constantly, for 2 minutes. Whisk in milk and Parmesan cheese. Cook, stirring constantly, for another 2 minutes until thickened. Remove from heat.

Add noodles, turkey, onions, bell peppers, and mustard to saucepan; toss to mix well. Spoon mixture into prepared dish and sprinkle with bread crumbs. Bake for 20 minutes or until browned and bubbly.

Lucia's Meat Loaf

Serves: 8

Meatloaf:

2 pounds lean ground beef
1 10-ounce box frozen chopped spinach,
    thawed and drained
1 pound mozzarella cheese, shredded
2 cloves garlic, minced
1 teaspoon basil
1 egg
1 cup Italian seasoned
    bread crumbs
Salt and pepper to taste

Marinara Sauce:

2 garlic cloves, chopped
2 tablespoons olive oil
1 teaspoon basil
1 pinch thyme
1 28-ounce can crushed tomatoes
Salt and pepper to taste
1 pinch red pepper

Preheat oven to 350°F. Spray one large or two small loaf pans with nonstick cooking spray.

Mix all meat loaf ingredients together to form one large loaf or two smaller ones. Put meat loaf in pan and bake for about 2 hours.

Meanwhile, make marinara sauce. Sauté garlic in olive oil. Add basil and thyme and stir a minute. Add all other ingredients and simmer about an hour. Let meat loaf rest about 10 minutes. Serve with marinara sauce.

Stuffed Mexican Meat Loaf

Serves: 6

2 pounds ground beef chuck
1 8-ounce can tomato sauce
2 tablespoons taco seasoning mix
1/3 cup chopped green pepper
1/3 cup finely chopped onion
1 1/2 slices white bread, torn into small
    pieces
1 large egg, slightly beaten
2 cups shredded Cheddar cheese
1/2 cup sour cream
3 Cheddar cheese slices, cut
    into triangles
Avocado slices for garnish
Cherry tomatoes for garnish

In a large bowl, combine ground beef, tomato sauce, taco seasoning mix, green pepper, onion, bread crumbs, and egg; mix thoroughly. Combine shredded cheese and sour cream.

Preheat oven to 375°F. Place half the meat mixture in a 9 1/4 x 5 1/4 x 2 3/4-inch loaf pan. Make a deep well the length of loaf; place cheese mixture in well. Place remaining meat mixture on top of cheese; seal well. Bake for 1 1/2 to 1 3/4 hours.

Pour off drippings. Top meat loaf with overlapping cheese triangles. Let meat loaf stand 8 to 10 minutes. Place on serving platter and garnish with avocado slices; place cherry tomato in center of each avocado slice.

Harvest Apple Meat Loaf

Serves: 8

> 2 1/2 pounds lean ground beef
> 1 1/2 cups herb-seasoned stuffing mix
> 2 cups peeled, finely chopped apples
> 3 eggs, slightly beaten
> 1 teaspoon salt
> 2 tablespoons prepared mustard
> 2 tablespoons horseradish
> 1 onion, finely chopped
> 3/4 cup ketchup

Preheat oven to 350°F.

Mix all ingredients together well in a large bowl. Pack into a large loaf pan. Bake about 1 hour and 15 minutes, or until cooked through. Let rest for 10 minutes before slicing.

Meat Loaf Tricks

Meat loaf will not stick to the pan if you place a slice of bacon on the bottom of the pan before patting the meat into the pan.

For a change of pace, don't just use ground beef for your meat loaf. Many supermarkets sell meat loaf mix, which is a package of three different ground meats—beef, veal, and pork—which, when used in any recipe, create a flavor that is more tasty and delicate than just using beef alone.

Chilies & Salsa Meat Loaf

Serves: 8

1 ½ pounds lean ground beef
1 ½ pounds bulk sausage
1 16-ounce can Mexican-style stewed
   tomatoes
1 8-ounce can chopped green chilies
2 eggs
3 tablespoons + 2 teaspoons tapioca
1 ½ teaspoons dried minced onions
½ teaspoon cumin
¼ teaspoon salt
1 ½ cups salsa
1 cup shredded jack or Cheddar cheese

Preheat oven to 350°F.

Mix all ingredients except salsa and cheese in a large bowl until well combined. Divide in half and shape into loaves. Place each in a 9 x 4-inch loaf pan. Top each with ¾ cup salsa. Bake for 1 ½ hours. If the sausage makes a lot of grease, drain it once or twice while cooking.

Top with cheese and return to oven until cheese melts. Remove to serving platter and let rest for 15 minutes before slicing.

Steak Stroganoff

Serves: 6

1 pound round steaks, thinly sliced
3 tablespoons butter, divided
½ cup chopped onions
½ pound mushrooms, sliced

2 tablespoons tomato paste
2 tablespoons water
½ teaspoon basil
1 tablespoon cornstarch
1 cup plain yogurt
¼ cup sherry or beef broth
3 cups cooked noodles

Trim the fat off the meat and slice into strips. Melt 2 tablespoons butter in skillet. Sauté onions until soft. Add beef. Brown for about 5 minutes. Remove beef and keep warm. Add remaining tablespoon of margarine and sauté mushrooms. Stir in tomato paste, water, and basil. Return meat to pan and simmer briefly.

In separate pan mix cornstarch with 1 tablespoon of yogurt, then stir in remaining yogurt and cook over medium heat until thickened. Add to meat mixture and heat thoroughly. Thin with sherry or broth as desired. Serve over cooked noodles.

Smothered Round Steak

Serves: 4

2 pounds round steak
2 teaspoons salt
½ teaspoon ground black pepper
1 teaspoon ground red pepper
1 teaspoon ground white pepper
¼ cup all-purpose flour
½ cup vegetable oil
3 medium onions, chopped
2 bell peppers, chopped

1 celery rib, chopped
1 cup beef stock or water

Season the roast with half of the salt and peppers. Dust with flour on all sides. Heat the oil in a Dutch oven or other large, heavy pot over medium-high heat. Add the steak, and brown well on all sides.

Remove the meat and pour off all but 1 teaspoon of the oil. Add half the onions, bell peppers, and celery, along with the other half of the seasonings, and the stock or water. Stir well and reduce the heat to the lowest setting. Return the roast to the pot and cover with the remaining vegetables. Cover and cook until the meat is very tender, about 1 hour and 15 minutes. Slice the meat, and serve with rice and gravy from the pot.

For an extra flavorful roast, try larding with slivers of garlic before smothering. (See sidebar entitled "Smothering.")

Tangy Round Steak

Serves: 4

1 1.06-ounce packet beef marinade mix
1 cup orange juice
1½ pounds round steak
1 tablespoon oil
2 tablespoons flour

In a 7 x 10-inch glass dish, combine marinade mix and orange juice. Stir to blend well. Cut meat into serving sized pieces. Pierce meat several times with a fork. Place meat in the marinade and turn once to coat both sides. Allow to stand in marinade for at least 15 minutes.

Remove meat from marinade and pat dry. Reserve marinade. Heat oil in skillet and add meat. Cook for 10 minutes over low heat. Turn meat once; continue to cook for another 5 to 10 minutes or until meat is tender.

Add flour to reserved marinade. Stir well, while simmering over low heat. Serve meat with sauce.

Smothering

Smothering is a multipurpose Cajun technique that works wonders with everything from game to snap beans. It's similar to what the rest of the world knows as braising: the ingredients are briefly browned or sautéed, then cooked with a little liquid over a low heat for a long time.

Bracciole

Serves: 8

Two 2-pound round steaks
Salt and pepper
1 cup pine nuts
½ pound prosciutto cut paper-thin
1 large clove garlic, quartered
3 tablespoons olive oil
3 tablespoons butter
½ cup minced onions
½ cup chopped carrots
2 cups chopped mushroom caps and
stems
1 cup Italian tomato purée
1 tablespoon Italian tomato paste
2 cups whole peeled Italian-style canned
tomatoes

Trim all fat from the steaks and pound them with a mallet or the edge of a heavy plate until they are very, very thin. Dust lightly with salt and pepper. Sprinkle the nuts over the meat, leaving about an inch margin all around. Cover with a blanket of prosciutto. Roll the steaks like jelly rolls and tie them securely with string.

In a Dutch oven, brown the garlic in the olive oil. Add the butter, and brown the beef rolls on all but one side. Add the onions, carrots, and mushrooms; turn the rolls to their unbrowned sides, and cook for 3 minutes. Combine the purée, tomato paste, and tomatoes, and add to the Dutch oven. When the liquid comes to a boil,

reduce the heat and simmer, covered, for 1½ hours.

Cut each roll into four pieces, and serve with the sauce.

Savory Beef

Serves: 8

3 tablespoons olive oil
2 pound round steak cut into ½-inch cubes
1 large onion, chopped
1 clove garlic, minced
3 tablespoons all-purpose flour
1 3-ounce can chopped mushrooms,
undrained
½ cup chopped celery
1 cup sour cream
1 8-ounce can tomato sauce
1 teaspoon salt
Freshly ground pepper to taste
Chopped celery for garnish
Chopped chives for garnish

In a large ovenproof saucepan, heat oil. Add beef and brown until beef is cooked through. Add the onion and garlic. Cook, stirring, until onions are transparent.

Add flour, stirring until beef cubes are coated. Add mushrooms with juice and celery. Stir the sour cream, tomato sauce, salt, and pepper into the meat mixture. Mix well.

Preheat oven to 325°F. Cover saucepan, and bake for 1¼ to 1½ hours until meat is tender. Sprinkle with chopped celery and chives.

Sicilian Steak

Serves: 6

2 pounds round steak
1/4 cup flour
1/2 teaspoon salt
1/8 teaspoon ground pepper
3 tablespoons olive oil
2 cups tomato, crushed
1/2 teaspoon oregano
1/8 teaspoon dry mustard
1 tablespoon chopped parsley
1 clove garlic, minced

Cut steak into serving pieces and pound thin. Mix flour, salt, and pepper, and dredge meat in mixture. Brown the meat with oil in large skillet. Pour off the liquid. Add tomatoes, oregano, mustard, parsley, and garlic. Cover and simmer about 1 hour.

Dijon Beef Stroganoff

Serves: 6

1 1/2 pounds boneless lean beef
Coarsely ground black pepper to taste
5 tablespoons butter, divided
1 medium-size onion, finely chopped
1/2 pound mushrooms, thinly sliced
3 tablespoons all-purpose flour
1 cup beef broth
1 tablespoon Dijon mustard
1/4 teaspoon ground nutmeg
1/2 cup whipping cream

1 pound egg noodles, cooked, buttered, and kept warm
Chopped parsley for garnish

Cut beef across grain in 1/4-inch-thick slanting slices. Sprinkle meat generously with pepper.

In a large skillet over medium-high heat, melt 1 tablespoon of the butter. Add onion and cook, stirring occasionally, until soft. Add half the meat and cook, stirring, for about 5 minutes or until well browned. Remove from pan and set aside. Repeat, using 1 more tablespoon of the butter and remaining meat; remove from pan.

Over medium heat in the same pan, melt remaining 3 tablespoons butter. Add mushrooms and cook, stirring, until soft. Blend in flour and cook, stirring, until bubbly. Gradually pour in broth and continue cooking and stirring until sauce boils and thickens. Stir in mustard, meat-onion mixture, nutmeg, and cream; stir until heated through. Serve over noodles and garnish with parsley.

Sassy Sirloin

Serves: 4

1 tablespoon black pepper
1/2 teaspoon onion powder
1 teaspoon ground whole thyme
1/4 teaspoon red pepper
1 1/2 pounds boneless sirloin steak

Combine spices in a small bowl; stir well.

(continued)

Trim fat off the steak. Press spice mixture into meat on both sides. Place steak on rack coated with cooking spray. Place rack in a shallow baking pan. Broil 5 inches from heat for 4 minutes on each side, or till desired doneness is reached. Cut steak diagonally across the grain, into ½-inch-thick slices.

Flank Steak with Peanut Sauce

Serves: 2

3 pound flank steak, trimmed of fat
2 tablespoons + 2 teaspoons soy sauce, divided
¼ teaspoon black pepper or to taste
¼ teaspoon crushed red pepper
1 tablespoon olive oil
¼ teaspoon garlic powder
¼ cup creamy peanut butter
1 tablespoon rice wine vinegar
½ cup water

Preheat broiler. Place steak on rack set in broiler pan. Brush top side with 1 tablespoon soy sauce. Season with black pepper; set aside. In a small saucepan, stir together the red pepper, oil, and garlic powder. Heat on medium for 1 minute. Add peanut butter, rice wine vinegar, 2 teaspoons soy sauce, and water. Cook until smooth, stirring constantly, for 2 minutes. Keep sauce warm.

Broil steak 3 inches from heat for about 7 minutes. Turn over; brush with remaining soy sauce and season with black pepper. Broil for 7 minutes more. Let stand for 5 minutes. To serve, slice thin across the grain; serve sauce in a small bowl beside meat dish.

Chicken Fried Steak

Serves: 2

1 egg
¼ cup milk
1 cup bread crumbs
1 teaspoon oregano
1 teaspoon seasoned salt
2 6-ounce cube steaks
¼ cup vegetable oil
Cheese (optional)

In a shallow bowl, beat egg and milk together. In another dish, combine bread crumbs, oregano, and seasoned salt. Dip cube steaks in egg mixture; turn to coat well. Dip steaks in seasoned mixture, turning once to cover.

In a heavy skillet, heat oil. Brown steaks in oil. Reduce heat, cover with lid slightly ajar, and cook for 10 to 15 minutes. Cook longer if necessary, until tender. If desired, melt cheese on top of steaks to add flavor.

Gingery Beef and Broccoli Stir-Fry

Serves: 4

1 pound flank steak
2 tablespoons vegetable oil
3 cups broccoli florets

½ cup water, divided
1 teaspoon crushed red pepper
¼ teaspoon garlic powder
¼ cup ketchup
2 tablespoons soy sauce
1½ teaspoons cornstarch
½ teaspoon ground ginger
Scallions for garnish
4 cups cooked white rice

Slice steak against the grain into large matchstick-sized pieces. In large skillet or wok, heat oil and stir-fry steak until just browned. Remove steak and set aside. In same skillet, combine broccoli, ¼ cup water, red pepper, and garlic powder. Cover and cook 5 minutes.

Meanwhile, in a small bowl combine remaining ingredients, including ¼ cup water, except scallions and rice; blend well. Return meat to skillet, and blend in ketchup mixture. Bring to a boil. Cook until sauce thickens and glaze develops. Garnish with chopped scallions. Serve with hot rice.

Wok Cooking

Make sure your wok is good and hot before you add any meat or vegetables, or else the food will stick. If you use vegetable oil to coat the wok, heat the surface to medium-high. If you choose a vegetable spray, heat only to medium, and spray it before you turn the heat on.

Beef & Mushroom Stir-Fry

Serves: 4

1½ teaspoons vegetable oil
1 12-ounce steak, cut into strips
1 small onion, chopped
1 small green pepper, chopped
¼ pound mushrooms
¼ teaspoon marjoram
¼ teaspoon thyme

¼ teaspoon pepper
¼ cup white wine
½ cup beef broth
1 teaspoon cornstarch
1 tablespoon cold water

Heat oil in wok over moderately high heat for 30 seconds. Add steak, and stir-fry until no longer pink. Remove and place on paper towel to absorb grease. Add onion and green pepper to wok, and stir-fry for one minute.

(continued)

Mix in mushrooms and herbs, and pepper, and stir-fry for 2 to 3 minutes. Raise heat to high and stir in white wine; boil uncovered for one minute. Add beef broth and simmer, covered, for 3 to 4 minutes. Stir cornstarch and water to form a smooth paste, and blend in. Stir until thickened, add beef, and cook for another minute.

Gingered Beef Stir-Fry

Serves: 4

> 1 tablespoon cornstarch
> 1 tablespoon dark soy sauce
> 1 tablespoon sesame oil
> $\frac{1}{2}$ teaspoon freshly ground white pepper
> 1 pound flank steak, sliced as thinly as possible across the grain
> 1 cup finely shredded gingerroot
> $\frac{1}{2}$ teaspoon salt
> $1\frac{1}{2}$ teaspoons sugar
> 3 tablespoons rice wine (or dry sherry)
> 1 cup peanut oil
> 2 cups lightly chopped and firmly packed fresh coriander leaves

Combine the cornstarch, soy sauce, sesame oil, and pepper. Marinate steak strips in the mixture for 30 minutes in the refrigerator. Meanwhile, in a small bowl, toss the ginger with the salt and set aside for 20 minutes; then squeeze ginger shreds to extract most of their moisture, and set aside. Combine the sugar and wine and set aside.

When the beef has marinated, heat the oil in a wok or skillet to a medium-hot temperature. Add the meat, stirring to separate the pieces. When the pieces change color, remove them to a colander to drain. (Some of the meat may still be pink.) Remove all but 3 tablespoons of the oil from the pan. (It can be strained and saved for another use.) Heat the 3 tablespoons of oil in the pan and add the ginger. Stir rapidly for 15 seconds. Add the beef, and cook and stir for another 15 seconds. Stir in the coriander leaves and the wine mixture, and cook just until the dish is heated through.

Japanese Beef Stir-Fry

Serves: 4

> $\frac{3}{4}$ pound beef flank steak, partially frozen
> 1 tablespoon peanut oil
> 1 large red bell pepper, cored, seeded, and thinly sliced
> 1 small onion, thinly sliced
> 1 tablespoon chopped fresh gingerroot or 1 teaspoon ground ginger
> 1 clove garlic, crushed
> $\frac{1}{8}$ teaspoon crushed hot red pepper
> 12 ounces fresh Chinese pea pods or 2 6-ounce packages frozen pea pods, thawed
> 1 large head escarole, about 1 pound, chopped
> 1 tablespoon soy sauce
> $\frac{1}{2}$ teaspoon light brown sugar, firmly packed

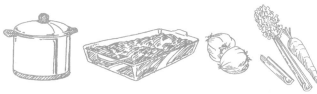

Using a sharp knife held almost parallel to the cutting surface, cut partially frozen flank steak into very thin slices. In a 12-inch skillet over medium-high heat, heat oil. Add beef; cook 2 to 3 minutes, stirring frequently, until browned. Using slotted spoon, remove meat to plate; keep warm.

To drippings in skillet, add red bell pepper, onion, ginger, garlic, and crushed red pepper. Cook about 4 minutes, stirring constantly, until vegetables are crisp-tender. Add pea pods, escarole, soy sauce, and brown sugar. Cook about 1 minute, stirring constantly, until pea pods are heated through and escarole is wilted. Stir beef into vegetables.

Italian Beef Stir-Fry

Serves: 4

12 ounces boneless beef top round steak
1 12-ounce package dried fettuccine or
    linguine
2 cups fresh or frozen broccoli florets
1 medium yellow summer squash, halved
    and sliced diagonally
1 teaspoon olive oil
2 cloves garlic, minced
1 cup cherry tomato halves
1/3 cup bottled Italian salad dressing
4 green onions, thinly sliced
1 tablespoon finely shredded Parmesan
    cheese

Trim fat from meat. Partially freeze meat. Thinly slice across the grain into bite-size strips. Cook fettuccine according to package directions; drain. Return fettuccine to pan. Cover to keep warm.

Spray a cold wok or large nonstick skillet with nonstick cooking spray; preheat over medium heat. Add broccoli and squash; stir-fry for 4 to 5 minutes or until vegetables are crisp-tender. Remove from wok.

Add oil to wok. Add meat and garlic to wok; stir-fry for 3 to 4 minutes or until meat is brown. Return cooked vegetables to wok. Add cherry tomatoes, salad dressing, and green onions. Toss to mix. Cover; heat through. Serve immediately over fettuccine. Sprinkle with Parmesan cheese.

Celery Sukiyaki

Serves: 6

1 1/2 pounds flank steak
3 tablespoons olive oil, divided
3 cups sliced diagonally celery
2 small onions, sliced, separated
    into rings
1 beef bouillon cube
3/4 cup boiling water
1 cup sliced water chestnuts
5 tablespoons soy sauce
1 1/2 teaspoons ground ginger
1/2 teaspoon black pepper
Hot cooked rice

Cut steak into thin diagonal slices. (For easier slicing, partially freeze first.) In large skillet, heat 2 tablespoons oil. Add steak

(continued)

strips, a few at a time. Brown on both sides. Remove and set aside.

Add celery and onion to skillet, along with 1 tablespoon oil. Sauté for 3 minutes. Dissolve bouillon cube in boiling water. Add to skillet along with water chestnuts, soy sauce, ginger, and black pepper. Stir well. Add browned steak; spoon juice over steak. Cover and simmer 10 minutes or until steak and vegetables are fork-tender. Serve over rice.

Slicing Meat

To slice meat for stir-fries, position a cleaver or large knife at a 45° angle to the meat and slice it across the grain into thin strips. Cut the strips into bite-size pieces, if necessary.

Western Trails Steak

Serves: 4

> 2 1-inch-thick sirloin steaks, about 12 ounces each
> 1 tablespoon black peppercorns, coarsely ground
> 2 cloves garlic, minced
> 4 cups coarse salt
> 3/4 cup water

Trim excess fat from steak. Press peppercorns and garlic into both sides of steak and let stand at room temperature for 1 hour. Make a thick paste of salt and water; cover top side of peppered steak with half the mixture. Heat the grill to high. If cooking steak over coals, cover salt side with a wet cloth or paper towels and place salt side down on grill. (Cloth or paper holds the salt in place; it will char as the steak cooks, but this does not affect the taste.) Cover the top side with remaining salt mixture and another piece of wet cloth or paper towel. If broiling, put salt side up, 3 inches from heat. Put salt on other side of steak when it is turned. Cook 15 minutes on each side for rare, 25 minutes for medium rare. Brush off the salt before serving.

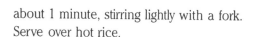

Chinese Pepper Steak With Cola

Serves: 6

1½ pounds boneless top round or sirloin steak
2 tablespoons olive oil
1 clove garlic, minced
1 teaspoon salt
1 cup canned beef broth, undiluted
1 cup thin strips green bell pepper
1 cup thinly sliced celery
¼ cup thinly sliced onions
¾ cup cola, divided
2 medium tomatoes
2½ tablespoons cornstarch
1 tablespoon soy sauce
Hot cooked rice

Trim all fat from the meat and cut into pencil-thin strips. In a deep skillet or Dutch oven, heat oil, garlic, and salt. Add the meat and brown over high heat, about 10 minutes, stirring occasionally with a fork. Add the beef broth. Cover and simmer for 15 to 20 minutes, or until the meat is fork-tender.

Stir in the green pepper strips, celery, onions, and ½ cup of cola. Cover and simmer for 5 minutes. Do not overcook; the vegetables should be tender-crisp. Peel the tomatoes, and cut into wedges; gently stir into the meat.

Blend cornstarch with the remaining ¼ cup of cola and the soy sauce. Stir mixture into the meat and cook until sauce thickens,

about 1 minute, stirring lightly with a fork. Serve over hot rice.

Easy Pepper Steak

Serves: 4

2 tablespoons oil
1 onion, sliced
2 green peppers, sliced
1 clove garlic, minced
1 cup beef bouillon
1 cup + 2 tablespoons soy sauce
1 tablespoon cornstarch
1½ teaspoons ginger
1½ cups cooked roast beef, julienned
3 cups cooked white rice

Heat oil in a large skillet over medium high heat. Sauté onions and peppers until almost softened. Add garlic and cook for another minute. Stir together remaining ingredients, except beef and rice. Add to skillet along with beef. Cook and stir until sauce is thick and meat is hot. Serve over hot white rice.

Beef & Edam Cheese Casserole

Serves: 6

¼ cup finely chopped onion
½ cup unsalted butter
1 pound sirloin steak, sliced thin
2 tomatoes, finely chopped
1 red bell pepper, cut in ½-inch strips

(continued)

½ green bell pepper, cut in ½-inch diced
    pieces
1 large egg, hard-boiled, chopped
¼ cup raisins
¼ cup black olives, pitted and halved
¼ cup sweet gherkins, chopped
¼ cup chopped mushrooms
2 tablespoons brandy, heated
2½ teaspoons flour
½ cup beef broth
¼ teaspoon Oriental chili paste
½ teaspoon chili sauce
½ teaspoon ketchup
Tabasco sauce to taste
Salt and pepper to taste
7 ounces Edam cheese, sliced ¼-inch thick
Sautéed sliced bananas as an
    accompaniment

In a skillet, cook onion in the butter over moderate heat until golden. Add the steak, tomatoes, and bell pepper. Cook, stirring, over medium-high heat, until veggies are softened. Add the egg, raisins, olives, gherkins, and mushrooms and cook the mixture, stirring, for 1 minute. Add the brandy, heated, and ignite. Shake skillet gently until flame goes out. Stir in flour and cook for 2 minutes, stirring. Stir in broth, chili paste, chili sauce, ketchup, Tabasco, and salt and pepper to taste. Simmer the mixture, stirring occasionally, for 5 minutes.

Preheat oven to 325°F. Line the sides of a shallow 2-quart casserole with some of the cheese slices. Pour the beef mixture into the

casserole, and cover it with the remaining Edam. Put the casserole in a larger pan, add enough water to reach 1 inch up the sides of the casserole, and cover the pan with aluminum foil. Bake in the middle of the oven for 15 minutes. Serve with sautéed bananas.

Goulash a la Budapest

Serves: 8

3 tablespoons butter
1 onion, chopped
2 tablespoons sweet Hungarian paprika
2 pounds beef round, cut in
    1½-inch cubes
3 tablespoons flour
Salt
¾ teaspoon marjoram, crumbled
4 cups beef broth
½ cup potato cubes
1½ tablespoons lemon juice

Melt the butter in a covered casserole. Add the onion; stir, and cook until soft. Stir in the paprika and cook slowly 1 to 2 minutes. Roll the meat in flour and add to the onion, cooking only long enough to brown lightly. Sprinkle with a little salt, and add marjoram. Pour in broth and bring to a boil. Cover and simmer for about 1 hour, or until tender.

Add the potato cubes and cook 15 to 20 minutes, until done. Remove from heat, stir in the lemon juice, and add more salt if necessary.

Pot Roast and Vegetables

Serves: 10

   4 pounds boneless shoulder
      pot roast
   2 tablespoons flour
   1 teaspoon salt
   2 tablespoons vegetable oil
   1 envelope onion soup mix
   1 teaspoon basil
   ¾ cup water
   1 16-ounce can tomatoes
   1 acorn squash, pared and cut into
      chunks
   1 pound zucchini, sliced

Preheat oven to 350°F. Dredge meat in flour and salt mixture and brown in oil in large Dutch oven. Pour off drippings. Stir onion soup mix and basil into ¾ cup water and add to meat. Cover tightly and cook in oven for 1 hour.

Add vegetables and cook approximately 1 hour or until tender.

Pot Roast Casserole

Serves: 10

   3½ pounds boneless beef round roast
   7⅛-ounce package beef barley soup mix
   5½ cups water
   1 medium rutabaga
   1 pound carrots
   1 pound green beans

About 4 hours before serving, in an 8-quart Dutch oven over medium heat, cook beef, fat side down, until brown on all sides. Add soup mix and water. Bring to a boil over high heat.

Cover and bake for 1½ hours at 350°F. Meanwhile, cut rutabaga into quarters; peel and cut quarters into 1½-inch chunks. Cut carrots lengthwise into quarters. Trim ends from beans.

When meat is cooked, remove 2 cups soup mix from pan and place in blender. Blend until smooth. Stir into liquid remaining in Dutch oven. Add rutabaga and carrots, cover, and bake for 1 hour. Add green beans, cover, and bake for 30 minutes.

Savory Pot Roast

Serves: 6

   2 tablespoons oil
   4 pounds beef pot roast, round, or chuck
      roast
   1 10¾-ounce can cream of mushroom
      soup
   1 package dry onion soup mix
   1¼ cups water, divided
   6 medium potatoes, quartered
   6 medium carrots, cut into 2-inch pieces
   2 tablespoons flour
   Fresh parsley for garnish

Heat oil in a 6-quart saucepan; add the roast and brown on all sides. Drain off fat. Stir in soup, dry soup mix, and 1 cup of

(continued)

water. Reduce heat to low. Cover and cook for 2 hours.

Add vegetables. Cover and cook for 45 minutes or until roast and vegetables are fork tender.

Remove vegetables and roast from pot. Stir together flour and remaining water until smooth. Gradually stir into soup mix in pot. Cook until mixture boils and thickens, stirring constantly. Garnish roast with fresh parsley.

All American Pot Roast

Serves: 8

> 1 onion
> 1 carrot
> 1 rib of celery
> 1 tablespoon oil
> 3 1/2 pound chuck roast
> 1 cup water
> 2 teaspoons salt
> 1/2 teaspoon pepper
> 1/2 teaspoon dried thyme
> 1 bay leaf
> 1/2 cup water
> 2 tablespoons all-purpose flour
> Salt and pepper to taste

Cut onion, carrot, and celery into 2-inch chunks. Heat oil in a large pot over medium heat. Brown roast on all sides, about 15 minutes. Remove meat from pot. Add vegetables to pot and cook until golden, about 10 minutes. Return meat to pot and add 1 cup of water, salt, pepper, thyme and bay leaf. Bring to

a boil. Reduce heat and simmer, covered, for about 2 1/2 hours, turning meat occasionally.

Remove meat to a platter. Cover loosely with aluminum foil to keep warm. Discard all the vegetables and the bay leaf. Skim fat from pan juices. Gradually add 1/2 cup water to the flour. Add the flour mixture to the pan and cook, stirring, until the gravy comes to a boil and thickens.

Red Wine and Garlic Pot Roast

Serves: 8

> 2 tablespoons olive oil
> 1 beef round or rump roast, about 4 pounds
> 2 medium carrots, diced
> 1 celery stalk, sliced
> 24 cloves garlic, peeled
> 2 cups dry red wine
> Salt to taste
> 1 teaspoon whole black peppercorns
> 2 bay leaves
> 1 1/2 teaspoons chopped fresh thyme leaves or 1/2 teaspoon dried thyme leaves
> 1 cup chicken broth
> 2 tablespoons butter

Heat the oil over medium heat on the stove top in a heavy pot with a lid or in a Dutch oven. Add the roast and surround it with carrots, celery, and garlic. Cover the pot tightly and reduce heat to low. Cook for 30 minutes. Remove cover; add the red wine,

salt, pepper, bay leaves, and thyme. Replace cover and continue to cook for 2½ to 3 hours.

Transfer the roast from the pot to a baking dish. Cover and keep warm in a 225°F oven for up to 15 minutes. Place the pot on top of the stove over medium heat and add the broth and butter. Cook, stirring vigorously until the butter is incorporated.

Remove the roast from the oven, slice into serving pieces and arrange on a serving platter. Strain the pan juices over the roast, pressing the vegetables against the sieve or strainer to extract all their juices. Serve with vegetables immediately and pass any extra sauce in a sauce boat.

Old-Fashioned American Pot Roast

Serves: 8

Pot Roast Basics

Simple pot roasts are frequently served with a whole carrot, turnip, onion, and a celery rib. These vegetables are referred to as aromatics, and dramatically improve the flavor of any pot roast. Serve them alongside the roast or incorporate into a rice or potato side dish.

2½ pounds boned bottom round roast
¼ teaspoon freshly ground
   black pepper
2 yellow onions, sliced
3 cloves garlic, minced
1 cup beef consommé
1 cup dry red wine
3 tablespoons tomato paste
½ teaspoon parsley
½ teaspoon sage
½ teaspoon rosemary
½ teaspoon thyme
½ teaspoon marjoram

½ teaspoon crumbled sweet basil
6 new potatoes, with skins
3 medium carrots, chopped
1 stalk of celery, minced
1 teaspoon butter
¼ pound thinly-sliced mushrooms
1 tablespoon minced parsley

Heat the broiler. Season the roast with pepper. Place the meat on the broiler pan rack and broil about 4 inches from the heat

(continued)

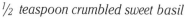

until brown on all sides—about 10 minutes or so. Reduce the oven temperature to 325°F.

Combine the onions, garlic, consommé, wine, tomato paste, and spices in a 4-quart Dutch oven. Add the beef and bring it to a simmer over moderate heat. Cover tightly and transfer to the oven, and cook for an hour and a half.

Add the potatoes, carrots, and celery, and continue baking for another hour, or until the meat is tender.

Slice the meat into ¼-inch-thick slices, and arrange them, overlapping slightly, on a heating platter, or a heated serving dish. Set the potatoes and carrots around the meat; keep warm.

Purée the onions, celery, and meat juices in a blender or food processor. Heat the butter in a heavy 10-inch skillet over moderate heat for about 30 seconds. Add the mushrooms and cook for about 5 minutes, until lightly browned. Stir in the puréed gravy. Keep warm over low heat until ready to serve. Spoon the sauce over the beef and sprinkle everything with parsley.

Slow Cooker Pot Roast

Serves: 6

1½ medium onions, chopped
2 cloves garlic, minced
2 tablespoons olive oil
3 pounds chuck roast
Pinch salt

¼ teaspoon coarsely ground pepper
1 teaspoon flour to cover the roast
1 16-ounce can stewed tomatoes
1 cup water
1 tablespoon Worcestershire sauce

Sauté onion and garlic with oil in a large Crockpot until transparent. Season the roast with salt and pepper and then dredge (lightly) in flour. Brown roast (on top of the onions and garlic) in the cook-pot on both sides, for about 10 minutes. Transfer to the slow cooker; add the stewed tomatoes, water, and Worcestershire sauce. Cook on setting 4 (of 5) for about 5 hours. When done, remove and purée the remaining tomatoes, juices, and onions. Return to pan; make gravy.

Dutch Oven Pot Roast

Serves: 8

5 pounds round bone pot roast
2 teaspoons salt
2 tablespoons shortening
½ cup bottled barbecue sauce
½ cup apple cider
8 medium carrots, peeled and cut into
    2-inch chunks
6 large potatoes, peeled and quartered
2 medium onions, sliced
8 ounces fresh okra

Rub meat with salt. Melt shortening in Dutch oven; add meat and cook over

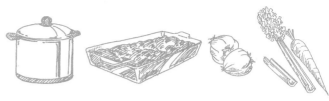

medium heat, turning once. Reduce heat; pour barbecue sauce and cider over meat.

Cover and simmer on top of range or in 325°F oven for 3 to 4 hours. Add carrots, potatoes, and onions 1½ hours before end of cooking time. Add okra 15 minutes before end of cooking time.

Winter Pot Roast and Vegetables

Serves: 6

> 2 pounds chuck, round, or rump roast beef
> 2 large cloves garlic, cut in slivers
> 1 teaspoon each salt and pepper
> ¼ cup olive oil
> 2 onions, finely chopped
> 3 carrots, finely chopped
> 1 stalk celery, finely chopped
> 2/3 cup beef broth
> 1 28-ounce jar pasta sauce
> 2 cups baby carrots
> 4 potatoes, peeled and cut into large chunks
> 2 onions, cut lengthwise in quarters

Make small slits in meat. Insert garlic slivers. Mix salt and pepper; sprinkle over all meat surfaces. Heat olive oil in a Dutch oven; add meat and brown on all sides. Remove meat and set aside. Add chopped vegetables; cook 10 minutes over low heat, stirring occasionally. Add beef broth and sauce; bring to a boil. Return meat to Dutch oven; cover and

cook 2 hours over low heat or until meat is very tender. Stir occasionally.

Add baby carrots, potatoes and onions. Simmer until vegetables are tender, about 30 minutes. Slice beef and serve on a platter surrounded by vegetables. Serve sauce over beef.

Louisiana Roast Beef

Serves: 8

> ¼ cup very finely chopped onions
> ¼ cup very finely chopped celery
> ¼ cup very finely chopped bell peppers
> 2 tablespoons unsalted butter
> 1 teaspoon salt
> 1 teaspoon white pepper
> ¾ teaspoon black pepper
> ¾ teaspoon minced garlic
> ½ teaspoon dry mustard
> ½ teaspoon ground cayenne pepper
> 4 pound boneless sirloin roast

In a small bowl combine the onions, celery, bell peppers, butter, and seasonings; mix well. Place roast in a large roasting pan, fat side up. With a large knife make 6 to 12 deep slits in the meat (to form pockets) down to a depth of about ½ inch from the bottom; do not cut all the way through. Fill the pockets to their depths with the vegetable mixture, reserving about 1 tablespoon of the vegetables to rub over the top of the roast.

Bake uncovered at 300°F until a meat thermometer reads about 160°F for medium

(continued)

doneness, about 3 hours. For a rarer roast, cook until thermometer reads 140°F. Serve immediately topped with some of the pan drippings if you like.

Cowboy Beef & Beans

Serves: 12

> 1 pound dry pinto beans
> 1 tablespoon lard
> 1 6-pound beef rump roast
> 1 cup green pepper strips
> 2 medium onions, sliced
> 2 cups tomato juice
> 1 8-ounce can tomato sauce
> $\frac{1}{2}$ cup water
> 2 teaspoons cider vinegar
> 2 tablespoons brown sugar
> 2 teaspoons salt
> 1 teaspoon dry mustard
> 1 teaspoon thyme

Rinse the beans. Place in a large oven-proof stockpot, cover with cold water, and soak overnight.

Bring beans to a boil, then reduce the heat and cook 1 hour; drain, discarding water.

Heat the lard in the stockpot. Brown the roast in hot fat evenly for about 10 to 15 minutes. Preheat oven to 350°F. Add peppers and onions to the pot, and cook until tender. Add beans and remaining ingredients. Cover and bake for $2\frac{1}{2}$ to 3 hours or until beans are tender and meat is done.

Stovetop Sauerbraten

Serves: 4

> 1 cup leftover beef gravy or 1 10$\frac{3}{4}$-ounce can prepared gravy
> 1 cup water
> $\frac{1}{4}$ cup cider vinegar
> $\frac{1}{3}$ cup finely crushed gingersnap cookies (about 6)
> 1$\frac{1}{2}$ tablespoons sugar
> 8 thin slices cooked roast beef

In a large skillet combine gravy, water, vinegar, gingersnaps, and sugar. Bring to boil and simmer until thickened, about 5 minutes. Add beef and cook until heated through. Serve over mashed potatoes.

Werewolf of London Beef Chow Mein

Serves: 4

> 1 tablespoon oil
> 1 onion, sliced
> $\frac{1}{2}$ cup bias-cut celery slices
> 1$\frac{1}{2}$ cups cubed cooked roast beef
> 1$\frac{1}{2}$ cups beef bouillon or broth
> $\frac{1}{4}$ cup soy sauce
> 3 tablespoons cornstarch
> 1 cup fresh bean sprouts

Heat oil in a large skillet and sauté the onion and celery until softened. Add beef and toss. Stir in beef broth. Blend together soy sauce and cornstarch until smooth. Add

to skillet, stirring constantly. Add bean sprouts and cook, stirring, until thickened and hot.

Serve with rice or noodles.

Indoor Barbecued Beef Brisket

Serves: 8

Salt and pepper to taste
1 4 to 5 pound beef brisket,
   fat trimmed
1 medium onion, diced
3 cloves garlic, crushed
1 jalapeño pepper, minced,
   seeds removed
2 cups bottled barbecue sauce
¼ cup white vinegar
¼ cup Worcestershire sauce
2 tablespoons brown sugar
1 teaspoon salt
2 tablespoons liquid smoke
   flavoring

Salt and pepper the brisket. In a large Dutch oven, sear the meat on all sides, over high heat. Reduce heat and add enough water to cover the meat. Add onion, garlic, and jalapeño. Bring to a boil. Reduce heat and simmer, covered, for 2 hours.

Remove the meat and reserve the liquid. Preheat oven to 250°F. Return brisket to pot. Combine barbecue sauce, vinegar, Worcestershire sauce, brown sugar, salt, and smoke flavoring. Pour mixture over meat. Cover and bake for 4 hours. While brisket is cooking, place reserved liquid in a saucepan and reduce by two-thirds over medium-high heat. Set aside and keep warm.

Remove brisket from pot and let stand for 15 minutes before slicing. Pour reduced liquid over the sliced brisket and serve.

Leftover Roasts

Whenever you make a roast and get tired of leftovers, cut up the remaining meat in slices or cubes and freeze for future use in salads, sandwiches, or stir-fries.

St. Patrick's Day Corned Beef & Cabbage

Serves: 10

>5 pounds corned beef, bottom round or brisket
>2 quarts water
>1 large onion, chopped
>¼ teaspoon garlic powder
>¼ teaspoon Tabasco sauce
>1 teaspoon dill weed
>3 bay leaves
>2 cinnamon sticks
>5 whole cloves
>1 orange, thinly sliced
>6 large potatoes
>1 large head (about 3 pounds) cabbage, cored

Place meat in a large ovenproof Dutch oven. Add the water and bring to a boil. Cover, reduce heat, and simmer for about 30 minutes.

Stir in onion, garlic powder, Tabasco, dill, bay leaves, cinnamon, cloves, and orange slices. Bring to a boil. Cover, reduce heat, and simmer for 3 to 3½ hours longer or until meat is very tender when pierced.

Spoon off the solidified fat. Remove the meat and strain liquid through a fine strainer or colander lined with cheesecloth. Return broth to pan, add meat, and bring to a boil. Cut the potatoes in half and carefully drop into boiling broth. Reduce heat and simmer for 10 to 12 minutes. Cut cabbage into wedges and carefully drop into broth; simmer for 5 more minutes.

New England Boiled Brisket Dinner

Serves: 6

>3½ pound beef brisket, whole, trimmed
>5 whole cloves garlic, peeled
>3 medium onions
>3 bay leaves
>12 whole peppercorns
>¼ teaspoon salt
>1 28-ounce can beef broth
>½ fresh lemon, peeled
>5 cups water
>2 leeks, white and yellow parts
>3 large carrots
>3 baking potatoes, quartered
>2 bulbs kohlrabi, peeled and cut into several pieces
>1 bulb fennel, quartered
>1 cabbage head, cut into ten wedges

In a large kettle, combine trimmed brisket, garlic, onions, bay leaves, peppercorns, salt, beef broth, lemon, and water. Make sure beef is covered with liquid; if not, add water to cover. Bring to a boil. Reduce heat to a simmer; cover and cook for 2 to 2½ hours. Remove from heat and allow to cool. Refrigerate overnight.

The following day, skim off all fat that has accumulated on the surface. Bring mixture to a boil. Reduce heat to a simmer. Add leeks, carrots, potatoes, kohlrabi, fennel and cabbage. Simmer for about 20 minutes. Cabbage should be tender but crisp.

Remove vegetables from kettle and arrange on a deep serving platter. Remove brisket and shred into pieces. Discard the bay leaves, lemon, and peppercorns. Serve brisket with about 1 cup of the broth.

New England Boiled Dinner

Serves: 6

1 2½- to 3-pound corned beef brisket
1½ teaspoons whole black peppercorns
2 bay leaves
6 medium carrots, cut into chunks
3 medium potatoes, quartered lengthwise
3 medium parsnips, peeled and cut into
    chunks
6 small onions
½ of a medium cabbage, cut in wedges

Mustard Sauce:
1½ cups milk
4 teaspoons cornstarch
2 tablespoons horseradish mustard

Trim fat from meat. Place meat in a Dutch oven; add juices and spices from package. Add enough water to cover meat. Add peppercorns and bay leaves. Bring to boiling; reduce heat. Simmer, covered, for 2 hours.

Add carrots, potatoes, parsnips, and onions to Dutch oven. Return to boiling; reduce heat. Simmer, covered, for 10 minutes. Add cabbage and cook about 20 minutes more or until vegetables are tender.

Remove meat and vegetables from liquid; discard liquid and bay leaves. Slice meat across the grain. Serve meat and vegetables with mustard sauce.

To make mustard sauce: Stir together milk and cornstarch in a small saucepan. Cook and stir until thickened and bubbly. Cook and stir for 2 minutes more. Stir in mustard. Heat through. Makes about 1½ cups.

Creamy Dijon Beef & Noodles

Serves: 6

1½ pounds boneless lean beef
Black pepper
5 tablespoons butter
1 medium-size onion, finely chopped
½ pound mushrooms, thinly sliced
3 tablespoons all-purpose flour
1 cup beef broth
1 tablespoon Dijon mustard
¼ teaspoon freshly grated nutmeg or
    ground nutmeg
½ cup whipping cream
Hot cooked, buttered noodles
Chopped parsley for garnish

Cut beef across grain in ¼-inch-thick slanting slices. Sprinkle meat generously with pepper.

In a wide frying pan over medium-high heat, melt 1 tablespoon of the butter. Add onion and cook, stirring occasionally, until soft. Add half the meat and cook, stirring, for

(continued)

about 5 minutes or until well browned. Remove from pan and set aside. Repeat, using 1 more tablespoon of the butter and remaining meat; remove from pan.

Over medium heat, melt remaining 3 tablespoons butter. Add mushrooms and cook, stirring, until soft. Blend in flour and cook, stirring, until bubbly. Gradually pour in broth and continue cooking and stirring until sauce boils and thickens. Stir in mustard, meat-onion mixture, nutmeg, and cream; stir until heated through. Serve over noodles and garnish with parsley.

Beef & Rib Bucco

Serves: 6

> 4 to 6 marrow-filled beef bones, cut in
>   3 to 4-inch lengths
> 6 pounds lean beef short ribs, cut in
>   3 to 4-inch lengths
> 3 quarts water
> 8 to 10 sprigs parsley
> 1 large onion, studded with
>   6 whole cloves
> 4 cloves garlic
> 1 bay leaf
> 1 teaspoon salt
> 1 teaspoon thyme leaves
> 6 medium-size new potatoes
> 6 small turnips, cut into chunks
> 6 medium-size carrots, sliced
> 6 leeks, sliced
> Prepared hot mustard or horseradish

Arrange beef bones in a large, deep, 10- or 12-quart heat-resistant casserole or Dutch oven. Place short ribs on top. Add water, parsley, onion studded with cloves, garlic, bay leaf, salt, and thyme. Bring to a boil. Cover, reduce heat, and simmer for 2 to 2½ hours or until meat is tender.

When meat is tender, add all vegetables except leeks and push them down into liquid. Cover and simmer for 30 to 40 more minutes or until vegetables are tender. During the last 15 minutes, add leeks to meat and vegetables.

With a slotted spoon, carefully lift vegetables and meat from broth and transfer to a warm serving platter; keep hot. If desired, shake marrow from bones onto platter before discarding bones.

Open-Face Beef Stroganoff Sandwiches

Serves: 4

> 1 4-ounce can mushroom stems and
>   pieces, drained
> 1½ cups leftover beef gravy or 18-ounce
>   jar prepared beef gravy
> ½ cup sour cream
> 8 thin slices roast beef
> 4 slices bread

In a large skillet over medium heat, stir mushrooms and gravy until hot. Stir in sour cream until smooth. Add roast beef slices and cook until heated through. Top each slice of bread with two roast beef slices and some gravy.

Beef and Bean Burritos

Makes: 12 burritos

> 2 tablespoons olive oil
> 1 onion, chopped
> 2 pounds lean ground beef
> 2 cloves garlic, minced
> 1 tablespoon chili powder
> 1 teaspoon cumin
> Salt and pepper to taste
> 1 8-ounce can tomato sauce
> 1 31-ounce can refried beans
> 12 large flour tortillas

Sauté onion in oil until tender. Add beef and garlic and cook until beef is no longer pink. Drain. Add chili powder, cumin, and salt and pepper. Stir in tomato sauce and simmer 5 minutes. Add refried beans and cook and stir until well blended. Set aside to cool completely.

Preheat oven to 350°F. Divide meat mixture into 12 portions. Soften tortillas according to package instructions, and place a portion of meat on each. Roll up, burrito style, and arrange in a 9 x 13-inch baking dish. Cover with a sheet of aluminum foil. Bake for 20 minutes or until burritos are slightly browned.

Slow-Cook Texas Barbecued Beef Sandwiches

Serves: 8

> 1 4-pound boneless chuck roast, trimmed
> $\frac{1}{2}$ cup water
> 1 14-ounce bottle ketchup
> 10 ounces cola
> $\frac{1}{4}$ cup Worcestershire sauce
> 2 tablespoons prepared mustard
> 2 tablespoons liquid smoke
> $\frac{1}{4}$ teaspoon hot sauce
> 8 hamburger buns

Cook roast with $\frac{1}{2}$ cup water in a 5-quart slow cooker on high 8 hours or until tender.

Drain roast, reserving 1 cup drippings in slow cooker. Shred the meat, removing and discarding fat, and return to slow cooker. Stir in ketchup and next 5 ingredients, and cook on high 1 hour. Serve on buns.

Quick Microwave Beef Stew

Serves: 3 to 4

> 2 to $2\frac{1}{2}$ cups cut-up cooked stew beef
>   (about 1 pound cooked beef)
> 4 medium carrots cut into $2\frac{1}{2}$-inch strips
> 3 medium potatoes, pared and cut into
> $1\frac{1}{2}$-inch pieces
> 1 cup sliced celery
> 1 envelope onion soup mix

(continued)

3 tablespoons unbleached flour
2¼ cups water

Mix all ingredients in 2½-quart casserole. Cover and microwave on high to boiling, 10 to 12 minutes; stir. Cover and let stand 5 minutes. Microwave again until vegetables are tender, 10 to 12 minutes more, stirring every 5 minutes.

Microwave Beef Burgundy Stew

Serves: 6

2 slices bacon
4 teaspoons unbleached flour
½ teaspoon instant beef bouillon
¼ teaspoon crushed dried basil
½ pound beef stew meat, cut into
  ½-inch cubes
7½ ounces canned tomatoes, cut up
¼ cup dry red wine
½ cup frozen pearl onions
8 small whole fresh mushrooms

In a 1-quart casserole microwave bacon, loosely covered, on high power for 2 to 2½ minutes or until done. Drain bacon, reserving drippings in casserole. Crumble bacon and set aside.

Stir flour, bouillon granules, and basil into drippings. Add beef, undrained tomatoes, and wine; mix well. Microwave, covered, on high power for 2 minutes. Cook, covered, on 50 percent power for 15 minutes, stirring twice. Stir in onions and mushrooms. Cook, covered, on 50 percent power for 12 to 18 minutes or until meat and vegetables are tender, stirring twice. Sprinkle crumbled bacon atop and serve.

Peeling Pearl Onions

Peeling onions is bad enough without feeling like you need a microscope to get the work done. When using raw onions, cook them first in boiling water for 3 minutes. Plunge into cold water. Remove them from the water and cut off the ends before easily removing the skins.

Bombay Beef Curry

Serves: 8

2 tablespoons butter
3 onions, sliced
2 cloves garlic, chopped
1 teaspoon ground cardamom
1 tablespoon ground coriander
1 teaspoon ground cumin
1 teaspoon dry mustard
1½ teaspoons salt
1 teaspoon pepper
2 tablespoons cider vinegar
3 pounds boneless stew beef, trimmed of
  excess fat and cut into 1-inch cubes
3 tomatoes, chopped
3 cups boiling water, in which 3 beef
  bouillon cubes have been dissolved
1½ cups uncooked white rice

In a heavy kettle, heat the butter until brown. Add the onion and garlic, and cook until translucent. Combine the dry seasonings and add them to the onion-garlic mixture. Add the vinegar. Add the beef and tomatoes. Simmer the mixture, tightly covered, for about an hour.

Add the bouillon and continue to simmer the meat for another hour.

Stir in the rice and cook, tightly covered, for 30 minutes, or until the beef and rice are tender and the liquid is absorbed.

Beef Burgundy

Serves: 10

1 teaspoon salt
½ teaspoon pepper
½ teaspoon thyme
⅔ cup flour
8 pounds lean boneless beef (chuck,
  round, etc.), cut into 2-inch cubes
6 slices bacon, chopped
6 tablespoons butter, divided
1 cup chopped onions
2 cloves garlic, minced
½ cup chopped carrots
2 tablespoons chopped parsley
2 tablespoons tomato paste
24 small whole peeled white onions
2 cups Burgundy wine, divided
1 cup beef stock
12 mushroom caps
Lemon juice

Mix the salt, pepper, and thyme with the flour. Dredge the beef cubes in the seasoned flour. In a large ovenproof skillet, sauté the chopped bacon until crisp. Add the beef and brown. Remove beef and bacon with a slotted spoon and set aside. Add 2 tablespoons of the butter to the skillet and sauté the chopped onions, garlic, carrots, and parsley for 3 minutes. Stir in the tomato paste. Set aside.

Preheat oven to 275°F. Rinse the skillet with a little wine. Melt the remaining butter and lightly brown the whole onions. Add about ½ cup of the wine, cover the skillet,

(continued)

and cook over low heat for 10 minutes. Mix the remaining wine with the stock and pour over the meat. Add the beef and chopped onion mixture back to the pan. Cover, and cook for 2 hours.

Raise the oven temperature to 350°F and continue to cook for 1 hour.

Add the mushrooms to the casserole, sprinkle with lemon juice, and bake, uncovered, for 20 minutes more.

Tangy Short Rib Barbecue

Serves: 8

> *5 pounds beef short ribs*
> *2 tablespoons vegetable oil*
> *1 cup chopped onions*
> *1¼ cups ketchup*
> *¾ cup water*
> *¼ cup Worcestershire sauce*
> *¼ cup red wine vinegar*
> *2 tablespoons brown sugar*
> *2 teaspoons salt*

Preheat oven to 450°F. Cut ribs into individual portions, about 2½ inches wide; trim excess fat. Place ribs on a rack in an aluminum foil-lined roasting pan; bake until browned, about 20 minutes.

Reduce oven temperature to 350°F. Remove beef and rack from the pan; pour off the fat. Return beef to the pan without the rack.

Heat oil in a saucepan; add onions and sauté 2 minutes. Stir in the ketchup, water, Worcestershire sauce, vinegar, brown sugar, and salt; bring to a boil. Reduce heat and simmer, uncovered, 2 minutes; pour over beef to coat. Cover and bake in 350°F oven until beef is fork-tender, about 2 hours, spooning sauce over beef once.

Arrange beef on a platter; serve with sauce from pan.

Barbecued Beef Ribs

Serves: 8

> *5 pounds beef short ribs, trimmed*
> *2 12-ounce bottles barbecue sauce*

Place ribs in a flat pan or dish. Pour sauce over ribs, turning to coat both sides; pierce meat with a large fork. Marinate for about 8 hours, turning once. Remove ribs from marinade and brush off excess sauce to avoid burning.

Broil or cook over coals for 10 minutes. Turn over, brush with more sauce, and cook 4 to 5 minutes more. Heat remaining sauce and serve with ribs.

Ribs may be cooked in a covered pan in a 350°F oven for 1½ hours, if desired.

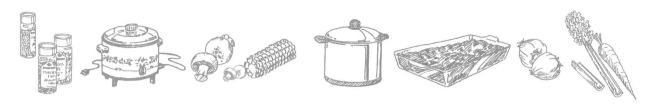

Pork

"The other white meat" lends itself quite well to many one-pot methods, whether it's cooked on top of the stove, slow-cooked in a Crockpot, or even baked in a casserole. The flavor of pork is especially enhanced by the addition of fruits and sweet spices, and the recipes here demonstrate this particularly well.

Salsa Pork and Potato Stew

Serves: 6 to 8

> 1 3-pound shoulder of pork (trimmed of all fat)
> 3 large onions, quartered
> 10 whole cloves
> 1 cinnamon stick
> 10 black peppercorns
> 3 to 4 cloves garlic, minced
> 1 teaspoon whole cumin seeds
> Assortment of whole, fresh chili peppers of your choice
> 5 medium new potatoes, peeled and quartered
> 2 tablespoons white vinegar

In the container of a large Crockpot, place the pork, onions, cloves, cinnamon, peppercorns, garlic, cumin, and chili peppers. Add enough cold water to cover all. Cover and cook on low setting 3 hours.

Stir, and add the potatoes to the mixture. Cook for about 1½ hours longer. Remove cloves, cinnamon, peppercorns and chili peppers, and five minutes before serving, add the vinegar.

Pork with Horseradish Sauce

 Serves: 6

> ½ teaspoon salt
> ½ teaspoon pepper
> ½ cup all-purpose flour
> 2 pounds lean boneless pork, cut into bite-size pieces
> 2 tablespoons butter
> 2 tablespoons oil
> 1 onion, chopped
> 1 carrot, thinly sliced
> 1 rib celery, thinly sliced
> ½ teaspoon powdered clove
> 2 cups hot water in which 2 beef bouillon cubes have been dissolved
> ½ cup cider vinegar
> ¼ cup prepared horseradish

(continued)

Combine the salt and pepper with the flour. Dredge the pork in the seasoned flour. In a heavy kettle, heat the butter and oil and brown the meat. Remove and set aside.

In the remaining fat, cook the vegetables until the onion is translucent. Stir in the clove. Put the meat back into the pot. Add the bouillon and vinegar; bring them to a boil. Reduce the heat, and simmer the stew, covered, for $1\frac{1}{2}$ hours, or until the pork is tender. Remove the casserole from the heat, stir in the horseradish, and serve.

Pork Schnitzel

Serves: 4

> 1 pound pork cutlets
> 1 teaspoon salt
> 1 teaspoon pepper
> $\frac{1}{2}$ cup flour
> 2 eggs, beaten
> $1\frac{1}{4}$ cups dry bread crumbs
> Oil for frying

Pound cutlets as thin as possible. Sprinkle with salt and pepper. Set up an assembly line with flour on one plate, eggs on another, and crumbs on a third. Coat each cutlet with flour, then egg, then bread crumbs.

Heat $\frac{1}{4}$ inch of oil in a large skillet over medium heat. Add as many cutlets as will fit without crowding. Cook until golden brown on each side, about $1\frac{1}{2}$ minutes. Drain cutlets on paper towels.

Pork Casserole with Cabbage

Serves: 8

> 2 pounds pork sirloin cut into $\frac{1}{2}$-inch cubes
> $\frac{1}{4}$ cup all-purpose flour
> 2 tablespoons caraway seeds
> $\frac{1}{4}$ cup olive oil
> 1 tablespoon paprika
> 1 small onion, chopped
> $\frac{1}{2}$ medium head white cabbage, shredded
> $\frac{1}{2}$ cup tomato purée
> $\frac{1}{4}$ cup white wine vinegar
> 1 cup cold water
> salt to taste
> $\frac{1}{2}$ cup sour cream

In a paper bag or sealable plastic bag, toss the meat cubes in flour and caraway seeds. In a large heavy skillet, heat the oil and sauté the meat with a lid on pan. Shake from time to time and cook until brown for 10 minutes.

Add the paprika and sliced onions. Toss a few minutes, then add cabbage, tomato purée, vinegar, and water. Season with salt. Simmer gently for $1\frac{1}{2}$ hours until the meat is tender. Add sour cream just before serving.

Cajun-Oriental Pork Chops

Serves: 6

> 6 thick pork chops
> 1 teaspoon salt
> 1 teaspoon red cayenne pepper
> $1\frac{1}{2}$ cups dry white wine

1 cup chopped bell pepper
1 cup chopped onions
1 clove garlic, chopped
3 tablespoons soy sauce
1 15-ounce can pineapple chunks
Hot cooked rice

Sprinkle the chops with salt and red pepper. Brown them slowly in a large heavy skillet. Add wine, bell pepper, onion, and garlic. Cover and simmer for 25 to 30 minutes.

Remove pork chops, and keep them warm. Add the soy sauce and syrup from the pineapple. Stir and simmer until fairly thick. Add the pineapple chunks and bring to a boil. Serve over pork chops and hot cooked rice.

Pork Stroganoff

Serves: 6

$\frac{1}{2}$ teaspoon salt
$\frac{1}{2}$ teaspoon pepper
$\frac{1}{2}$ cup all-purpose flour
2 pounds lean boneless pork, cut into
*   2-inch chunks*
4 tablespoons butter
2 cloves garlic, minced
2 onions, finely chopped
$1\frac{1}{2}$ cups hot water, in which 2 chicken
*   bouillon cubes have been dissolved*
2 teaspoons Worcestershire sauce
$1\frac{1}{2}$ cups sour cream
$\frac{1}{4}$ cup chopped parsley for garnish

Combine the salt and pepper with the flour. Dredge the pork chunks in the seasoned flour. In a large saucepan, heat the butter until brown. Cook the garlic until the butter is translucent. Add the meat and cook until browned.

Add the onion, bouillon, and Worcestershire sauce. Bring the liquid to a boil, reduce the heat, and simmer the meat, covered, for 30 minutes, or until it is tender.

Stir in the sour cream and cook the dish only long enough to heat it through, approximately 10 minutes. Adjust the seasonings. Garnish the dish with parsley.

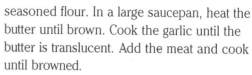

Pork Chops

Pork chops from the shoulder tend to be less expensive than chops from the loin, but they also have more bone by weight and therefore less meat. When choosing the type of pork chop for your one-pot creation, let the prices and your taste decide.

Hungarian Pork Chops

Serves: 6

½ teaspoon salt
½ teaspoon pepper
½ cup all-purpose flour
6 shoulder pork chops, 1-inch thick each
4 tablespoons butter
4 medium onions, chopped
2 cloves garlic, chopped
2 tablespoons paprika, or more, to taste
1 cup hot water, in which 1 chicken
    bouillon cube has been dissolved
1 cup sour cream
1 tablespoon dried dill

Mix the salt and pepper with the flour. Reserve 2 tablespoons of the mixture for later. Dredge the pork chops in the seasoned flour. In a heavy skillet, heat the butter until brown. Add the chops and brown for about five minutes on each side. Remove them and set aside.

In the remaining fat, cook the onion and garlic until translucent. Add the paprika and bouillon to the onion mixture and, over high heat, deglaze the pan. Put the chops back into the pan. Bring the liquid to a boil. Reduce the heat, and simmer the chops, covered, for 45 minutes, or until they are tender. Remove them and keep them warm.

Stir the reserved flour into the sour cream. When smooth, add the dill. Add the sour cream to the skillet and, over medium heat,

cook the sauce, stirring constantly, until it is thickened and smooth. Pour the sauce over the chops and serve.

Pork Chops in Wine Sauce

Serves: 4

1 teaspoon sage
1 teaspoon rosemary
2 cloves garlic, chopped
1 teaspoon salt
1 teaspoon freshly ground pepper
4 1-inch-thick pork chops, about ⅓ pound
    each
2 tablespoons butter
1 tablespoon olive oil
¾ cup dry white wine

Combine sage, rosemary, garlic, salt, and pepper. Press a little of this mixture firmly into both sides of each of the pork chops. Melt butter and oil in a heavy 10-inch skillet. Brown chops on both sides, turning carefully with tongs. Remove and pour off all but a small amount of fat from pan. Add two-thirds of the wine and bring to boil. Return chops to pan. Cover, reduce heat, and simmer until chops are tender when pressed with tip of knife, about 25 to 30 minutes. When ready to serve, remove chops to heated plate. Add remaining wine to skillet and boil down to a syrupy glaze. Pour over chops.

Cheesy Pork & Rice Skillet

Serves: 6

  1 12-ounce package ground pork sausage
  1 16-ounce package coleslaw mix
  1 tablespoon vegetable oil
  1 tablespoon all-purpose flour
  1 8-ounce carton sour cream
  1 6-ounce package long-grain and wild rice
     mix, cooked
  1 10-ounce can diced tomatoes and green
     chilies, with juice
  2 cups shredded Cheddar cheese

Brown sausage in a large skillet, stirring until it crumbles. Drain sausage; set aside. Wipe skillet clean. Sauté coleslaw mix in hot oil in skillet until crisp and tender; drain. Preheat oven to 375°F.

Stir flour into sour cream. Layer rice, sausage, coleslaw mix, sour cream mixture, tomatoes and green chilies, and cheese in a lightly greased 13 x 9-inch baking dish. Bake for 30 minutes or until thoroughly heated.

Polish Pork Stew

Serves: 4

  1 pound sauerkraut
     (fresh or canned)
  1 tablespoon bacon fat
  ½ cup chopped onions
  ½ pound mushrooms, sliced or chopped
  1 medium apple, peeled, cored, and
     chopped
  1½ cups canned tomatoes
  1 cup chicken stock
  ½ pound kielbasa, cut into 1-inch pieces
  1 cup diced cooked pork
  ⅛ teaspoon paprika
  Salt to taste
  1½ teaspoons sugar
  1 tablespoon flour

Drain the sauerkraut and rinse it under running cold water. Set aside. In a large skillet, heat the fat for one minute. Add the onions and sauté until they become translucent. Add the mushrooms and sauté for 2 minutes. Add the apple and sauté for 1 minute. Add the sauerkraut, tomatoes, and stock and bring to a boil. Reduce the heat, and let simmer gently. Add the kielbasa and pork, and cook over low heat for 10 minutes, stirring often. Stir in the paprika, salt, sugar, and flour and mix thoroughly. Simmer for 1½ hours, covered. If the mixture appears dry, add a little more stock.

Barbecued Ribs Oriental

Serves: 6

  5 pounds pork spare ribs
  1½ teaspoons salt, divided
  1 beef bouillon cube
  ¾ cup boiling water
  1 teaspoon olive oil

(continued)

Chinese Glossary

Hoisin Sauce: A thick, dark brown jam-like semi-sweet sauce available in jars or cans in Chinese grocery stores or in the Oriental food section of large supermarkets like Safeway. It's made with soybeans and spices. There is no substitute.

Five-Spice Powder: This is a fine powder usually made from ground star anise, fennel seed, Sichuan peppercorns, cloves, and cinnamon. The pungency varies depending on the mix of ingredients and age of the powder. A fresh, well-made mix should be quite pungent. It's also available in Chinese grocery stores or in large supermarkets in the Oriental food section.

Chinese Rice: To make Chinese-style rice without a rice cooker: Put 1 cup of rinsed Chinese rice and 1.2 cups of cold water into a saucepan (i.e. 20 percent more water than rice). Cover and bring to a simmer over slow heat. Let the rice cook, undisturbed for 12 to 15 minutes. Turn off the heat and let the rice sit for at least 5 minutes before serving.

1 8-ounce can crushed pineapple, undrained
$\frac{1}{4}$ cup dark brown sugar, firmly packed
1 teaspoon onion powder
$\frac{1}{4}$ teaspoon garlic powder
2 tablespoons Worcestershire sauce
2 tablespoons cornstarch
$\frac{1}{4}$ cup cold water

Preheat oven to 375°F. Cut ribs to form individual portions; sprinkle with 1 teaspoon salt. Place ribs on a rack in a shallow baking pan; bake until almost tender, 1$\frac{1}{2}$ to 2 hours. Drain off fat.

Meanwhile, dissolve bouillon cube in boiling water in a medium-size saucepan. Add oil, pineapple with juice, brown sugar, onion powder, garlic powder, Worcestershire sauce, and remaining salt; bring to a boil. Reduce heat and simmer, uncovered, 5 minutes.

Combine cornstarch with cold water in a small bowl; stir into sauce mixture. Cook and stir until thickened. Spoon sauce over drained, baked ribs.

Increase oven temperature to 425°F; bake until nicely glazed, about 30 minutes.

Spareribs in a Pot

Serves: 6 to 8

One rack of ribs, 8 to 10 pounds

Sauce:

6 tablespoons hoisin sauce
2 teaspoons five-spice powder, depending
    on pungency the powder
3 tablespoons dry mustard
3 tablespoons dry cooking sherry
3 large cloves garlic, minced
2 tablespoons very finely chopped fresh
    gingerroot, peeled
1 tablespoon white sugar
¼ cup + 2 tablespoons ketchup
¼ cup soy sauce

Have your butcher cut through the cartilaginous "heel" end of the rack of ribs with a meat saw, but leave it attached to the rack.

At home, prepare the rack by first trimming off as much of the fat as you can. Then cut the heel off the rack following the joint where it attaches to the rib bone structure. Cut the rack into individual ribs and cut the "heel" into riblets. Wash and dry thoroughly.

Mix all of the sauce ingredients in a bowl and slather the sauce over the ribs.

Put the ribs into a large, heavy duty roasting pan so they do not overlap. Then marinate them for 3 to 4 hours or overnight. Bring ribs to room temperature and then bake in a 300°F oven for 2 hours. Baste

with a bulb baster from time to time. Try not to disturb the ribs while they're cooking so the sauce will stick to each rib evenly.

To serve, remove ribs from the roasting pan and place on a warm serving platter.

Tip the pan so the fat runs to one end and scrap any remaining sauce over the ribs.

Spare Ribs

When deciding how many ribs to buy at the supermarket, the rule of thumb is to allow 1 pound for each serving. Loin ribs are the meatiest spare ribs, and are therefore more expensive, but you may need only ¾ pound of ribs per serving.

Sausage

No matter what kind of sausage you choose—hot or sweet, Italian or Polish—this favorite meat adds a nice zip to a one-pot dish. Sausage is a common ingredient in one-pot meals. Experiment with different kinds of sausage, adding a few slices to any of the other one-pot recipes in the book you think might benefit from it.

Sausage Skillet Supper

Serves: 4

4 small red potatoes, cut in $\frac{1}{2}$-inch cubes
4 Italian-style sausages, cut into $\frac{1}{4}$-inch slices
1 onion, diced
1 green bell pepper, cut into lengths
1 red pepper, cut into lengths

In saucepan, cover potatoes and sausage with water; simmer, covered, until sausage is fully cooked, about 20 minutes. Drain off water; add vegetables to potatoes and sausage in saucepan. Simmer 10 minutes, stirring occasionally.

Polish Reuben Casserole

Serves: 8

2 $10\frac{3}{4}$-ounce cans condensed cream of mushroom soup
$1\frac{1}{3}$ cups milk
$\frac{1}{2}$ cup chopped onion
1 tablespoon prepared mustard
2 16-ounce cans sauerkraut, rinsed and drained
1 8-ounce package uncooked medium-width noodles
$1\frac{1}{2}$ pounds Polish sausage, fully cooked, cut into $\frac{1}{2}$-inch pieces
2 cups (8 ounces) shredded Swiss cheese
$\frac{3}{4}$ cup whole-wheat bread crumbs
2 tablespoons butter, melted

Preheat oven to 350°F.

Combine soup, milk, onion, and mustard in medium bowl; blend well. Spread sauerkraut in greased 13 x 9-inch pan. Top with uncooked noodles. Spoon soup mixture evenly over top. Top with sausage, then cheese. Combine crumbs and butter in small bowl; sprinkle over top. Cover pan tightly with aluminum foil. Bake 1 hour or until noodles are tender.

Sausage & Potato Melange

Serves: 4

1 pound fully cooked sausage, thinly sliced
About 6 tablespoons butter
1½ pounds potatoes, sliced into ¼-inch-
  thick slices
1 large onion, sliced
½ cup chopped celery
½ cup chopped dill pickle

¼ cup dill pickle liquid
1 tablespoon sugar
½ teaspoon caraway seeds
½ teaspoon dry mustard
Salt and pepper to taste
Chopped parsley for garnish

In a wide frying pan over medium heat, cook sausage until browned. With a slotted spoon, remove sausage and set aside.

In the same pan, melt 3 tablespoons of the butter. Add potato slices, a few at a time, to be sure each slice gets coated with butter; turn frequently, adding more butter as needed to coat potatoes thoroughly. Add onion and cook, turning often, until onion and potatoes are golden. Gently stir in celery, dill pickle, and browned sausage.

Combine pickle liquid, sugar, caraway seeds, and mustard; pour over potato mixture. Cover, reduce heat to low, and cook for 20 to 25 minutes or until potatoes are tender when pierced; turn often. Season to taste with salt and pepper. Garnish with parsley.

Sauerkraut Casserole

Serves: 4

1 pound mild Italian sausage, cut into
  1-inch slices
1 large onion, chopped
2 apples, peeled and quartered
1 27-ounce can sauerkraut, undrained
1 cup water
½ cup brown sugar, packed
2 teaspoons caraway seeds
Fresh parsley (optional)

In a large ovenproof skillet, cook sausage and onion until sausage is brown and onion is tender; drain. Preheat oven to 350°F.

Stir in apples, sauerkraut, water, brown sugar, and caraway seeds. Remove from heat. Cover and bake for 1 hour. Garnish with snipped parsley if desired.

Easy Bean and Sausage Casserole

Serves: 8

1 10-ounce package frozen lima beans
1 21-ounce can baked beans
1 15-ounce can kidney beans, drained
1 15-ounce can Great Northern beans,
  drained
1 small onion, chopped
1 pound smoked sausage, cut in 1-inch pieces
¾ cup ketchup
2 tablespoons packed brown sugar
½ teaspoon salt

(continued)

¹/₂ teaspoon dry mustard
¹/₈ teaspoon pepper

Preheat oven to 400°F. Rinse frozen lima beans with cold water to separate. Mix lima, baked, kidney, and Northern beans, along with onion and sausage in ungreased 2¹/₂-quart casserole. Mix remaining ingredients; stir into bean mixture. Cover and bake 40 to 50 minutes or until hot and bubbly.

Ratatouille

Serves: 8

1 pound Italian sausage, cut into
*   1¹/₂ inch pieces*
Cooking oil
2 medium onions, sliced
1 medium green pepper, cut into strips
2 cloves garlic, sliced
2 pounds zucchini, sliced
3 medium tomatoes, peeled, seeded, and
*   cut in chunks*
1 teaspoon salt
¹/₄ teaspoon pepper
¹/₂ cup shredded Cheddar cheese

In a large skillet, fry the sausage; set aside, and discard drippings. Add the cooking oil to the pan; cook onion, green pepper, and garlic. Add the zucchini; cook about 10 more minutes. Add tomatoes and salt and pepper. Return the sausage to the pan. Cook about 15 minutes, stirring occasionally, then sprinkle cheese on top. Cook until cheese is melted.

Italian Sausage & Veal Dish

Serves: 6

2 tablespoons olive oil
3 mild Italian sausages, about 3 ounces
*   each, casings removed and cut*
*   in ³/₄-inch slices*
1³/₄ pounds boneless veal, cut into
*   1³/₄-inch cubes*
1 medium-size onion, chopped
¹/₂ pound mushrooms, quartered
1 cup beef broth
1 medium green bell pepper, seeded and
*   chopped*
¹/₂ cup dry sherry, or additional beef broth
1 cup sour cream
1 tablespoon all-purpose flour
Salt, pepper, and ground nutmeg to taste

Heat oil in a wide frying pan over medium-high heat. Add sausages and veal and cook, stirring occasionally, until well browned. Add onions and mushrooms and cook until onions are soft.

Stir in broth, bell pepper, and sherry. Bring to a boil. Cover, reduce heat, and simmer for about 1 hour or until meat is tender when pierced. Increase heat to high and cook, uncovered, until liquid is reduced to about 1 cup.

Combine sour cream and flour; gently stir into veal mixture until well blended and heated through. Season to taste with salt, pepper, and nutmeg.

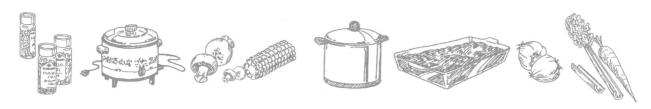

Ham

Ham is not just for Sunday dinners anymore! Especially when you can follow these one-pot recipes to streamline meal preparation and cut down on cooking time; after all, it's no longer necessary to turn on the oven and heat up the kitchen on hot summer days in order to enjoy a delicious succulent ham. Ham can be on the menu any day of the week.

Farmer's Supper

Serves: 6

1 ½ tablespoons olive oil
5 medium potatoes, peeled and thinly
    sliced
Salt and freshly ground pepper to taste
½ cup chopped onion
½ cup chopped green pepper
2 cups ham cut in julienne strips
6 eggs
½ cup Cheddar cheese, grated

Melt oil in large skillet. Spread half of the potato slices in skillet and sprinkle with salt and pepper to taste. Top with half the onion and green pepper; sprinkle with seasonings again. Arrange half of the meat on top; repeat layers. Cover and cook over low heat 20 minutes, or until potatoes are tender.

Break eggs on top; cover and cook until eggs are desired doneness, about 5 minutes. Remove from heat. Top with cheese and cover a minute or two until cheese starts to melt.

Casserole of Pumpkin with Ham

Serves: 6

3 cups peeled and thin sliced fresh
    pumpkin
Salt and pepper to taste
Dash of cinnamon and allspice
1 cup canned chicken broth
4 tablespoons olive oil
2 large onions, peeled and sliced
½ pound ham steak, diced
1 10-ounce box frozen whole kernel corn
Toasted pumpkin seeds for garnish

Slice peeled pieces of pumpkin as you would apples for pie. Put the sliced pumpkin in a 2 quart baking dish. Sprinkle with salt, pepper, some cinnamon and some allspice. Add broth; dot with oil; top with onions. Mix diced ham and corn; spread over top of onions. Cover and bake at 350 degrees for 40 minutes or until pumpkin is fork tender. Top with toasted pumpkin seeds. Serve hot.

Creamy Potato and Ham Casserole

Serves: 4

- 1 12-ounce can evaporated skimmed milk
- 1/2 teaspoon salt
- 1 tablespoon cornstarch
- 1/4 teaspoon pepper
- 1/4 teaspoon nutmeg
- 1/2 cup white wine
- 3 large baking potatoes, washed, sliced thin, but not peeled
- 1 cup grated Swiss cheese
- 2 tablespoons grated Parmesan cheese
- 1 small onion, chopped
- 4 ounces thin sliced deli ham
- 1 teaspoon oregano

Preheat oven to 350°F. In a medium saucepan, heat the milk, salt, cornstarch, pepper, and nutmeg until milk comes to a boil and the sauce thickens. Add the wine. Remove from heat and set aside.

Coat a 1 1/2-quart casserole dish with nonstick cooking spray. Layer half the potato slices in the bottom of the dish. Cover with cheeses, onion, ham, and oregano. Cover with remaining potatoes. Pour sauce over the top. Bake for 1 hour.

If desired, place casserole under broiler for 5 minutes to brown the top.

Piperade

Serves: 8

- 4 slices bacon, cut in small pieces
- 2 small green peppers, seeded and cut in julienne strips
- 2 medium-size tomatoes, peeled, seeded, and diced
- 2 cups (about 1/2 pound) coarsely chopped cooked ham
- 1/4 cup chopped parsley
- 16 eggs
- 1/4 cup water
- 1 teaspoon salt
- 1/4 teaspoon pepper

In a 12-inch frying pan over medium-low heat, cook bacon until crisp and browned. With a slotted spoon, remove bacon and set aside.

Increase heat to medium and add green pepper to pan drippings. Cook pepper until soft but still bright green. Stir in tomatoes, ham, and parsley; cook until heated through. With a slotted spoon, remove vegetable-ham mixture and set aside; keep warm.

Combine eggs, water, salt, and pepper; mix well. Pour into frying pan, reduce heat to low, and cook eggs, gently lifting cooked portion to allow uncooked portion to flow underneath. When eggs are almost set, distribute vegetables and ham over surface and continue cooking, gently shaking pan, until eggs are set to your liking. Sprinkle with bacon and serve from pan.

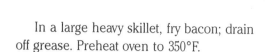

Creamy Corn & Bacon Casserole

Serves: 6

1 pound bacon, diced
2 cups bread crumbs
¼ cup minced onion
½ cup chopped green pepper
2 16.5-ounce cans cream-style corn

In a skillet, fry the bacon until lightly browned. Remove and set aside. Pour ⅛ to ¼ cup of the bacon drippings over bread crumbs; set aside. Discard all but 2 tablespoons of remaining drippings. Preheat oven to 350°F.

Sauté onion and green pepper in drippings until tender. Stir in corn and bacon. Spoon into a 1-quart baking dish; sprinkle with crumbs. Bake for 20 to 25 minutes or until bubbly and heated through.

Zucchini Bake

Serves: 4

4 slices bacon, chopped
3 cups cubed zucchini
1 small green pepper, chopped
1 onion, sliced
¼ cup long-grain rice (not Minute Rice)
3 tomatoes, sliced
4 slices Cheddar cheese
1 teaspoon sugar
¼ teaspoon salt
¼ teaspoon pepper

In a large heavy skillet, fry bacon; drain off grease. Preheat oven to 350°F.

Layer in casserole dish: zucchini, green pepper, onion, bacon, rice, tomato, and cheese, in that order. Sprinkle sugar, salt, and pepper. Bake for 1½ hours.

Full-flavor Herbs

Crushing dried herbs before you add them to a recipe will result in a stronger flavor. You can pinch them between your fingers or use a spoon to crush them on a plate before adding to the dish.

Veal

In a game of *Family Feud*, it's highly unlikely that veal would ever show up on the board given the category of "Popular Meats That Go in One-Pot Meals." But that would be a shame; veal benefits greatly from slow-cooking in a broth with a variety of spices that will complement it, and not overpower this tender meat, a fact you'll discover after cooking one of the following dishes.

Casserole of Veal

Serves: 8

2 tablespoons unsalted butter
1 cup thinly sliced onions
1 clove garlic, minced
⅓ cup all-purpose flour
½ teaspoon salt or to taste
½ teaspoon freshly ground pepper
¼ teaspoon paprika
3 pounds boneless veal stew meat, cut into 2-inch cubes
2 tablespoons unsalted butter
1 tablespoon olive oil
½ cup port, Marsala or other sweet red wine
1 16-ounce can tomatoes, drained and roughly chopped
½ cup chicken broth
½ teaspoon thyme, crumbled
18 pitted black olives
Salt and freshly ground pepper to taste
Garnish: Freshly chopped parsley

Preheat oven to 325 degrees. In Dutch oven or large casserole, heat butter; sauté onions and garlic over medium heat until soft and lightly golden; remove to bowl and set aside. Combine flour, salt, pepper and paprika; add veal cubes and toss to coat all over.

Add remaining butter and oil to casserole; sauté veal over medium high heat until golden. Add wine to deglaze pan, scraping brown particles up from bottom; add tomatoes, broth and thyme. Bring to boil, cover and bake 1½ hours or until veal is tender. Add olives, cover and continue to bake 10 minutes longer to heat through. Taste and adjust seasoning with salt and pepper. Serve garnished with chopped parsley.

Saltimbocca alla Genovese

Serves: 6

2 pounds veal scallops, sliced 1/4-inch thick, pounded thin
Salt and pepper

Fresh sage, dried sage, or ground sage
½ pound thin slices of prosciutto
Flour
4 tablespoons butter
Freshly ground pepper
1 cup Marsala or dry white wine
½ cup hot beef bouillon

Trim the veal scallops so they are all approximately the same size. (Save trimmings for sauces.) Sprinkle a little salt and pepper on each slice of meat. Place 2 or more leaves of fresh or dried sage on each veal slice, or sprinkle a scant ¼ teaspoon ground sage on each.

Cut prosciutto to the same size as veal slices. Top each veal slice with a prosciutto slice. Roll up and secure with toothpicks or tie with kitchen thread. Coat each veal roll lightly with flour, shaking off excess flour.

Divide butter between 2 large frying pans; heat it without browning. Over medium heat, cook veal rolls about 5 minutes, or until golden brown on all sides. Reduce heat and add ½ cup marsala and ¼ cup beef bouillon to each frying pan. Cover frying pans and cook for 5 to 10 minutes longer; cooking time depends on the size and thickness of the rolls. Shake the pans frequently to prevent sticking. If necessary, add a little more beef bouillon; there should be 1 to 2 tablespoons sauce for each veal scallop.

Transfer the cooked veal scallops to a heated serving dish and spoon the sauce over it. Serve immediately and very hot.

Osso Bucco

Serves: 6

6 tablespoons butter, divided
2 large onions, chopped
1 carrot, finely chopped
7 to 8 pounds meaty veal shanks with
*   marrow in bones, cut in 2-inch lengths*
*   (12 to 18 pieces)*
Salt
½ cup all-purpose flour
1½ cups dry white wine
1 to 1½ cups chicken broth

In a Dutch oven over medium-high heat, melt 1 tablespoon of the butter. Add onions and carrot and cook until onions are soft. Remove from pan and set aside.

Sprinkle the veal shanks with salt. Dust with flour and shake off excess. In pan over medium-high heat, melt remaining 5 tablespoons butter. Cook shanks, a few at a time, until well browned on all sides. Return vegetables and meat to pan, standing shanks on end with marrow sides up.

Pour in the wine and ¾ cup of the broth; bring to a boil. Cover, reduce heat, and simmer for 2 to 2½ hours or until meat is very tender when pierced. If sauce becomes too thick, add more broth.

With a slotted spoon, carefully remove meat and transfer to a warm serving platter; keep hot. Bring sauce to a boil, scraping brown particles free from pan; add broth as needed.

Lamb

Lamb is the meat most likely to be served in one of two ways: as chops or a roast. You can break with convention by trying any one—or all—of the following recipes that use lamb as the cornerstone of the dish. In fact, when a recipe calls for chops, try using lamb stew chunks instead, adjusting the cooking time accordingly: longer for large stew pieces, shorter for smaller ones.

Dilled Lamb

Serves: 6

> 3 pounds stewing lamb, trimmed of excess
>   fat and cut into bite-size pieces
> Cold water
> 1 bay leaf
> 6 sprigs fresh dill
> 6 sprigs parsley
> 1 1/2 teaspoons salt
> 6 peppercorns
> 1 teaspoon sugar
> 2 tablespoons butter
> 2 tablespoons flour
> 2 cups reserved stock
> 1/4 cup fresh dill
> 1 teaspoon white vinegar
> 2 teaspoons sugar
> Juice of 1 lemon
> 1 egg yolk, lightly beaten

Place the lamb in a heavy kettle. Add just enough cold water to cover the lamb. Over high heat, bring it to a boil, uncovered, and skim the surface. Reduce the heat to simmer. Add the bay leaf, 6 sprigs dill, parsley, salt, peppercorns, and sugar. Cook the meat, covered, for 1 1/2 hours, or until tender. Remove the bay leaf, dill, and parsley sprigs.

Drain the meat, reserving the stock. Arrange the lamb on a serving platter and keep it warm. In the same kettle, heat the butter. Stir in the flour, and cook the mixture over gentle heat for a few minutes. Gradually add the stock and cook the sauce, stirring constantly, until it is thickened and smooth.

Add the dill, vinegar, sugar, and lemon juice, stirring to blend the mixture well. Into the egg yolk, stir a little of the sauce, then stir the yolk mixture into the bulk of the sauce; do not allow it to boil. Pour the sauce over the warm lamb and serve.

Lamb Chop Skillet Dinner

Serves: 8

> 8 large lamb chops, $1/3$ pound each,
>   trimmed
> $1/2$ cup flour
> 2 tablespoons oil
> 2 tablespoons butter
> 1 large eggplant, peeled and cut into
>   8 slices
> 8 small onions
> 8 small potatoes
> 8 small firm whole tomatoes, peeled
> $1/2$ cup diced green peppers
> $1 1/2$ teaspoons salt
> $1/2$ teaspoon paprika
> $1/2$ teaspoon marjoram
> $1/4$ teaspoon basil
> $1/2$ teaspoon crumbled mint leaves
> 1 cup tomato sauce

Dredge the lamb chops in the flour. Heat the oil and butter in a large heavy skillet. Brown the chops on both sides in the hot oil, about four minutes per side. Add the eggplant slices to the skillet and cook for five minutes. Add the onions, potatoes, and tomatoes and sprinkle with the diced peppers. Add the salt, paprika, marjoram, basil, and mint leaves and stir into the vegetable mixture. Top with dabs of the tomato sauce. Cover, reduce the heat to low, and cook for 45 minutes to an hour, stirring occasionally.

Lamb Shanks

If lamb shanks are not readily available where you live, you can substitute veal shanks, which tend to be commonly available year-round. Cooking time remains the same, although the flavor may be more delicate, so you may want to add extra spice to compensate.

Orange Lamb Shanks

Serves: 6

> 5 large oranges
> 1 teaspoon salt
> $1/2$ teaspoon paprika
> 6 lamb shanks (about 5 pounds), with
>   bones cracked
> 2 tablespoons olive oil

(continued)

Doubling and Tripling Recipes

If you find a one-pot recipe that you really like, you may want to prepare two or three times the original recipe in order to freeze the dish in individual containers to cook for a busy dinner. Most of the recipes in *The Everything One-Pot Cookbook* can be doubled or tripled without affecting the quality of the dish. However, before you try a new dish on company, make it in its original quantity so you can see how the dish is supposed to look and taste. And be sure to allow extra time for preparation and cooking when you increase the quantity of a recipe.

1 clove garlic, minced
1 large onion, thinly sliced
2 teaspoons ground allspice
2 teaspoons cinnamon
1 tablespoon cornstarch
2 tablespoons water

Grate 2 teaspoons orange peel from 2 or 3 of the oranges. Squeeze 1 cup juice from the 2 or 3 oranges. Remove and discard peel and white membrane from remaining oranges and cut oranges into thin, crosswise slices. Set aside.

Sprinkle salt and paprika over lamb. Heat oil in a 6-quart Dutch oven over medium heat. Add lamb shanks, a few at a time, and cook, turning, until well browned. Add garlic and onion; cook until soft.

Stir in orange peel, orange juice, allspice, and cinnamon. Bring to a boil. Cover, reduce heat, and simmer, turning meat occasionally, for 2 to 2½ hours or until lamb is very tender when pierced. With slotted spoon, transfer meat to a warm platter.

Skim off and discard fat from pan. Mix cornstarch with water. Add cornstarch mixture to pan and cook, stirring constantly, until mixture boils and thickens. Spoon over lamb. Garnish with orange slices.

Tomato Lamb Shanks

Serves: 4

> 2 tablespoons olive oil
> 4 lamb shanks (about 1 pound each),
>   with bones cracked
> 2 cloves garlic, minced
> 1 large onion, sliced
> 1 large green pepper, seeded and thinly
>   sliced
> $3/4$ teaspoon thyme
> 1 teaspoon savory leaves
> 1 teaspoon salt
> $1/4$ teaspoon pepper
> 1 12-ounce can tomato juice
> $1/2$ cup dry red wine
> 3 tablespoons all-purpose flour
> 3 tablespoons water

Heat oil in a 5-quart Dutch oven over medium heat. Add shanks, a few at a time, and cook until well browned. Remove from pan and set aside.

To the pan juices, add garlic, onion, and green pepper. Cook, stirring, until vegetables are soft. Stir in thyme, savory, salt, pepper, tomato juice, and wine; add lamb. Bring to a boil. Cover, reduce heat, and simmer for 2 to $2 1/4$ hours or until meat is very tender when pierced.

Skim off and discard fat. Stir flour into water in a small bowl. Stir flour mixture into pan juices. Over medium heat, cook, stirring, until sauce boils and thickens.

Greek Lamb with Orzo

Serves: 6

> $1/4$ cup olive oil
> 3 pounds stewing lamb, cut into bite-size
>   pieces
> 2 onions, chopped
> 2 cloves garlic, chopped
> 1 teaspoon basil
> 1 bay leaf, crumbled
> 1 teaspoon thyme
> 2 teaspoons salt
> $1/2$ teaspoon freshly ground black pepper
> Juice and zest of 1 lemon
> 2 ripe tomatoes, peeled, seeded, and
>   chopped
> 1 6-ounce can tomato paste
> 6 cups water
> 1 1-pound box orzo

In a large heavy saucepan or kettle, heat the olive oil for about a minute. Add the lamb and brown it. Remove and reserve the meat.

In the same kettle, cook the onion and garlic until translucent. Replace the lamb and add all remaining ingredients except orzo. Bring the liquid to a boil, reduce the heat, and simmer the lamb, covered, for 1 hour, or until it is fork-tender. Remove the lamb pieces to a large serving bowl and keep it warm.

Over high heat, return the sauce to a boil. Add the pasta, stirring. Cook, uncovered, stirring often, for 12 minutes. Pour the sauce over the lamb.

Spring Lamb

The term spring lamb is used to describe a lamb that is no more than a year old, though it of course is derived from the days when a spring lamb was only available in the spring. Today, you can purchase spring lamb year-round; the color should be light pink and the texture should be smooth.

Acapulco Peanut Lamb

Serves: 6

$^1/_4$ cup olive oil
3 pounds stewing lamb, trimmed of excess
    fat and cut into bite-size pieces
Salt and freshly ground black pepper to
    taste

2 medium onions, chopped
1 clove garlic, minced
3 tomatoes, chopped
1 tablespoon sugar
$1^1/_2$ cups unsalted peanuts
$^1/_4$ cup chopped parsley
$^1/_2$ teaspoon nutmeg
$^1/_4$ teaspoon oregano
$^1/_4$ teaspoon thyme
$1^1/_2$ cups hot water, in which
    2 chicken bouillon cubes have
    been dissolved

Preheat oven to 325°F. In a flameproof casserole, heat the olive oil for about a minute. Add the lamb and brown it for 7 minutes, and season with salt and pepper. Remove and set aside. Discard all but 3 tablespoons of the fat.

In the reserved fat, cook the onion until translucent. Add the garlic, tomatoes, and sugar, and cook the mixture until the tomato liquid has evaporated. Add the peanuts to the tomato-onion mixture, together with the parsley and seasonings. Add the bouillon, stirring thoroughly.

Put the lamb into the mixture. Bake, covered, for $1^1/_2$ hours, or until the meat is tender.

Lamb Roasted with Coffee

Serves: 6

4½ pound leg of lamb
1 tablespoon butter or oil
Salt and freshly ground black pepper
1 cup coffee, medium strength, mixed with
    2 tablespoons light cream and
    1 teaspoon sugar
2 tablespoons flour
Additional light cream or milk
1 teaspoon red currant jelly

Preheat oven to 400°F. Rub meat with butter or oil; season well with salt and pepper. Place in roasting pan and roast for 10 minutes. Reduce heat to 350°F and continue roasting for 1 hour, basting every 20 minutes.

Then add the white, sweetened coffee to the pan and continue roasting for another hour, or until cooked to your liking, basting as before. When done, remove meat and keep warm.

Strain the pan juices, then skim fat off the top and return 2 tablespoons of the juices to the roasting pan along with the flour. Cook over moderate heat for a few minutes, stirring all the time. Make a smooth sauce with the degreased juices from the pan and red currant jelly, made up to 2 cups with additional light cream or milk, scraping the bottom of the roasting pan well to incorporate any crusty bits with all their flavor. Adjust seasoning, simmer 5 to 10 minutes, then serve with the meat.

Tangy Lamb & Mushroom Pilaf

Serves: 4

1½ pounds boneless lean lamb
¼ cup lemon juice
3 tablespoons olive oil, divided
2 tablespoons firmly packed brown sugar
1 clove garlic, minced or pressed
1 tablespoon tomato-based chili sauce
½ teaspoon oregano leaves
1 pound mushrooms, sliced
1 cup brown rice
Chicken broth
¼ cup currants

Remove and discard excess fat from lamb; cut lamb into ¾-inch cubes. Combine lemon juice, 2 tablespoons of the oil, sugar, garlic, chili sauce, and oregano; pour over meat. Cover and chill for 2 to 4 hours.

Heat remaining 1 tablespoon oil in a wide frying pan over medium heat. With a slotted spoon, lift meat from marinade (reserve marinade), drain briefly, and brown lamb in oil, a few pieces at a time. Remove lamb with a slotted spoon and set aside.

To the pan juices, add mushrooms and cook until soft. Stir in rice and lamb. To reserved marinade, add enough broth to make 2½ cups; stir into rice mixture. Cover, reduce heat, and simmer for about 1¼ hours or until lamb and rice are tender and liquid is absorbed. Just before serving, stir in currants.

Chapter 3

*Poultry
Dishes*

A chicken in every pot is the battle cry for one-pot enthusiasts everywhere. Easy to prepare and quick to cook, no matter which of the following recipes you choose, one-pot chicken dishes are family-pleasers and appropriate for almost every occasion, from a fancy buffet dinner to an informal weekend supper.

Easy Sunday Afternoon Chicken

Serves: 6

4 boneless, skinless chicken breasts
1 10-ounce can cream of chicken soup
½ can water
Stuffing
1½ teaspoons curry powder
2 tablespoons lemon juice
1 cup grated Cheddar cheese
1 cup mayonnaise
1 8-ounce package herb stuffing mix

Preheat oven to 350°F. Lay chicken breasts in bottom of 9 x 12-inch casserole. Pour soup mixture over chicken. Mix remaining ingredients into stuffing mix. Top with stuffing mix. Bake 1 hour. If stuffing gets too brown, cover loosely with aluminum foil.

Sunday Afternoon Chicken and Rice Casserole

Serves: 6

3½-pound chicken, halved
Salt and pepper to taste

1 large onion, peeled and chopped
1 4-ounce can mushrooms, drained
4 tablespoons butter, cut into small pieces
1 cup uncooked long-grain rice
3 cups chicken stock, boiling

Preheat oven to 350°F.

Place half of the chicken in a Dutch oven and season with salt and pepper. Cover with the onions, mushrooms, and half of the butter. Cover with remaining chicken; season with salt and pepper and dot with butter. Cover and bake for about 45 minutes.

Remove chicken pieces; add rice and stir into cooking fat. Add the boiling stock. Place chicken over mixture. Re-cover and bake for about an hour, or until rice and chicken are tender and almost all liquid has been absorbed.

Honey Baked Chicken

Serves: 6

¼ cup butter
¼ cup honey
1 tablespoon prepared mustard
1 teaspoon curry powder
3½ pound chicken, cut into serving pieces

Preheat oven to 350°F. In a 9 x 13 x 2-inch pan, melt the butter. Add honey, mustard, and curry powder; mix well. Coat the chicken on both sides with the honey mixture in the pan. Place the chicken pieces in the pan, skin side down. Bake for 30 minutes on each side. Baste occasionally.

Lemon Chicken

Serves: 6

> 4 medium baking potatoes
> 3 pounds frying chicken, cut into serving
>   pieces
> 2 tablespoons butter, melted
> 2 tablespoons oil
> 2 tablespoons lemon juice
> $1/4$ teaspoon pepper
> 1 teaspoon salt
> 1 teaspoon dried oregano leaves

Preheat oven to 400°F. Peel and cut potatoes into wedges, cutting lengthwise through potato. Brush chicken on both sides with butter. Beat oil, lemon juice, pepper, salt, and oregano leaves in a small bowl. Brush on both sides of chicken pieces. Place chicken skin side down in a 10 x 15-inch jellyroll pan. Pieces should not touch. Bake for 15 minutes. Baste with juices. Bake 15 minutes longer.

Turn pieces over and place potato wedges in pan. Baste chicken and potatoes with juices. Bake for 25 to 30 minutes or until chicken and potatoes are browned and tender. Serve with cooked rice.

Chicken Fat Conservation

Since chicken fat is great for frying potatoes and adding to recipes for additional flavor, store some ahead of time. When preparing a soup or stew, skim the fat off the top and store in baby food jars in the freezer. Thaw by placing in a pan of simmering water, and it's ready to use.

Orange Chicken on Rice

Serves: 6

> 3 pounds meaty chicken pieces
> 1 teaspoon salt, divided
> $1/4$ cup butter
> 2 tablespoons flour
> 1 tablespoon brown sugar
> $1/2$ teaspoon curry powder
> $1/8$ teaspoon cinnamon
> 1 1-inch piece gingerroot, sliced

(continued)

1¹/₂ cups orange juice
¹/₂ cup raisins
¹/₂ cup chopped pecans
2 oranges, cut into wedges, skinned
4 cups hot cooked rice

Sprinkle chicken with ¹/₂ teaspoon salt. Heat butter in large skillet and brown chicken pieces. Remove chicken from pan. Combine flour, ¹/₂ teaspoon salt, brown sugar, curry powder, and cinnamon. Stir into pan drippings to make a smooth paste. Add ginger and orange juice. Cook, stirring constantly, until sauce bubbles and begins to thicken. Return chicken to pan and add raisins. Cover and cook over low heat for 40 to 50 minutes, until chicken is tender and cooked through. Add pecans and orange slices. Heat through. Spoon cooked rice onto large platter and top with chicken pieces and some of the sauce. Serve remaining sauce on the side in a gravy boat.

Easy Baked Chicken

Serves: 4

4 tablespoons butter, divided
1 large onion, thinly sliced and separated into rings
6 to 8 pieces (breasts, legs, and thighs) broiler-fryer chicken (about 2 pounds total)
2 teaspoons paprika
1 teaspoon salt
¹/₄ cup ketchup
¹/₄ cup dry white wine
6 cloves garlic, peeled

Dot the butter (about 2 tablespoons) over the bottom of a shallow 3-quart casserole or 9 x 13-inch baking dish. Place in a cold oven while you preheat oven to 350°F. After 5 minutes, take out the dish and scatter the onion rings over the bottom of the casserole. Melt remaining butter in a small dish in the microwave. With a brush, spread the butter over chicken pieces and arrange them over onions. Sprinkle chicken with paprika and salt.

Blend ketchup and wine; carefully pour into casserole. Tuck in whole garlic cloves. Bake, covered, for about 45 minutes. Uncover and bake for 15 more minutes or until thigh meat near bone is no longer pink when slashed. Discard garlic and serve chicken with pan juices.

Chicken and Wild Rice Casserole

Serves: 6

1 package mixed long grain and wild rice
¹/₄ cup butter
¹/₃ cup chopped onion
¹/₃ cup flour
¹/₂ teaspoon salt
¹/₈ teaspoon pepper
1 cup evaporated milk
1 cup chicken broth
2 cups cubed cooked chicken
¹/₃ cup diced pimiento
¹/₃ cup fresh parsley
¹/₄ cup slivered almonds

Cook contents of rice package according to package directions. Melt butter in a large saucepan and sauté onion until tender. Stir in flour, salt, and pepper. Gradually stir in milk and chicken broth. Cook, stirring constantly, until thickened. Add chicken, pimiento, parsley, almonds, and cooked rice. This can be frozen in plastic bags at this point if desired.

To serve, defrost, place into a greased 2-quart casserole and bake, uncovered, at 400°F for 30 minutes.

Lemon Chicken Casserole

Serves: 4

$1/4$ cup flour
1 tablespoon chopped fresh dill or
    1 teaspoon dried dill
$1/4$ teaspoon salt
$1/8$ teaspoon pepper
1 chicken ($2 1/2$ to 3 pounds), cut in pieces
2 tablespoons butter
1 clove garlic, minced
2 cups chicken broth
$1/4$ cup freshly squeezed lemon juice
$1/4$ teaspoon grated lemon peel
2 ribs celery, chopped
1 medium zucchini, sliced $3/4$-inch thick
$1/2$ pound small, whole fresh mushrooms
1 lemon, sliced

In a plastic bag, combine flour, dill, salt, and pepper. Add chicken and shake until well coated. In a large skillet, melt butter; add garlic and cook until golden. Add chicken and brown on both sides.

Remove and set aside. Drain fat from skillet. In same skillet, stir in any remaining flour mixture; gradually add broth, scraping up bits from bottom of pan. Stir in lemon juice, lemon peel, and celery. Bring to boil. Return chicken to skillet; cover and simmer 15 minutes until chicken is tender.

Add zucchini and mushrooms. Cook 10 minutes longer. Remove to serving platter. Garnish with lemon slices, if desired.

Reducing Saltiness, Part 1

One-pot dish tasting too salty? Add a teaspoon each of cider vinegar and sugar to a one-pot dish to help cut down on the salty flavor in the recipe.

Chicken Parmesan Casserole

Serves: 8

2 cups parboiled (converted)
long-grain rice
8 green onions, sliced
8 skinless, boneless chicken breast halves
(2 pounds total)
1 tablespoon cooking oil
2 cloves garlic, minced
2 teaspoons dried Italian seasoning,
crushed
2 tablespoons cornstarch
4$\frac{1}{2}$ cups milk
2 3-ounce packages cream cheese, cut up
3 cups loose-pack frozen cut broccoli
1 cup grated Parmesan cheese (4 ounces)
$\frac{2}{3}$ cup diced fully cooked ham
Salt and pepper to taste
1 cup sliced almonds

Cook rice according to package directions, omitting salt; stir in half of the onions. Rinse chicken; pat dry with paper towels. Heat oil in large skillet. Cook chicken, garlic, and Italian seasoning in hot oil over medium heat for 8 to 10 minutes or until chicken is tender and no longer pink, turning once. Remove from skillet; reserve drippings.

Cook and stir remaining onions in drippings in skillet until tender. Stir in cornstarch; add milk all at once. Cook and stir over medium heat until slightly thickened and bubbly. Reduce heat; stir in cream cheese until nearly smooth. Remove from heat; stir in broccoli, Parmesan cheese, and ham. Preheat oven to 350°F.

Spoon rice mixture into two 2-quart square baking dishes. Arrange chicken over rice; sprinkle with salt and pepper. Spoon broccoli mixture over chicken; top with almonds. Bake, covered, about 10 minutes or until heated through.

Rula's Chicken Casserole

Serves: 6

1 8-ounce package uncooked macaroni
4 hardboiled eggs, chopped
2 cups cooked, chopped chicken
2 cups milk
$\frac{1}{2}$ pound Cheddar or Swiss cheese, grated
1 10$\frac{3}{4}$-ounce can cream of
mushroom soup
1 10$\frac{3}{4}$-ounce can cream of chicken soup

In a 2-quart casserole, mix all ingredients. Stir well. Refrigerate overnight, covered.

Take out 1 hour before cooking. Bake 1 hour at 350°F or until top is golden brown.

Easy Chicken Casserole

Serves: 6

Vegetable oil
4 boneless chicken breasts, halved and
skin removed
1 cup grated Swiss or Monterey Jack
cheese

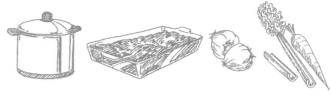

1 10¾-ounce can cream of mushroom
   soup
¼ cup wine, sherry or white
¼ cup buttered bread crumbs

Preheat oven to 350°F. Lightly grease a 2-quart casserole with oil.

Place the chicken in the casserole and sprinkle with cheese. Mix the soup and the wine and pour over all. Cover with crumbs and bake covered for 30 to 45 minutes or until chicken is tender.

Kansas Style Chicken Casserole

Serves: 6

1 8-ounce package egg noodles, cooked
3 tablespoons olive oil
1½ cups chopped celery
½ cup chopped green pepper
¼ cup chopped onion
1 10¾-ounce can cream of chicken soup
⅔ cup milk
½ cup sour cream
2 cups shredded Cheddar cheese
2 cups chopped cooked chicken
1 3-ounce can mushroom pieces, drained
1 4-ounce jar pimientos, drained and diced
½ teaspoon salt
¼ teaspoon nutmeg
⅛ teaspoon pepper
½ cup toasted slivered almonds

In a large ovenproof 3-quart skillet, heat oil. Add celery, peppers, and onion. Cook until tender. Stir in soup, milk, sour cream, and cheese. Heat on low until cheese melts. Preheat oven to 350°F.

Combine noodles with cheese sauce, chicken, mushrooms, pimiento, and seasonings. Top with almonds. Bake for 40 minutes or until hot and bubbly.

Hot Chicken Salad Casserole

Serves: 5

1½ cups cooked, diced chicken
1 10½-ounce can cream of chicken soup
1 cup diced celery
¼ cup minced onion
¼ cup slivered almonds
½ cup mayonnaise
¼ cup lemon juice
2 tablespoons black pepper
Salt to taste
3 hard-cooked eggs, chopped
1 8-ounce bag potato chips

In a large bowl, combine chicken, chicken soup, celery, onion, almonds, mayonnaise, lemon juice, pepper, and salt. Combine well. Fold in chopped eggs. Don't mix too much.

Preheat oven to 350°F. Spray an 8½ x 10½ x 2½-inch casserole dish with nonstick cooking spray.

(continued)

Pour mixture into pan. Crush potato chips and generously sprinkle them on top of casserole. Bake for 1 hour or until heated through.

Baked Breast of Chicken Galahad

Serves: 4

> 4 8-ounce chicken breast halves, boned and skinned
> Garlic salt
> $\frac{1}{2}$ cup butter, melted
> 1 teaspoon paprika
> 3 tablespoons lemon juice
> 1 cup sour cream, room temperature
> $\frac{1}{2}$ cup sherry or broth
> 1 8-ounce can mushroom pieces, drained
> Dash of pepper

Preheat oven to 375°F. Place chicken in a lightly greased 9 x 13-inch baking dish. Sprinkle chicken with garlic salt to taste. Mix together melted butter, paprika, and lemon juice in a small dish. Brush chicken well with butter mixture and place in pan. Bake, tented with aluminum foil, about 30 minutes or until tender, brushing with remaining butter mixture occasionally to keep from drying.

In a bowl, blend together sour cream, sherry or broth, mushrooms, and pepper. Pour over chicken for last 15 minutes.

Chicken-n-Chips Bake

Serves: 6

> 2 cups cubed cooked chicken
> 2 cups sliced celery
> $\frac{1}{2}$ cup blanched almonds (optional)
> $\frac{1}{2}$ teaspoon salt
> $\frac{1}{2}$ teaspoon monosodium glutamate
> 2 teaspoons grated onions
> 2 tablespoons lemon juice
> 1 cup mayonnaise
> $\frac{1}{2}$ cup shredded Cheddar cheese
> 1$\frac{1}{2}$ cups crushed or whole potato chips

Preheat oven to 425°F.

In a lightly greased shallow 1$\frac{1}{2}$-quart baking dish, combine the chicken, celery, almonds, salt, monosodium glutamate, onions, lemon juice, and mayonnaise. Sprinkle with cheese and potato chips. Bake for 15 minutes or until heated through.

Chicken Bake (with Ham and Bacon)

Serves: 6

> 6 thin ham slices
> 6 chicken breasts, boned and skinned
> 6 slices bacon
> 1 10$\frac{3}{4}$-ounce can cream of chicken soup
> $\frac{1}{2}$ cup milk
> 1 8-ounce container sour cream

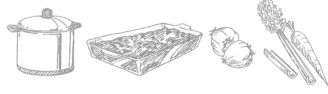

Preheat oven to 350°F. Place ham slices on chicken breasts and wrap each with a slice of bacon. Secure bacon with a toothpick. Place chicken in a 9 x 13-inch baking dish.

Combine soup, milk, and sour cream. Pour over chicken breasts. Cover dish with aluminum foil. Bake for about an hour.

Oven Fried Chicken

Serves: 4

1/3 cup oil
1/3 cup butter
1 cup all-purpose flour
1 teaspoon salt
2 teaspoons ground black pepper
1 teaspoon garlic salt
1 teaspoon dried marjoram
1 3 1/2 broiler-fryer chicken, cut into serving pieces

Place oil and butter in a jellyroll pan. Place pan in preheating oven (375°F) to melt butter. Set pan aside.

In a large paper sack, combine flour and seasonings. Roll the chicken pieces in oil/butter mixture, then drop them in the sack and shake to coat. Place on a dish.

Return the chicken pieces to the pan, skin side down, and bake for 45 minutes. Turn pieces over and bake for 10 minutes longer.

Oriental Chicken & Vegetable Medley

Serves: 6

1 2 1/2 to 3-pound broiler-fryer chicken, deboned, cubed
1/4 cup all-purpose flour
1/2 teaspoon paprika
1/4 teaspoon salt
1/4 teaspoon ground black pepper
2 tablespoons olive oil
1 medium onion, chopped
2 cloves garlic, minced
1 tablespoon grated gingerroot
3/4 cup chicken broth
1 pound fresh asparagus, cut into 1-inch pieces
3 small yellow summer squash and/or zucchini, cut into 1-inch chunks
2 medium red sweet peppers, cut into 1-inch strips
12 ounces fresh mushrooms, thickly sliced (3 cups)
1/4 cup dry sherry
2 tablespoons soy sauce
2 teaspoons cornstarch
2 to 3 cups hot cooked orzo, rice, or noodles

Skin chicken, if desired. Rinse chicken; pat dry with paper towels. Combine flour, paprika, salt, and black pepper in a plastic bag. Add chicken, a few pieces at a time, shaking to coat well. Heat oil in a 12-inch skillet. Cook

(continued)

chicken in hot oil about 15 minutes or until chicken is lightly browned, turning to brown evenly. Remove chicken; set aside.

Add 1 tablespoon additional oil, if necessary. Add onion, garlic, and gingerroot to skillet; cook and stir until onion is tender. Carefully stir in broth. Return chicken to skillet. Bring to boiling; reduce heat. Simmer for 25 minutes.

Add asparagus, squash, green peppers, and mushrooms. Return to boiling; reduce heat. Simmer, covered, about 10 minutes or until chicken is tender and no longer pink. Remove chicken and vegetables from skillet. Cover and keep warm.

Stir together sherry, soy sauce, and cornstarch in a small bowl. Stir into skillet. Cook and stir until thickened and bubbly; cook and stir for 1 minute more. Return chicken and vegetables to skillet. Stir to coat evenly; heat through. Serve with hot pasta or rice.

Spanish Chicken & Rice

Serves: 6

> 2 teaspoons olive oil
> 1 large onion, chopped
> 1 medium green pepper, chopped
> 2 cloves garlic, minced
> 1³⁄₄ cups chicken broth
> 1 cup long-grain rice
> ¹⁄₄ cup dry white wine
> 1 bay leaf
> ¹⁄₈ teaspoon ground saffron

> 1 cup frozen peas, thawed
> ¹⁄₂ cup sliced pimiento-stuffed olives
> ¹⁄₄ cup snipped parsley
> 1 2¹⁄₂-pound broiler-fryer chicken, cut into individual serving pieces
> 1 tablespoon olive oil
> ¹⁄₄ teaspoon garlic salt
> ¹⁄₈ teaspoon paprika

Heat the 2 teaspoons oil in a medium saucepan. Cook onion, green pepper, and garlic in hot oil until vegetables are tender. Add broth, uncooked rice, wine, bay leaf, and saffron. Bring to boiling; reduce heat. Simmer, covered, for 10 minutes. Discard bay leaf. Stir in peas, olives, and parsley. Transfer mixture to a 3-quart rectangular baking dish.

Skin chicken, if desired. Rinse chicken; pat dry with paper towels. Preheat oven to 350°F. Heat the 1 tablespoon oil in a large skillet. Cook chicken in hot oil for 10 minutes, turning to brown on all sides. Arrange chicken over rice in baking dish. Sprinkle chicken with garlic salt and paprika. Cover dish with foil. Bake for 35 to 40 minutes or until chicken is tender and no longer pink.

Simple Cassoulet

Serves: 6

> 8 ounces skinless, boneless chicken thighs
> 2 medium carrots, sliced into ¹⁄₂-inch pieces
> 1 medium green or red sweet pepper, cut into ¹⁄₂-inch pieces

1 large onion, chopped

3 cloves garlic, minced

2 15-ounce cans cannellini beans, rinsed and drained

1 14½-ounce can Italian-style stewed tomatoes

8 ounces fully cooked smoked turkey sausage, halved lengthwise and cut into ½-inch slices

1½ cups chicken broth

⅓ cup dry white wine or chicken broth

1 tablespoon snipped parsley

1 teaspoon dried thyme, crushed

¼ teaspoon ground red pepper

1 bay leaf

Rinse chicken and pat dry with paper towels. Cut into 1-inch pieces. Layer carrots, sweet pepper, onion, garlic, beans, undrained tomatoes, chicken, and sausage in a 3½ to 5-quart Crockpot.

Combine broth, wine, parsley, thyme, red pepper, and bay leaf in a bowl. Add mixture to cooker. Cover; cook on low for 7 to 8 hours or cook on high for 3½ to 4 hours. Discard bay leaf.

Saffron Chicken Pot Pies

Makes: 9 pot pies

5 cups cubed cooked chicken

2 carrots

1 5-ounce package frozen baby peas

1 medium pinch saffron

4 cups chicken stock

4 tablespoons butter

½ cup flour

1 teaspoon onion powder

1 teaspoon black pepper

1 teaspoon salt

½ teaspoon rosemary, crushed

½ teaspoon thyme

½ teaspoon sage

Pastry for 2 large pie crusts

Dice carrots into ¼-inch cubes. In a large bowl toss together the chicken, carrots, and peas. Crumble saffron into chicken stock. Preheat oven to 375°F.

In a medium-large saucepan melt butter over medium heat until bubbling but not browning. Whisk in flour and cook for 5 minutes, stirring continuously. Slowly stir in chicken stock until well blended. Add spices and cook until mixture thickens, stirring constantly. Pour sauce over chicken mixture and toss.

Spoon chicken mixture into 9 individual pie pans or two large pie dishes. Top with pastry crust and cut vents. Bake for about 40 minutes until crust is golden and filling is bubbling.

Easy Chicken & Cheese Casserole

Serves: 4

1 onion, chopped

2 ribs celery, chopped

2 tablespoons butter

1 large jar Cheez Whiz

(continued)

2 cups cooked rice
1 16-ounce package frozen chopped
    broccoli
4 cups cooked diced chicken or turkey

Preheat oven to 375°F.

Sauté onion and celery in butter until tender. Remove the jar top and place the jar of cheese in the microwave for a minute at medium until melted. Blend all ingredients together and put into a greased casserole dish. Bake for 30 minutes.

Poached Chicken

Serves: 4

1 sliced onion
3 carrots, cut in strips
3 celery stalks, cut in strips
1 tablespoon margarine
2½ pounds skinned chicken,
    in parts
3 to 4 cups chicken stock
¼ cup dry vermouth or white wine
    (optional)
1 bay leaf
3 sprigs dried parsley
½ teaspoon thyme
⅛ teaspoon salt
⅛ teaspoon pepper

In a 2-quart casserole, cook the onion, carrots, and celery in margarine over medium heat for about 5 minutes. Add chicken to casserole and cover. Cook for another 5 minutes. Add chicken stock, vermouth or wine, and seasonings. Simmer (do not boil) for 25 minutes or until chicken juices run yellow when flesh is poked with a fork.

Chicken Margarita

Serves: 6

1 3½-pound chicken
1 tablespoon ground cumin
1 tablespoon chili powder

Easy Pie Crust

Ready-made pie crusts are a great time saver, and your guests and family will never know the difference. Whether you choose a frozen pie crust or fresh shell from the refrigerated case, you'll never need to wrestle with a rolling pin again.

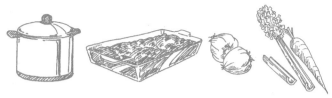

Juice of 3 limes
10 cloves garlic, chopped fine
3 tablespoons olive oil, divided
½ cup tequila (white/gold)
½ cup water
1 tablespoon chopped fresh cilantro for garnish
Hot cooked rice

Remove skin from chicken; cut chicken into parts. Combine cumin, chili powder, lime juice, garlic and 1 tablespoon oil in a bowl. Marinate the chicken in the mixture for 20 minutes.

Heat remaining oil in a heavy skillet; brown chicken on all sides. Add marinade, tequila, and water. Cover skillet and poach gently until chicken is cooked through, about 25 minutes.

Transfer chicken pieces onto a platter. Reduce sauce over high heat until of a good coating consistency and pour over chicken. Garnish with cilantro. Serve with rice.

Simmered Broccoli Lemon Chicken

Serves: 4

1 tablespoon oil
4 boneless chicken breast halves
1 10-ounce can cream of broccoli soup
¼ cup milk
2 teaspoons fresh lemon juice
⅛ teaspoon pepper
4 thin lemon slices

Heat oil in a skillet. Sauté chicken breasts about 10 minutes, until browned on both sides. Pour off fat. Combine soup, milk, lemon juice, and pepper. Pour over chicken. Top each chicken piece with a slice of lemon. Reduce heat to low and cover. Simmer 5 to 10 minutes until chicken is tender, stirring occasionally.

Quick Chicken Piccata

Serves: 4

4 boneless chicken breast halves, skinned
Salt and freshly ground pepper to taste
2 tablespoons butter
1 teaspoon olive oil
½ cup chicken broth
¼ cup vermouth
2 tablespoons fresh lemon juice
1 tablespoon capers, drained and rinsed
Lemon slices for garnish

Pat chicken dry. Season with salt and pepper. Melt butter with oil in large heavy skillet over medium-high heat. Add chicken and cook until springy to the touch, about 4 minutes per side. Remove from skillet; keep warm.

Increase heat to high. Stir broth and vermouth into skillet. Boil until reduced by half, scraping up any browned bits. Remove from heat. Mix in lemon juice and capers. Place chicken on plates and pour sauce over chicken. Garnish chicken with lemon slices.

Curried Chicken

Serves: 4

½ teaspoon pepper
⅛ teaspoon salt
½ cup flour
2½ pounds skinned chicken, cut up
¼ cup oil
1 onion, chopped
1 green bell pepper, chopped
1 clove garlic, minced
6 ounces tomato paste
2 cups water
1½ teaspoons curry powder
½ teaspoon thyme
3 teaspoons raisins

Combine pepper and salt with flour. Coat chicken with seasoned flour. Brown chicken in oil. Add onion, green pepper, and garlic and cook until soft. Drain off fat. Add tomato paste, water, and remaining seasonings. Simmer 30 minutes or until chicken juices run yellow when flesh is poked with a fork. Add raisins and heat for another 5 minutes.

Chicken Marsala

Serves: 4

1 tablespoon butter
4 boneless chicken breast halves
⅛ teaspoon salt

⅛ teaspoon freshly ground black pepper
2 tablespoons shallots or scallions, finely chopped
½ cup Marsala wine
½ cup chicken stock
2 cups chopped, seeded, and peeled tomatoes
¼ cup finely chopped fresh parsley

Melt butter in skillet. Brown chicken parts on both sides. Sprinkle with salt and pepper; remove from skillet. Add chopped shallots, wine, stock, and tomatoes to skillet. Simmer until liquid is partially reduced, about 10 minutes.

Return chicken to skillet, spooning sauce over chicken. Cover and simmer until chicken is tender, about 30 minutes. Serve sauce over chicken. Sprinkle with chopped parsley.

Chicken Paprikash

Serves: 8

2 3- to 3½-pound broilers
¼ cup chicken fat
1 clove garlic, halved
2 tablespoons butter
½ cup chopped onions
1 cup sliced or diced carrots
1 cup diced green peppers
½ teaspoon salt
3 or 4 tablespoons fresh Hungarian paprika

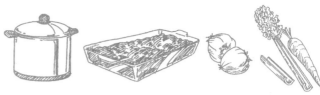

3 tablespoons flour
2 cups warm chicken stock or consommé
1 cup sour cream

Cut the chicken meat from the broilers into stew-size pieces. Heat the chicken fat in a large skillet and stir-fry the garlic for 3 minutes. Discard the garlic. Brown the chicken slowly, turning frequently, then remove and keep warm.

Add the butter to the skillet and sauté the onions, carrots, and peppers over low heat for 5 minutes. Stir in the salt and paprika and cook for 2 minutes. Stir in the flour, slowly add the warm stock or consommé, and stir over low heat. When thickened and bubbling, simmer for 10 minutes. Return the chicken and continue to simmer for 30 minutes. Add sour cream. Stir, and heat through without boiling.

Busy Day Guadalajara Chicken and Rice Skillet

Serves: 4

3 boneless chicken breast halves
1 tablespoon oil
1 15-ounce jar salsa
³⁄₄ cup chicken broth
¹⁄₂ cup chopped green pepper
1 cup quick-cooking rice
¹⁄₂ cup shredded Cheddar cheese

Cut the chicken into 1-inch cubes. Heat oil in a large skillet and sauté chicken until cooked. Stir in salsa, chicken broth, and green pepper and bring to a boil. Stir in the uncooked rice. Sprinkle with the cheese, cover, and remove from heat. Let stand 5 minutes until rice is cooked.

Skillet Chicken and Rice

Serves: 6

2 pounds chicken pieces, skinned
3 cups fresh mushrooms, sliced
4 carrots, peeled, sliced in ¹⁄₂-inch pieces
³⁄₄ cup long-grain rice
¹⁄₂ cup onion, chopped
1 teaspoon chicken bouillon granules
1 teaspoon poultry seasoning
2 cups water
¹⁄₄ teaspoon salt

Spray a 12-inch skillet with nonstick cooking spray. Brown chicken pieces on all sides over medium heat about 15 minutes. Remove chicken.

Drain fat from skillet, if necessary. Add mushrooms, carrots, rice, onion, bouillon, poultry seasoning, water, and salt. Place chicken atop rice mixture. Cover; simmer 30 minutes or till chicken and rice are done.

Fiesta Chicken

Serves: 4

1 8-ounce can tomato sauce
½ cup orange juice
½ cup finely chopped onion
2 tablespoons raisins
2 tablespoons chopped pimento
½ teaspoon crushed oregano
½ teaspoon chili powder
1 clove garlic, minced
Several dashes bottled hot pepper sauce
4 chicken breast halves
2 teaspoons cornstarch
1 tablespoon water
¼ cup snipped parsley
3 cups hot cooked rice

In a large skillet combine tomato sauce, orange juice, onion, raisins, pimiento, oregano, chili powder, garlic, and hot pepper sauce. Bring to boiling; reduce heat. Cover and simmer 5 minutes. Stir in chicken; return to boiling. Cover and simmer 12 to 15 minutes more or till chicken is tender and no longer pink.

Meanwhile combine cornstarch and water. Stir into skillet. Cook and stir till thickened and bubbly. Cook and stir 2 minutes more. Toss parsley with rice. Serve chicken mixture over rice.

Chicken Jerusalem

Serves: 6

6 boneless, skinless, chicken breasts
Paprika
¼ cup butter
2 green onions, chopped
¾ cup white wine
¾ cup water
1 cup fresh sliced mushrooms
2 14-ounce cans artichoke hearts
Hot cooked noodles
Parsley
Grated Parmesan cheese

Toss chicken with paprika and in a large skillet brown in butter. Add chopped green onions, wine, and water. Simmer for 45 minutes.

Add mushrooms and artichoke hearts. Cook slowly 15 minutes. Serve over noodles sprinkled with parsley. Sprinkle with Parmesan cheese.

Chicken with Garlic, Garlic & More Garlic

Serves: 4

8 chicken legs and thighs, skinned
2 tablespoons olive oil
1 large onion, coarsely chopped
4 ribs celery, sliced into ½-inch pieces
2 teaspoons dried parsley
1 teaspoon tarragon
½ cup dry vermouth

½ teaspoon salt
1 teaspoon black pepper
Dash nutmeg
40 cloves garlic, unpeeled

Preheat oven to 325°F.

Brush the chicken pieces with oil. In a large casserole, combine onion, celery, parsley, and tarragon. Arrange the chicken over the vegetables and herbs, and pour the vermouth over all. Sprinkle the chicken with salt, pepper, and nutmeg. Remove skins from garlic cloves. Spread the garlic cloves throughout the casserole. Cover tightly with aluminum foil or a lid. Bake the chicken 1½ hours.

Chicken Pepperoni

Serves: 6

½ pound pepperoni
1 pound boneless chicken breast
⅓ cup flour
½ teaspoon tarragon
½ teaspoon basil
½ teaspoon oregano
½ teaspoon garlic powder
½ teaspoon onion powder
½ teaspoon fresh pepper
2 8-ounce cans tomato sauce
½ pound linguine, cooked

Dice pepperoni into ¼-inch cubes. Cook in frying pan over medium heat until mostly degreased. Remove pepperoni from pan and set aside.

Cut chicken into bite-sized pieces. Combine flour with tarragon, basil, oregano, garlic powder, onion powder, and pepper. Coat chicken pieces with flour mixture. Brown chicken in pepperoni fat (and olive oil, if needed). Remove chicken from pan. Stir tomato sauce and remaining flour mixture together in pan. Stir in chicken and pepperoni. Add ⅓ to ½ cup water to cover meat. Allow to simmer 30 to 45 minutes or until chicken is tender. Serve over a bed of pasta.

Safe Chicken Handling

Today, with everyone so aware of salmonella and other bacteria that can easily be transmitted through raw chicken, the following standards bear repeating:

- Always wash your hands before and after handling raw chicken.
- Thoroughly wash all cutting boards and utensils you've used to prepare raw chicken.
- Make sure chicken is thoroughly cooked (to 170°F) before serving.
- If chicken smells funny, throw it out.

Arroz con Pollo

Serves: 4

4 chicken breast halves, skin removed
$\frac{1}{4}$ teaspoon salt
$\frac{1}{4}$ teaspoon pepper
$\frac{1}{4}$ teaspoon paprika
1 tablespoon vegetable oil
1 medium onion, chopped
1 small red pepper, chopped
3 cloves garlic, minced
$\frac{1}{2}$ teaspoon dried rosemary
1 14$\frac{1}{2}$-ounce can crushed tomatoes
1 10-ounce package frozen peas
Hot cooked rice

Season chicken with salt, pepper, paprika. In skillet, heat oil and brown chicken. Drain. Put chicken in Crockpot. In a small bowl combine onion, pepper, garlic, rosemary, and tomatoes. Pour over chicken. Cover and cook on low 7 to 9 hours or on high 3 to 4 hours.

One hour before serving add the peas. Serve over rice.

Chicken Cacciatore

Serves: 6

1 large onion, thinly sliced
3 pounds chicken, cut up
2 6-ounce cans tomato paste
4 ounces sliced mushrooms
1 teaspoon salt
2 cloves garlic, minced
1 teaspoon oregano

$\frac{1}{2}$ teaspoon celery seed
1 bay leaf
$\frac{1}{2}$ cup water
Hot cooked spaghetti

Place onions in bottom of Crockpot. Add chicken pieces. Stir together remaining ingredients except spaghetti. Pour over chicken. Cook on low 7 to 9 hours or high 3 to 4 hours. Serve over spaghetti.

Balsamic Chicken and Mushrooms

Serves: 4

2 tablespoons flour
Salt and pepper to taste
4 boneless, skinless chicken breast halves
3 tablespoons olive oil
6 cloves garlic, peeled
$\frac{3}{4}$ pound small mushrooms, quartered
3 tablespoons balsamic vinegar
$\frac{3}{4}$ cup chicken broth
1 bay leaf
$\frac{1}{4}$ teaspoon thyme
1 tablespoon butter

Season the flour with salt and pepper and dredge the chicken breast halves in it. Shake off excess flour. Heat the oil in a heavy skillet and cook the chicken over moderately high heat until nicely browned on one side, about 3 minutes. Add the garlic cloves. Turn the chicken pieces over and scatter the mushrooms over all.

Continue cooking, shaking the skillet and redistributing the mushrooms so they cook evenly. Cook about 3 minutes. Add the balsamic vinegar, broth, bay leaf, and thyme. Cover tightly and cook over moderately high heat about 10 minutes. Turn the pieces occasionally as they cook. Transfer the chicken to a warm platter and cover with aluminum foil.

Let the sauce cook, uncovered, over moderately high heat about 7 minutes. Swirl in the butter. Remove the bay leaf. Pour the sauce and mushrooms over the chicken and serve.

Japanese Grilled Chicken

Serves: 4 to 6

½ cup Italian dressing
½ cup teriyaki sauce
4 to 6 boneless chicken breast halves

Combine the Italian dressing and teriyaki sauce. Marinate the chicken in this mixture overnight. Grill over hot coals.

Authentic Kung Pao Chili Chicken

Serves: 4

3 boneless chicken breast halves
1½ tablespoons peanut oil
1 dried red chili
⅓ cup shelled peanuts
2 tablespoons water
2 tablespoons dry sherry

1 tablespoon soy sauce
1 tablespoon chili bean sauce
1 teaspoon sugar
2 garlic cloves, minced
2 scallions, chopped
1 teaspoon grated ginger
2 teaspoons rice or cider vinegar
1 teaspoon sesame oil
4 cups cooked white rice

Dice the chicken into 1-inch cubes. Heat the oil in a wok or skillet and add the chili. Add the chicken and peanuts and stir-fry until the chicken is cooked. Add the remaining ingredients, except the sesame oil and rice, and bring to a boil. Cook for a few minutes. Add the sesame oil and serve over rice.

Spicy Aromatic Chicken

Serves: 4

4 whole chicken legs
3¼ cups tomato sauce
½ cup chicken stock
⅛ teaspoon cayenne pepper
2 teaspoons curry powder
2 cloves garlic, minced
Freshly ground pepper to taste
1½ cups sliced mushrooms
3 cups hot cooked white rice

Remove the skin from the chicken legs. In a medium saucepan heat the tomato sauce on low heat. Add the chicken legs, stock, cayenne, curry, garlic, and pepper. Cover and

(continued)

simmer on low until chicken is tender, about 1 1/2 hours.

Gently remove the chicken meat from the bones and return to the pot. Add the mushrooms and simmer for an additional 10 minutes. Serve over hot rice.

The Three C's (Chicken, Cheese & Chilies) Enchiladas

Serves: 6

1 tablespoon butter
1 tablespoon olive oil
2 cloves garlic, minced
4 cups cooked chicken, cut into
    bite-sized pieces
1 cup chicken broth
1 4-ounce can chopped green chilies
2 teaspoons Dijon mustard
1 15-ounce can cannellini beans, rinsed
    and drained
1 cup heavy cream
6 large flour tortillas
6 ounces Monterey Jack cheese, shredded

Preheat broiler or oven. Heat the butter and oil in a large skillet over medium-high heat. When butter has stopped foaming, add garlic and chicken. Sauté, stirring, until chicken has started to brown. Add chicken broth and stir to loosen any browned particles. Add undrained chilies, mustard, and cannellini beans. Simmer,

uncovered for 5 minutes, until thickened slightly. Add cream and simmer for another 5 minutes.

Meanwhile, warm tortillas according to package directions. Place one tortilla in a 9 x 11-inch (or similar) baking dish. Using a slotted spoon, place 1/6 of the chicken/bean mixture in a line down the center of the tortilla. Sprinkle with about 1 tablespoon of cheese and quickly roll up, folding the sides in. Push the rolled tortilla to one end of the baking dish. Repeat with remaining tortillas. Pour remaining sauce over all the rolls and sprinkle with the remaining cheese. Place in broiler or oven to melt cheese.

Bayou Chicken

Serves: 6

2 1-ounce packages béarnaise sauce mix
1/2 cup dry white wine
1/2 teaspoon tarragon
1/2 teaspoon ground turmeric
1/2 teaspoon garlic powder
3 shallots, minced
1 pound cooked ham, cut in 1-inch chunks
1 red bell pepper, chopped
1 pound red potatoes, scrubbed, cut in
    1/2-inch cubes
1 9-ounce package frozen artichoke halves
    and quarters, thawed
1 pound skinless chicken breast
    tenderloins, cut in chunks

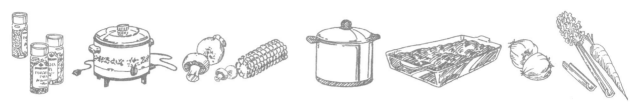

In a Crockpot, mix both packages of béarnaise sauce mix, wine, tarragon, turmeric, and garlic powder until well blended. Add shallots, ham, red pepper, potatoes, artichokes, and chicken. Stir gently. Cover, set heat on low setting, and cook for 6 hours.

Chinese Citrus Chicken Thighs

Serves: 4

8 skinless chicken thighs
$\frac{1}{2}$ cup dry white wine
$\frac{1}{4}$ cup red wine vinegar
$\frac{1}{4}$ cup fresh orange juice
2 tablespoons fresh lime juice
3 tablespoons low-sodium soy sauce
2 tablespoons fresh minced
 thyme leaves
1 clove garlic, minced
1 tablespoon honey
1 teaspoon fresh ginger, minced
1 teaspoon ground cumin
1 jalapeño pepper, chopped and seeded

Remove the surface layer of fat from the thighs. Rinse. Towel dry. In a large nonstick skillet, combine all remaining ingredients. Over medium-high heat, bring the mixture to a boil, then add the chicken (bones up). Reduce the heat to low; cover and simmer for 15 minutes. Remove the cover, turn the chicken pieces over, raise the heat to medium, and cook until the liquid is evaporated and the chicken is glazed, about 10 to 15 minutes. Adjust heat as necessary.

Chicken & Vegetable Stew

Serves: 4

3 skinned and boned chicken
 breast halves
4 small potatoes
1 large onion
2 tablespoons butter
2 carrots, sliced
2 celery stalks, sliced
1 $14\frac{1}{2}$ ounce can chicken broth
$\frac{1}{2}$ teaspoon garlic salt
$\frac{1}{2}$ teaspoon pepper
1 teaspoon dried basil
1 tablespoon all-purpose flour
$\frac{1}{4}$ cup water
1 cup frozen English peas, thawed

Cut chicken and potatoes into $\frac{1}{2}$-inch cubes. Cut onion into 8 wedges. Melt butter in a large Dutch oven over medium-high heat; add chicken, and cook, stirring occasionally, until browned. Add vegetables, chicken broth, and next three ingredients; bring to a boil. Cover, reduce heat, and simmer 30 minutes. Combine flour and water, stirring until smooth; stir into stew. Bring to a boil; boil, stirring constantly, 1 minute or until mixture thickens. Remove from heat; stir in peas.

Chicken & Salsa Casserole

Serves: 4

> 2 to 3 cups cooked chicken, pulled into
>   bite-sized pieces (use your fingers)
> 1 16-ounce jar medium-hot salsa
> 1 4-ounce can diced green chilies, drained
> 1 8-ounce can mushroom stems and
>   pieces, drained
> 1/2 cup + 2 tablespoons sour cream
> 2 cups cooked rice

Preheat oven to 350°F.

Place chicken in the bottom of a greased 1 1/2 quart casserole dish. Mix together salsa, chilies, and mushrooms. Spread all but 3/4 cup of mixture over chicken. Add sour cream and rice to remaining salsa mixture. Spread over mixture in casserole dish. Bake for 30 minutes, until hot and bubbly.

Barbecued Chicken & Beans Casserole

Serves: 4

> 1 16-ounce can pork and beans
> 1 3 1/2 pound broiler-fryer chicken,
>   quartered
> 1/4 cup ketchup
> 2 tablespoons peach preserves
> 2 teaspoons instant minced onion
> 1/4 teaspoon soy sauce
> 1/4 cup brown sugar

Preheat oven to 325°F.

Place beans in an ungreased 2-quart casserole. Add chicken quarters. Mix together remaining ingredients; pour over chicken and beans. Cover and bake for 1 3/4 hours.

Szechuan Sesame Chicken

Serves: 6

> 2 whole chicken beasts, skinned and
>   boned
> 1/4 cup sesame paste
> 3 tablespoons green tea, brewed
> 2 tablespoons wine vinegar
> 2 1/2 teaspoons soy sauce
> 3 tablespoons peanut oil
> 2 teaspoons crushed red pepper
> 3 slices fresh ginger, minced
> 1 scallion (white part only), chopped
> 1 clove garlic, minced fine
> 1 1/2 tablespoons dry sherry or
>   Chinese rice wine
> 1/2 teaspoon cayenne pepper
> 2 tablespoons Szechuan peppercorns
> Lettuce leaves

In a 4-quart pot, poach the chicken breasts in a little boiling water for 10 minutes until white and opaque.

Remove the chicken breasts from the pot; drain and cool them. Slice the chicken, then cut the slices into julienne pieces.

In the same pot, combine the sesame paste and green tea. Add the vinegar and soy sauce; blend well. Add all remaining ingredients except lettuce. Mix thoroughly. Toss the chicken strips in this sauce, to coat. Refrigerate until 20 minutes before serving.

Pass the chicken and the lettuce leaves separately, and let each guest place a small portion of the chicken in the middle of a lettuce leaf and roll it up like an egg roll to eat using fingers.

Green Curried Chicken

Serves: 6

- 1½ cups unsweetened coconut milk, divided
- 1½ tablespoons green curry paste
- 2½ pounds boneless chicken sliced into 1-inch strips
- 1 cup sliced bamboo shoots
- ¼ cup fish sauce
- 1 tablespoon sugar
- 1 small bunch mint leaves, chopped (about ¼ cup) or Oriental basil leaves
- 2 fresh green chili peppers, seeded and thinly sliced on the diagonal
- 4 cups hot cooked white rice

In a large saucepan, heat ¼ cup of coconut milk with the green curry paste. Stir until it is well blended and a thin coat of oil appears on the surface. Add the chicken and continue cooking over medium heat for 5 minutes, stirring constantly.

Stir in the remaining coconut milk and the bamboo shoots, fish sauce, and sugar. Cover and simmer for 8 to 10 minutes, or until chicken is cooked. Remove cover and stir in mint leaves and chili peppers. Cook, stirring, for 3 to 5 minutes. Serve with rice.

Reducing Saltiness, Part 2

If you've added too much salt to a one-pot dish, cut up some raw potatoes and add them to the dish. Leave them in for 5 to 10 minutes, or longer, tasting the dish occasionally. When the saltiness has been reduced, discard the potatoes.

Chicken Gumbo

Serves: 8

> 1 4-pound broiler-fryer chicken, cut into serving pieces
> 12 cups hot water, in which 6 chicken bouillon cubes have been dissolved
> 2 large onions, chopped
> 3 large carrots, scraped and chopped
> 2 ribs celery, chopped, with their leaves
> 2 bay leaves
> Pinch of cayenne pepper
> $3/4$ teaspoon thyme
> 1 teaspoon sugar
> 1 teaspoon salt
> 6 peppercorns
> 3 tablespoons chicken fat
> 1 clove garlic, chopped
> $1\frac{1}{2}$ cups uncooked long-grain rice
> 4 tomatoes, peeled, seeded, and chopped
> 1 10-ounce package frozen okra, thawed

In a large stockpot, combine the chicken, bouillon, vegetables, and seasonings. Bring the liquid to a boil, reduce the heat, and simmer the chicken, covered, for 2 hours, or until the meat falls from the bones. Remove the chicken from the pot, discard the skin and bones, and dice the meat. Set aside.

In a skillet, heat the chicken fat. Cook the garlic in the fat until it is golden. Add the rice, and toast it for 3 minutes, stirring to coat each grain, until lightly browned. Add the rice and tomatoes to the stockpot; simmer the gumbo, covered, for 15 minutes. Add the okra and cook for 5 minutes, or until it is tender.

Apple & Onion Chicken Curry

Serves: 8

> $1/2$ cup all-purpose flour
> $1/2$ teaspoon salt
> $1/2$ teaspoon pepper
> 1 teaspoon ground ginger
> 2 3-pound broiler-fryer chickens, cut into serving pieces
> 2 tablespoons butter
> 2 tablespoons oil
> 2 onions, chopped
> 1 clove garlic, chopped
> 1 tart apple, peeled, cored, and diced
> 1 tablespoon curry powder
> 1 cup hot water, in which 1 chicken bouillon cube has been dissolved
> 1 cup warm milk
> Grated rind and juice of 1 lemon

Combine flour with salt, pepper, and ginger. Dredge the chicken in the flour mixture. In an ovenproof casserole, heat the butter and oil. Sauté the chicken until lightly browned. Remove the chicken from the dish and set it aside.

Preheat oven to 350°F. In the same dish, cook the onion and garlic until translucent. Stir in the apple and curry powder.

Gradually add the water and then the milk, stirring constantly, until the mixture is thickened and smooth. Stir in the lemon rind and juice.

Add the chicken back to the dish, spooning the sauce over it. Bake, covered, for 1 hour, or until chicken is tender.

Yogurt Chicken

Serves: 8

2 cups plain lowfat yogurt
Juice of 1 lime
1 clove garlic, minced
1 1/2 teaspoons ground cardamom
1 teaspoon chili powder
1 teaspoon ground coriander
1 teaspoon ground ginger
2 tablespoons olive oil
1 teaspoon salt
1 teaspoon freshly ground black pepper
2 3-pound broiler-fryer chickens, cut into
*   serving pieces*
2 tablespoons butter
2 tablespoons olive oil
2 tablespoons all-purpose flour

In a mixing bowl, combine and blend thoroughly yogurt, lime juice, garlic, cardamom, chili powder, coriander, ginger, olive oil, salt, and pepper. In a shallow baking dish, place the chicken pieces, and pour the marinade over them; cover. Refrigerate for 6 hours, turning occasionally.

Remove the chicken from the marinade with a slotted spoon. Reserve the marinade. Dry the chicken on paper towels. In an ovenproof casserole, heat the butter and oil and brown the chicken, about 7 minutes on each side.

Preheat oven to 350°F. Remove the chicken from the pan and set it aside. In the same pan, add the flour, stirring into the fat. Gradually add the reserved marinade, stirring constantly, until the sauce is thickened and smooth. Return the chicken to the pan. Bake the casserole, covered, for 1 hour, or until the chicken is tender.

Chicken & White Bean Chili

Serves: 4

2 tablespoons olive oil
2 medium onions, chopped
1 teaspoon minced garlic
1 15- or 19-ounce can cannellini beans
1 14 1/2-ounce can chunky tomatoes
2 5-ounce cans or one 12 1/2-ounce can
*   chunk-style chicken, drained and flaked*
1 10-ounce package frozen peas and carrots
1 6-ounce can tomato juice
1 tablespoon chili powder
1/2 teaspoon seasoned salt
1/4 teaspoon ground cumin
1 cup shredded Cheddar or Monterey Jack
*   cheese (4 ounces)*

Heat oil in a large saucepan. Cook and stir onions and garlic in hot oil for 3 minutes. Stir in undrained beans, undrained tomatoes, chicken, peas and carrots, tomato juice, chili powder, seasoned salt, and cumin.

Bring to boiling; reduce heat. Simmer; covered, about 5 minutes or until mixture is heated through. Spoon into soup bowls. Sprinkle each serving with shredded cheese.

2 tablespoons diced pimiento
1 cup chopped lettuce
$\frac{1}{4}$ cup thinly sliced radishes
1/4 cup shredded Cheddar cheese (1 ounce)
1 2$\frac{1}{4}$-ounce can sliced pitted ripe olives, drained
Sour cream (optional)
Thinly sliced green onion

Preheat oven to 350°F. Place tortillas in a single layer directly on the middle oven rack. Bake about 6 minutes or until golden and crisp, turning halfway through baking time. Cover to keep warm.

Meanwhile, cook chicken and chili powder in a large skillet until chicken is no longer pink. Stir in salsa. Cover and keep warm.

Drain beans, reserving liquid. Place beans in a small saucepan; stir over low heat until heated through. Mash beans with a potato masher or fork, adding enough reserved bean liquid to make a spreadable consistency. Heat through.

To serve, spread each warm tortilla with a thin layer of beans. Place each tortilla, bean side up, on a dinner plate. Top with some of the chicken mixture, pimiento, lettuce, radishes, cheese, olives, sour cream, and green onion.

Substituting Beans

If you keep the ingredients for easy Chicken & White Bean Chili—and other recipes—on hand, you can whip up an easy supper without having to make a special trip to the supermarket. But if you need to stop in a convenience store on the way home from work, or if you don't feel like battling the lines at the super-market and can't find cannellini beans (also called white kidney beans), navy or Great Northern beans can be substituted.

South-of-the-Border Chicken Tostadas

Serves: 4

4 8-inch flour tortillas
1 pound ground chicken
1 teaspoon chili powder
1 8-ounce bottle medium or hot salsa
1 15-ounce can black beans or pinto beans

Creamy Chicken & Corn

Serves: 6

10 ears sweet corn
1 3-pound spring chicken

2 tablespoons cooking oil
1 large onion, finely chopped
½ bell pepper, chopped
1 large tomato, diced
1 teaspoon salt
1 teaspoon sugar
1 teaspoon black pepper
¼ cup milk, if needed

Cut corn off cob, and then scrape ears with the back of a knife, scraping the milky pulp into a heavy iron pot. In a separate pan brown the chicken in oil a few pieces at a time, until all sides are done. Add the chicken to the corn. Add the onion, bell pepper, tomato, salt, sugar and pepper to the pot. Stir mixture frequently while cooking over low heat for 30 minutes. If mixture is too dry, add a small amount of milk.

Marinated Ginger Chicken

Serves: 4

1 2½ to 3 pound frying chicken, cut into
    serving pieces
½ cup lemon juice
½ cup vegetable oil
¼ cup soy sauce
1 teaspoon grated gingerroot or
    1 tablespoon ground ginger
1 teaspoon onion salt
¼ teaspoon garlic powder

Place chicken in shallow baking dish. In small bowl, combine the lemon juice, oil, soy sauce, ginger, onion, and garlic powder. Pour over chicken. Cover and refrigerate at least 4 hours or overnight, turning occasionally. Grill or broil as desired, basting frequently with marinade.

Microwave Chicken Breasts with Rice

Serves: 2

1 2½-ounce jar dried beef
2 medium stalks celery, chopped
1 small onion, chopped
1 tablespoon butter
2 cups cooked rice
2 tablespoons chopped parsley
1 1-ounce jar pine nuts
2 medium chicken breasts, boned and
    halved
½ teaspoon seasoned salt
1 teaspoon paprika

Snip beef into small pieces. Combine beef, celery, onion, and butter in 2-quart casserole. Cover and microwave on high until onion is crisp-tender, 3 to 4 minutes. Stir in rice, parsley, and pine nuts. Arrange chicken breasts skin sides up with thickest parts on the outside of rice mixture. Sprinkle with seasoned salt and paprika. Cover and microwave 5 minutes; turn casserole a half turn. Microwave until chicken is done, 8 to 11 minutes.

Chicken Jambalaya

Serves: 10

 2 tablespoons vegetable oil
 1 chicken fryer (3 to 4 pound),
   cut up
 4 cups chopped onion
 $^3/_4$ cup chopped green pepper
 $^3/_4$ cup minced shallots
 1 tablespoon minced garlic
 3 tablespoons minced parsley
 $^1/_2$ cup chopped baked ham
 1 pound cubed lean pork
 6 creole (Polish or French garlic) smoked
   sausage, sliced
 $^1/_4$ teaspoon basil
 $^1/_8$ teaspoon mace
 $3^1/_2$ teaspoons salt
 $^1/_2$ teaspoon black pepper
 $^1/_4$ teaspoon cayenne pepper
 $^1/_2$ teaspoon chili powder
 2 bay leaves
 $^1/_4$ teaspoon thyme
 $^1/_8$ teaspoon cloves
 $1^1/_2$ cups long-grain white rice
 3 cups water

In heavy 7- or 8-quart pot, heat oil on high. Brown the chicken, turning frequently to brown evenly. As chicken browns, remove to a platter. When all chicken is browned and removed, add the veggies, parsley, ham, and pork to the pot. Reduce heat to medium and cook, stirring frequently 15 minutes or until meat is browned.

Add sausage and seasonings and continue cooking and stirring 5 minutes more. Add chicken, rice, and water. Mix gently. Raise heat to high and bring to boil. Cover and cook on very low heat 45 minutes, stirring occasionally.

Uncover last 10 minutes and raise heat to medium. Stir gently as rice dries out. Remove bay leaves before serving.

Coriander Chicken

Serves: 4

 1 small chicken, cut into serving pieces, or
   4 to 6 boneless breasts and/or thighs
   of chicken
 1 tablespoon butter
 2 tablespoons olive oil
 4 large cloves garlic, crushed
 1 teaspoon turmeric
 Salt and pepper to taste
 Sprig of fresh cilantro leaves, chopped
   fine, or 2 teaspoons ground coriander
 $^1/_4$ pound purple olives, pitted (Greek or
   Italian)
 1 lemon, sliced
 Hot cooked rice or couscous

Brown the chicken in butter and oil in a large, heavy skillet over moderate heat. Add the garlic, turmeric, salt, pepper, and cilantro. Cook for about 10 minutes, turning the chicken pieces occasionally to distribute sauce evenly. Stir in enough water to cover, about 1 cup, and simmer over low heat, adding more water if necessary until the chicken is tender.

Add olives and lemon and cook over somewhat lower heat for 8 to 10 more minutes, or until sauce is reduced. Serve over rice or couscous.

Note: Use less water (½ to ¾ cup) if you use boneless chicken.

Ginger Garlic Chicken Baked Stir-Fry

Serves: 6

¼ cup soy sauce
1 tablespoon dry sherry
1 teaspoon minced fresh ginger or
*   ½ teaspoon ground ginger*
1 large clove garlic, minced
3 whole chicken breasts (about 1 pound
*   each), split, skinned, and boned*
2 teaspoons cornstarch
1 teaspoon olive oil
2 large green peppers, seeded and cut in
*   1-inch squares*
2 stalks celery, diagonally cut in ½-inch-
*   thick slices*
1 4-ounce can water chestnuts, drained
*   and sliced*
1 8-ounce can pineapple chunks, drained
*   well*

In a shallow, 2-quart ovenproof casserole or 7 x 11-inch baking dish, combine soy sauce, sherry, ginger, and garlic. Place chicken in a heavy plastic bag or large bowl. Pour marinade over chicken, cover, and refrigerate for 4 hours, turning occasionally.

Preheat oven to 325°F. Lift chicken from marinade and set aside. Reserve 2 tablespoons of the marinade; discard the remainder. Cover and bake chicken for about 35 minutes. Remove from oven; remove chicken from pan. Drain off and save juices, and add enough water to make ½ cup.

Add saved ½ cup broth and cornstarch to reserved 2 tablespoons marinade and set aside. Heat oil in casserole over medium heat; add peppers, celery, water chestnuts, and pineapple; stir-fry just until pieces are glazed (about 2 minutes).

Stir broth mixture once or twice and gradually pour into vegetables, cooking and stirring until sauce thickens. Return the chicken to the casserole, cover, and return casserole to oven for 15 more minutes or until meat near thigh bone is no longer pink when slashed.

Hunter-Style Chicken

Serves: 4

1 tablespoon butter
1 tablespoon olive oil
3½ pounds chicken, cut up for frying
6 shallots, peeled and diced
1 10-ounce package mushrooms, sliced
2 tablespoons flour
1 tablespoon pesto
¼ cup tomato sauce
1 ounce brandy
10 ounces white wine
16 ounces (2 cups) chicken stock

(continued)

Salt and pepper to taste
1 tablespoon chopped fresh parsley
Lemon juice to taste
dash balsamic vinegar

Using a heavy pot with a lid, fry the chicken skin side down in the butter and oil over medium heat; fry until brown, about 8 minutes. Turn the chicken over and brown the other side. Remove the chicken and set aside.

In the same pan, combine the diced shallots and mushrooms. Let the shallots get soft and lightly browned. Add flour and let it brown, about 5 minutes. Pour off all excess fat. Add the pesto and cook a few moments more. Add tomato sauce and cook 5 minutes.

Add the brandy, wine, and chicken stock. Let this come to a boil, and simmer 5 minutes, stirring occasionally. Add the previously browned chicken and any juices it may have left with it, and simmer in the sauce for about an hour, till tender.

Season with salt, pepper, and parsley. If the sauce tastes a bit oily, try adding some fresh lemon juice or a dash of balsamic vinegar.

Savory Stuffed Chicken

Serves: 8

8 slices bacon, diced
1 large onion, chopped
1 10-ounce package frozen chopped
    spinach, thawed and drained well
1 egg, lightly beaten
1/2 cup seasoned croutons, lightly crushed
1/2 teaspoon garlic salt
4 whole chicken breasts, split, skinned,
    and boned

In a wide ovenproof skillet over medium heat, cook bacon until crisp. Pour off all but 2 tablespoons of the drippings. Add onion and cook until soft. Add the spinach, egg, croutons, and garlic salt; toss gently. Set aside.

With a small sharp knife, cut a pocket in the thick side of each breast. Place several tablespoons of the stuffing into each chicken breast, securing with a toothpick.

Preheat oven to 325°F. Place the chicken into the skillet, and loosely cover with a piece of aluminum foil. Bake for 45 minutes, or until stuffing is hot.

Spicy Cinnamon Chicken

Serves: 6

2 tablespoons olive oil
2 tablespoons butter
1 broiler-fryer chicken (3 to 3 1/2 pounds),
    cut in pieces
2 large onions, chopped
1 green pepper, seeded and diced
1 cup brown or white rice
Hot water
3 chicken bouillon cubes
1/2 teaspoon thyme leaves
1/4 teaspoon pepper
1/4 teaspoon ground cinnamon

¹/₄ teaspoon ground allspice
1¹/₂ teaspoons salt
1 8-ounce can stewed tomatoes
Chopped parsley

Heat oil and butter in a 6-quart Dutch oven over medium heat. Add chicken pieces, a few at a time, and cook, turning occasionally, until well browned. Remove pieces and set aside.

Discard all but 4 tablespoons of the pan juices. Add onions and green pepper and cook for about 3 minutes or until onion is slightly soft. Stir in rice and cook for 5 more minutes.

Combine hot water (2 cups for white rice; 2²/₃ cups for brown rice), bouillon cubes, thyme, pepper, cinnamon, allspice, and salt; pour over rice. Cover, reduce heat, and simmer until rice is almost tender (20 minutes for white rice; 45 to 50 minutes for brown rice).

Stir in tomatoes and arrange chicken pieces on top. Cover and simmer for about 25 more minutes or until meat is cooked through. Sprinkle with parsley.

Slow-Cooking Sticky Fingers Chicken

Serves: 8

4 teaspoons salt
2 teaspoons paprika
1 teaspoon cayenne pepper
1 teaspoon onion powder
1 teaspoon thyme

1 teaspoon white pepper
¹/₂ teaspoon garlic powder
¹/₂ teaspoon black pepper
1 large roasting chicken, at least
    4¹/₂ to 5 pounds
1 cup chopped onion

In a small bowl, thoroughly combine all the spices. Remove giblets from chicken, clean the cavity well, and pat dry with paper towels. Rub the spice mixture into the chicken, both inside and out, making sure it is evenly distributed and down deep into the skin. Place the chicken in a resealable plastic bag, seal, and refrigerate overnight.

Preheat oven to 250°F. Stuff chicken cavity with onions, and place in a shallow baking pan. Roast, uncovered, for 5 hours (yes, 250°F for 5 hours). After the first hour, baste chicken occasionally (every half hour or so) with pan juices. The pan juices will start to caramelize on the bottom of pan and the chicken will turn golden brown. If the chicken contains a pop-up thermometer, ignore it. Let chicken rest about 10 minutes before carving.

Quick Chicken Vinaigrette

Serves: 4

4 boneless, skinless chicken breast halves
Salt and pepper
1 clove garlic, crushed
2 tablespoons olive oil
2 tablespoons tarragon vinegar
¹/₃ cup dry sherry

(continued)

Preheat oven to 350°F. Sprinkle chicken with salt and pepper. Crush garlic into oil and vinegar in a skillet. Sauté chicken breasts until golden brown, turning frequently. Remove and place in a baking dish. Pour sherry over chicken and bake for 10 minutes.

Chicken a la King

Serves: 5

$\frac{1}{2}$ cup butter
$\frac{1}{2}$ cup all-purpose flour
2 cups chicken broth
$\frac{3}{4}$ cup light cream
2 egg yolks, beaten
$\frac{1}{2}$ cup pimientos
1 cup sliced mushrooms
$\frac{1}{4}$ cup chopped and blanched green peppers
3 cups diced cooked chicken
2 tablespoons sherry
Salt and black pepper to taste
Paprika

Melt butter in top of double boiler. Add flour and cook one minute. Add chicken broth and cream. Bring to a boil. Cook for 15 minutes. Remove from heat and add beaten egg yolks, pimiento, mushrooms, green peppers, and chicken. Season with sherry, salt, pepper, and paprika to taste.

Curried Chicken Salad

Serves: 8

1 4-pound roaster chicken
1 large carrot, sliced
1 large onion, quartered
1 or 2 stalks celery with leaves, chopped
2 teaspoons salt
3 cups boiling water
1 cup mayonnaise
1 teaspoon curry powder
$\frac{1}{4}$ teaspoon pepper
$\frac{1}{4}$ cup cream
$\frac{1}{2}$ cup diced green pepper
1 cup slivered green celery

Cut the chicken into sections and wash them quickly under running cold water. Put the carrot, onion, celery with leaves, and salt in a large pot of boiling water and simmer for 5 minutes. Add the chicken pieces slowly to keep the liquid simmering, cover the pot tightly, and continue to simmer until tender, up to 2 hours. Let the chicken cool in the broth, then remove it.

Discard skin and bones. Dice the chicken meat. In a large bowl combine the mayonnaise, curry powder, and pepper; blend well, then stir in the cream. Add the chicken and raw vegetables and mix thoroughly. Chill in the refrigerator, then serve on a bed of lettuce.

Cold Thai Lemon Chicken

Serves: 8

1 medium onion, chopped
1 pound whole chicken beast
5 to 6 celery leaves
$^1/_4$ cup Chinese lemon sauce
1$^1/_2$ tablespoons dark soy sauce
Lettuce leaves
$^1/_4$ cup finely chopped cilantro leaves and
    stems
juice of 1 lemon

In a saucepan, combine the onion, chicken breast, and celery leaves with just enough water to cover. Bring to a slow boil; cover and simmer over medium heat for 10 minutes. Remove from the heat and allow the chicken to cool in the liquid. When it is cool, skin and bone the chicken and slice it. In the same pot, mix the lemon sauce and soy sauce together. Place the chicken slices in the mixture and marinate for 45 minutes.

On a serving dish, arrange the chicken slices on a bed of lettuce leaves; sprinkle with the chopped cilantro. Sprinkle the lemon juice over the chicken slices.

California Chicken and Wild Rice Salad

Serves: 6

1 package mixed white and wild rice
1 tablespoon fresh lemon juice
3 cups cooked chicken, cut into bite-sized pieces
4 scallions, chopped
1 cup Italian dressing
2 ripe avocados
$^1/_2$ cup toasted pine nuts or
    sliced almonds
1 cup cherry tomatoes

Prepare rice according to package directions. When the rice is ready, stir in chicken and scallions; add dressing and toss well. Pour into a serving dish and chill.

Dice avocados and toss with lemon juice. Garnish salad with avocados, nuts, and cherry tomatoes.

Chicken Pasta Salad

Serves: 6

1 16-ounce package frozen broccoli
$^1/_4$ teaspoon salt
1 whole cooked chicken, boned, skinned,
    and diced
1 8-ounce package pasta shells, cooked
2 large tomatoes, cubed
$^1/_2$ cup coarsely chopped red onions
$^1/_2$ teaspoon black pepper
1 cup Italian salad dressing

In saucepan, steam broccoli over boiling water for about 5 minutes. Remove broccoli from pan; sprinkle with salt. Place chicken, broccoli, pasta, tomatoes, and onion in a large bowl; sprinkle with pepper. Add Italian dressing and mix gently but thoroughly. Chill in refrigerator. Serve cold.

Enchiladas de Pollo y Queso

Serves: 6

5 tablespoons butter, divided
1 cup chopped onions
$\frac{1}{2}$ cup chopped bell peppers
2 cups chopped cooked chicken
4 ounces green chili peppers, chopped
$\frac{1}{4}$ cup all-purpose flour
1 tablespoon chili powder
$\frac{1}{2}$ teaspoon ground coriander seed
$\frac{1}{2}$ teaspoon ground cumin seed
$2\frac{1}{2}$ cups chicken broth
1 cup sour cream
$1\frac{1}{2}$ cups shredded Monterey Jack cheese
12 6-inch tortillas

In a skillet, melt 2 tablespoons butter, and cook onions and green pepper in it until softened. Remove to a bowl. Stir chopped chicken and green chilies into onion-pepper mixture. Melt remaining 3 tablespoons of butter. Blend in flour and seasonings. Whisk in chicken broth. Cook, stirring, until sauce boils. Remove from heat; stir in sour cream and $\frac{1}{2}$ cup cheese. Stir $\frac{1}{2}$ cup sauce into chicken mixture.

Preheat oven to 350°F. Dip each tortilla in remaining hot sauce to soften and spoon chicken mixture into center of tortilla. Roll up and arrange in 13 x 9 x 2-inch pan; repeat with all tortillas. Pour remaining sauce over tortillas. Sprinkle with remaining cheese. Bake uncovered for about 25 minutes.

Chili Pepper Primer

Do you know your poblano from your jalapeño? Here's how to tell the difference:

Jalapeño: The jalapeño is short, fat, and dark green. It's the most popular fresh chili pepper sold in supermarkets and can be eaten raw or sautéed.

Poblano: Like the jalapeño, the poblano is dark green, but shaped like a cone and has a milder flavor. The flavor comes out when roasted.

Anaheim: The anaheim, also known as the New Mexico chili pepper, can range from three to six inches long. Its shade of green is a little lighter than either the jalapeño or poblano, and it's also the chili with the least bite.

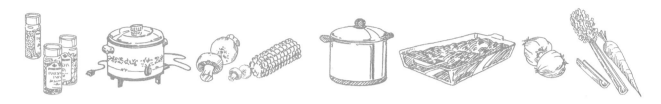

Turkey

According to the Butterball Brigade, more people are serving roast turkey year-round than before, and not just at Thanksgiving. But since the preparation involved in serving up a traditional turkey dinner is still very labor intensive, I think that turkey would become even more popular if one-pot dishes featuring turkey are promoted; here are a few to get you started.

Turkey Tetrazzini

Serves: 4

6 tablespoons butter
6 tablespoons flour
1½ cups chicken or turkey broth
1½ cups evaporated milk
4 ounces Cheddar cheese, shredded
Salt and pepper to taste
5 cups diced cooked turkey
1 12-ounce package egg noodles or
    spaghetti, cooked and drained
1 cup fresh peas
1 8-ounce package mushrooms, sliced
Seasoned bread crumbs

Melt butter in a large saucepan. Add flour, stir until well blended, and cook a few minutes. Remove from heat and slowly stir in broth and milk, stirring until well blended and smooth. Cook over low heat until thickened. Add cheese and stir until melted. Season with salt and pepper.

Preheat oven to 350°F. Mix sauce with chicken, noodles, peas, and mushrooms. Place in a 2-quart casserole dish and sprinkle with bread crumbs. Bake about 40 minutes until hot and bubbly.

Oven Barbecued Turkey Legs

Serves: 3

¼ cup flour
1 teaspoon salt
½ teaspoon chili powder
¼ teaspoon pepper
6 small turkey legs, about ⅓ pound each
¼ cup corn oil
½ cup bottled barbecue sauce
½ cup water
1 chicken bouillon cube, crushed

In a small flat dish, mix the flour with salt, chili powder, and pepper; dredge turkey legs with flour mixture. Heat oil in a large

(continued)

ovenproof skillet; brown turkey, turning to brown all sides, about 10 minutes.

Preheat oven to 325°F. Combine barbecue sauce, water, and crushed bouillon; spoon over turkey. Cover skillet with aluminum foil; bake for 1 hour.

Uncover and bake for another hour, until turkey is tender, basting frequently.

Potato Pot Pie

Serves: 6

8 ounces mushrooms, sliced

$\frac{1}{4}$ cup onion, chopped

1 cup + 2 tablespoons Miracle Whip salad dressing, divided

$\frac{1}{4}$ cup flour

1 teaspoon dried basil leaves

$\frac{1}{2}$ teaspoon salt

$\frac{1}{2}$ teaspoon pepper

1 $\frac{1}{4}$ cups milk

2 cups cooked, chopped chicken or turkey

1 10-ounce package frozen mixed vegetables, thawed and drained

1 $\frac{1}{2}$ cups shredded Cheddar cheese, divided

2 cups potatoes, mashed with $\frac{1}{2}$ cup Miracle Whip

In an ovenproof 2-quart skillet, cook mushrooms and onions in 2 tablespoons dressing over medium-high heat. Add flour and seasonings; gradually add milk, stirring until thickened. Stir in 1 cup dressing, chicken or turkey, mixed vegetables,

and 1 cup cheese; cook 5 minutes. Remove from heat.

Top casserole with potato mixture; broil until golden. Sprinkle with remaining cheese; broil until cheese begins to melt.

Chinese Turkey & Noodle Stir-Fry

Serves: 4

1 bunch scallions

2 teaspoons minced garlic

1 tablespoon grated fresh ginger

2 tablespoons olive oil

1 pound ground turkey

$\frac{1}{4}$ cup soy sauce

1 5-ounce can sliced water chestnuts

$\frac{1}{2}$ teaspoon crushed red pepper flakes

3 cups boiling water

$\frac{1}{2}$ pound wide egg noodles, uncooked

Chop scallions, separating green part from white part. Sauté garlic, ginger, and white part of scallions in oil in a large, deep skillet or wok for 30 seconds. Add meat and sauté, breaking up with a spoon. Cook until no longer pink, about 5 minutes.

Add soy sauce, water chestnuts, and red pepper flakes, and stir until well combined. Add boiling water and noodles and stir well. Cover and cook over medium heat until noodles are tender, about 7 to 10 minutes, stirring once or twice to make sure noodles are cooking evenly. Garnish with chopped green scallions.

Easy Turkey Vegetable Stir-Fry

Serves: 4

- 2 tablespoons butter
- ½ pound mushrooms, sliced
- 1 10-ounce package frozen peas
- 1 6-ounce package frozen snow peas
- ¾ cup chicken broth, divided
- ½ cup sliced canned water chestnuts, drained
- 3 cups cooked turkey cut in bite-size pieces
- ⅓ cup sliced green onions (including tops)
- 4 teaspoons cornstarch
- 2 tablespoons soy sauce
- 4 cups hot steamed rice
- ¾ cup slivered almonds for garnish

In a wide frying pan over medium heat, melt butter. Add mushrooms and cook until soft. Add peas, snow peas, and ½ cup of the broth. Cover and cook, stirring, for about 4 minutes or until peas are thawed.

Stir in water chestnuts, turkey, and onions; continue cooking and stirring for about 2 more minutes. Combine cornstarch, soy sauce, and remaining ¼ cup broth. Stir into turkey mixture and cook until sauce boils and thickens. Serve over steamed rice and garnish with almonds.

Hearty Turkey & Sausage Loaf

Serves: 8

- 1 pound ground turkey
- 1 pound turkey sausage
- 1 cup shredded carrots
- 1 onion, finely chopped
- 1 cup fresh bread crumbs
- 1 egg
- ⅓ cup milk
- ¼ cup fresh chopped parsley
- ⅓ cup ketchup
- 1 tablespoon brown sugar
- ½ teaspoon dry mustard

Preheat oven to 350°F. Spray a 9 x 13-inch baking pan with nonstick cooking spray. In a large bowl mix meats, carrots, onion, bread crumbs, egg, milk, and parsley until well blended. Shape into a large loaf in the baking pan. Mix remaining ingredients and spread over loaf. Bake 45 minutes to an hour or until cooked through. Allow to rest 10 minutes before slicing.

Coconut Turkey Curry

Serves: 6

- 1 onion, coarsely chopped
- 1 teaspoon minced garlic
- ½ teaspoon ground ginger
- 2 teaspoons curry powder
- ⅓ cup flour

(continued)

2 cups chicken or turkey broth, divided
5 cups cubed cooked turkey or chicken
Salt and pepper
1 16-ounce can coconut cream,
    unsweetened
1 cup milk

Purée the onions, garlic, ginger, curry powder, flour, and 1/2 cup of the broth until smooth. In a large saucepan, combine puréed mixture and all remaining ingredients except turkey or chicken. Cook, stirring often, till thickened. Add the meat and heat gently.

Serve with white rice and small dishes of raisins, peanuts, chutney, coconut, bacon, and green onions.

Easy Thanksgiving Anytime

Serves: 6

3 cups leftover stuffing or 1 6-ounce
    package stuffing mix,
prepared according to package directions
2 cups cooked and cubed turkey
1 10 1/2-ounce can cream of mushroom
    soup
1/2 cup chopped celery
1/2 cup chopped onion
1 teaspoon poultry seasoning
1/2 teaspoon pepper

Heat oven to 350°F. Combine all ingredients. Add turkey broth or water if mixture is too dry.

Place in lightly greased 1-quart casserole dish. Bake for 35 to 45 minutes or until hot and lightly browned on top. Garnish with cranberry jelly sauce, if desired.

Curry Powder

Curry powder is not one spice, but a combination of anywhere from 15 to 50 different spices. Madras curry has a fuller, richer flavor than national brands, but there are even differences between the kinds of curry powder you find in the supermarket. Become a curry connoisseur!

Chapter 4

*Fish
Dishes*

It's popularly believed that most kinds of fish are too delicate for cooking in one pot. However, as you can see by the following recipes, the more delicate kinds of fish—flounder, sole, and other fish often served in fillets rather than steaks—can stand up in one-pot meals as well as the heartier types of fish like swordfish and salmon.

Sometimes, a more delicate touch with the spatula is necessary, but any of the recipes given in the *Everything One-Pot Cookbook* that don't specify a particular kind of fish will be fine with everything from the most delicate flounder to the sturdiest swordfish.

Poached Cod with Spicy Buttermilk Sauce

Serves: 4

> 1½ pounds cod fillets
> ¾ teaspoon turmeric
> Black pepper to taste
> 3 cups buttermilk
> 1 tablespoon lemon juice
> ½ teaspoon salt
> 2 teaspoons cumin

Sprinkle the fillets with turmeric and black pepper. Pour the buttermilk into a heavy skillet and poach the fish for 5 minutes. Remove the fish. Add the lemon juice and salt to the pan. Heat the buttermilk over high heat for 5 minutes. Stir in the cumin, reduce the heat, and return the fish to the pan. Cook for another 5 to 10 minutes until the fish is done. Spoon the sauce over the fish to serve.

A Thousand Layers of Fish

Serves: 4

> Olive oil
> 1½ pounds of cod, haddock, or flounder
> 3 lemons, sliced very thinly with a mandolin
> 1 head of butter lettuce, torn into full leaves
> 4 large tomatoes, cut in half and sliced thinly

Lightly grease a deep 4-quart baking dish with olive oil.

Layer ingredients in the baking dish in the following order: fish, lemons, lettuce, tomatoes. Drizzle each layer with a little olive oil. Repeat the layers to use up all the ingredients except a few lemon slices. Put a cover of lettuce over the last layer and tuck the ends down the sides as far as you can reach (about ½ inch or so). This will help to seal

in the juices while cooking. Preheat oven to 225°F.

Dip a few lemon slices in olive oil and use them to make a decorative arrangement on the lettuce. Bake for 1 1/2 hours.

Let the casserole rest for 10 minutes to allow the juices to retract before serving. Slice into 2-inch-square slices. Spoon the cooking juices over each slice.

Chinese Sweet and Sour Fillets

Serves: 6

1 1/2 pounds fish fillets: cod, haddock, or flounder
2 eggs, beaten with 1 tablespoon water
1/2 cup flour
2 inches peanut oil in deep fryer with basket
1 cup chicken stock
1/2 cup white vinegar
1/2 cup French vermouth or pale dry sherry
1/2 cup sugar
1 cup thinly sliced carrots
1 tablespoon soy sauce
1 tablespoon cornstarch
2 or 3 firm tomatoes, quartered
2 green peppers, seeds removed, cut coarsely
1/2 cup drained canned or frozen pineapple chunks
4 cups hot cooked rice

Cooking with Lemons

Use lemons that have not been sprayed with pesticides. Select lemons that have a smooth, thin outer peel and very little white pith. The pith is bitter and if there's too much of it, it will impart an unpleasant sharpness. When using the whole lemon, include the outer peel. In cooking, slice the lemons as thinly as possible so they can "melt" during cooking.

Cut the fillets into pieces about the size of large shrimp. Blend the beaten eggs with the flour into a smooth batter. Dip the fish pieces into the batter, coating evenly, and deep-fry in the hot oil until golden brown. Remove the fish and drain on paper towels. In a large saucepan combine the stock, vinegar, wine, and sugar. Bring to a brisk boil, add the carrots, and boil for 5 minutes. Reduce the heat to simmer.

(continued)

Combine the soy sauce and cornstarch and stir this mixture into the simmering carrots. Add the quartered tomatoes, cut peppers, and pineapple chunks and stir. Add the fried fish pieces and stir carefully with a wooden spoon to distribute all the ingredients evenly. Simmer until the sauce clears somewhat and thickens, about 8 to 10 minutes. If more liquid seems to be needed, stir in your choice of stock or sherry. Serve over rice.

Sautéed Fillets and Bananas in Wine Sauce

Serves: 4

> $1/2$ cup flour
> $1/2$ teaspoon salt
> $1/4$ teaspoon ground black pepper
> $1/4$ teaspoon paprika
> 1 pound fish fillets: cod, flounder, or haddock
> $1/4$ cup olive oil
> $1/2$ cup dry sherry or vermouth
> $1/2$ teaspoon ground ginger or anise
> 2 tablespoons lemon juice
> 2 tablespoons brown sugar
> 4 bananas, peeled and sliced lengthwise
> $1/4$ cup chopped walnuts, pecans, peanuts, or almonds

Combine the flour with the salt, pepper, and paprika. Pat the fillets as dry as possible and dredge them with the seasoned flour. Heat the oil in a large skillet, but do not let it smoke. Put the fish into a single layer in the skillet over moderate heat, and cook until the undersurface is golden brown. Reduce the heat, turn the fish carefully, and cook the second side until the fish is translucent.

Remove the fillets from the skillet, drain on paper towels, and arrange them on a large warmed platter. To the oil in the skillet add the sherry, ginger or anise, lemon juice, and brown sugar; stir to blend. Add the sliced bananas and simmer for 3 minutes, basting them with the skillet mixture. Surround the fillets with the banana slices, cover with pan sauce, and garnish with the chopped nuts.

Indian Fish Curry

Serves: 6

> 2 cups vegetable bouillon
> 2 pounds fish fillets: cod, haddock, or flounder
> 2 tablespoons butter
> 1 onion, chopped
> 1 green pepper, chopped
> 1 rib celery, chopped
> 2 teaspoons curry powder
> 2 tablespoons flour
> Salt and pepper to taste
> $1/2$ cup chopped fresh parsley for garnish

In a shallow pan or skillet, bring the bouillon to a boil. Reduce the heat so the liquid simmers. Place the fish in the liquid and simmer for 5 minutes. Remove the fish to a serving dish and keep it warm. Strain the broth.

In the same pan, heat the butter until brown. Add the onion, pepper, and celery and cook until translucent. Stir in the curry powder and then the flour. Add the reserved broth and cook the mixture, stirring constantly, until it is thickened and smooth. Adjust the seasoning to taste. Pour the sauce over the warm fish and garnish the plate with parsley.

Steamed Ginger Fish

Serves: 4

> 2-inch piece gingerroot, julienned
> 5 scallions, julienned
> 2 pounds fish fillets (your favorite)
> 1/2 teaspoon soy sauce
> 2 teaspoons sesame oil
> 1/4 cup + 2 tablespoons rice wine vinegar
> 12 sprigs fresh cilantro
> Chinese bamboo steamer

Place half the ginger and scallions on a deep plate that will fit inside the steamer. Cover with the fish fillets and strew the remaining ginger and scallions on top. Sprinkle with soy sauce, sesame oil, and vinegar. Allow to marinate at room temperature, covered, for 20 to 30 minutes.

Pour an inch or two of water into the bottom of the steamer and bring to a boil. When it boils, put in the plate of fish. Add cilantro. Cover and steam over high heat until done, about 20 minutes. Serve with the juices that have accumulated in the plate.

Red Snapper a la Ritz

Serves: 4

> 1 pound red snapper fillets
> 1 sleeve low-fat Ritz crackers
> 1 green pepper, cut into chunks
> 1 tablespoon honey

Preheat oven to 350°F. Place fillets in a shallow baking dish or glass pie plate in one layer. In a blender, grind the crackers to crumbs and place in a bowl. Finely chop green pepper in blender. Add to crumbs. Add the honey and mix well. Top fillets with crumb mixture to cover. Bake for 20 minutes or until fish flakes.

Poached Trout

Serves: 6

> 3 cups water
> 1 cup dry white wine
> 2 tablespoons finely snipped chives
> 2 tablespoons minced fresh basil leaves
> 1 tablespoon chopped fresh dill
> 1 tablespoon chopped fresh rosemary
> 1 tablespoon chopped fresh tarragon
> 1 teaspoon salt
> Freshly ground pepper to taste
> 1 strip lemon zest, 2 inches by 1/2 inch
> 2 fresh brook trout (about 12 inches each), cleaned, heads and tails left on
> 3 tablespoons unsalted butter, melted
> Lemon wedges for garnish

(continued)

In a large pot or Dutch oven, bring the water, wine, herbs, spices, and lemon zest to a boil. Reduce the heat and simmer 10 minutes. Gently lower the trout into the liquid. Simmer, partially uncovered, until firm to the touch, about 10 minutes (or 10 minutes per inch of thickness of the fish).

Using two spatulas, lift each trout out and place it on a dinner plate. Blend the butter with 2 teaspoons of the cooking liquid (with as much of the herbs as you can retrieve), and spoon over the fish. Serve immediately with lemon wedges alongside.

Salmon in Red Wine with Apricots

Serves: 4

1 1/4 pounds salmon fillets
1/4 cup all-purpose flour
2 tablespoons olive oil
1 cup dry red wine
1/2 cup fish stock
1 cup dried apricots
Salt to taste
Freshly ground pepper to taste
2 tablespoons unsalted butter

Preheat oven to 375°F. Pat the salmon dry on towels. Dust in flour, shaking off the excess. Heat the oil in a 12-inch oven-proof skillet or roasting pan over medium heat on the stove. Add the salmon and brown on all sides. Remove to a plate and discard oil. Add the wine and stock to the skillet and bring to a boil.

Replace salmon in the skillet. Add the apricots and sprinkle with salt and pepper. Place, uncovered, in the oven. Cook 7 minutes. When done, transfer skillet to the stovetop and remove the fish to a carving board.

Cook the liquid in the roasting pan over high heat, stirring, until it thickens slightly. Remove from heat and whisk in the butter. Cut the salmon into 1/2-inch slices, arrange on a serving platter and spoon sauce over the top.

Northwest Salmon Vegetable Pie

Serves: 4

4 ounces uncooked spaghetti
1 beaten egg
1/3 cup grated Parmesan cheese
3 tablespoons butter, divided
1 cup broccoli florets
1 medium carrot, thinly sliced
1 small onion, cut into thin wedges
1/3 teaspoon crushed dried oregano or savory
1 clove garlic, minced
Dash salt
1 12 1/2-ounce can skinless, boneless salmon, drained and flaked
2 beaten eggs
1/3 cup half-and-half, light cream, or milk

For the spaghetti crusts, cook pasta according to package directions; drain. Immediately toss together pasta, 1 beaten

egg, Parmesan cheese, and 1 tablespoon of the butter. Divide pasta mixture evenly among 4 greased individual au gratin dishes. Press pasta mixture on the bottoms and up the sides of dishes to form crusts. Set aside.

Melt the remaining 2 tablespoons butter in a large skillet. Cook broccoli, carrot, onion, oregano, garlic, and salt in the hot butter until vegetables are crisp-tender. Gently stir salmon into the vegetable mixture. Divide salmon mixture evenly among the 4 spaghetti crusts. Preheat oven to 350°F. Combine the 2 beaten eggs and the half-and-half. Pour evenly over the salmon mixture. Cover with aluminum foil. Bake for 15 minutes. Remove foil; bake for 5 to 10 minutes more or until set. Let stand 5 minutes before serving.

Salmon with Horseradish Sauce

Serves: 2

> 1 quart chicken stock
> 1 rib celery, sliced
> 1 medium carrot, peeled and julienned
> 1 medium leek, julienned
> 1 small turnip, julienned
> 2 6-ounce salmon fillets, skinned
> 2 sprigs fresh parsley, chopped
> Rock or coarse (kosher) salt
> Imported cornichon pickles
> Horseradish sauce (see below)

Hard-Boiled Eggs

Hard-boiled eggs make a great garnish to add extra oomph to the tops of many one-pot dishes. To make a perfect hard-boiled egg, poke a hole with a needle in the round part of the egg. Boil water then remove the pot from the flame. Add eggs and boil gently 9 to 10 minutes. Pour water out of the pan, and shake eggs in the pan to crack them. Drop eggs into a bowl of water and ice. Peel under water for easier peeling. This will prevent green-tinged egg yolks and a sulfur smell.

Horseradish Sauce:

> 1 tablespoon butter
> 1 tablespoon flour
> 1 cup chicken stock
> 1 tablespoon heavy (whipping) cream
> 2 tablespoons prepared horseradish
> Salt to taste

In a 3-quart pan, heat the chicken stock to a simmer. Add the celery, carrot, leek, and turnip and cook until tender-crisp. Remove the vegetables from the stock and keep warm.

(continued)

139

Poach the salmon fillets in the stock for 4 minutes; turn and poach for 3 minutes more until firm. The salmon should not flake or fall apart.

Transfer the salmon to warm soup plates. Surround and sprinkle attractively with the poached vegetables and chopped parsley. Ladle stock over salmon. Garnish plates with the coarse salt, pickles, and horseradish sauce.

To prepare the horseradish sauce: In a saucepan over medium heat, melt the butter. Stir in the flour with a wooden spoon or wire whisk. Stir until smooth. Add the stock gradually, stirring/whisking constantly until sauce is smooth. Whisk in the cream and horseradish. Salt to taste. Stir until the sauce is smooth and thickened.

Louisiana Crawfish Étouffée

Serves: 4

½ cup flour
½ cup oil or butter
1 large onion, finely chopped
1 large celery stalk, finely chopped
3 large cloves garlic, minced
2½ cups fairly rich shrimp broth
1 tablespoon lemon juice
½ cup crawfish fat (substitute 3 to 4 tablespoons crawfish liquid or crawfish stock)
1 teaspoon salt (omit if using crawfish stock)

1 tablespoon fresh parsley (or 1 teaspoon dried)
½ teaspoon cayenne pepper
½ teaspoon black pepper
½ teaspoon thyme
1 bay leaf
1 pound frozen crawfish, all liquid included
2 large scallion tops, sliced
Hot cooked rice

Make a medium dark roux by whisking the flour into the oil over medium heat and stirring constantly until the mixture is the color of chocolate. Add the onion along with the celery and garlic, and sauté over medium-low heat until vegetables are tender, about 10 minutes. Slowly add the shrimp broth, and bring to a boil. Reduce heat to a simmer, and add lemon juice, crawfish fat/stock/liquid, and the herbs and spices. Simmer 15 minutes.

Add the crawfish and any liquid, and bring to a rapid simmer. Reduce to a low simmer, add the scallions, and simmer just until the crawfish are tender, about 10 minutes. Adjust seasonings. To serve, mound some rice on a plate, and ladle some of the étouffée on top.

Scallops au Gratin

Serves: 6

2 to 2½ pounds fresh or frozen raw scallops
2 cups fine bread crumbs, divided
4 tablespoons melted butter, divided

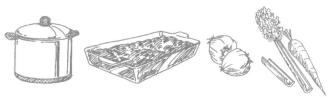

³⁄₄ cup diced green pepper
³⁄₄ cup diced celery
Salt and pepper
¹⁄₂ cup grated Cheddar cheese
1¹⁄₂ cups light cream or half-and-half

Barely cover the scallops with cold water in a saucepan and bring them slowly to the boiling point. Remove from the heat and drain. Preheat oven to 350°F.

Mix 1¹⁄₂ cups of the bread crumbs with 2 tablespoons of the melted butter. Divide the mixture into thirds, and spread one-third in a thin layer in a buttered freezer-to-oven casserole.

If the scallops are large, they may be cut into smaller pieces. Build up alternating layers of bread crumbs, scallops, and green pepper combined with celery, seasoning lightly as you go. Create the top layer out of the remaining bread crumbs mixed with the remaining butter and all the grated cheese.

Slowly pour in the cream or half-and-half, distributing it evenly. Bake for 25 to 30 minutes.

Coquilles St. Jacques Provençal

Serves: 6

2 pounds scallops
Salt and pepper to taste
2 tablespoons minced onion
6 tablespoons butter, divided
¹⁄₂ pound sliced fresh or frozen
   mushrooms

2 large tomatoes, peeled and chopped
¹⁄₂ cup dry white wine
1 tablespoon minced chives
1 clove garlic, minced

Pat the scallops dry. If they are large, cut them into smaller pieces. Sprinkle scallops lightly with salt and pepper and sauté along with the minced onion in 4 tablespoons of the butter until the onions look transparent, about 5 minutes, turning the scallops to brown all sides lightly. Remove the scallops and onions.

Add the remaining butter to the pan and sauté the mushrooms for 2 minutes. Add the tomatoes, wine, chives, and garlic and simmer for 5 minutes.

Scallop Sauté

Serves: 6

2 pounds bay or sea scallops
Flour
1 tablespoon olive oil
³⁄₄ cup butter
2 bunches green onions, chopped
1 white onion; chopped
2 pounds mushrooms, sliced
2 tablespoons minced shallots
2 cloves minced garlic
1 tablespoon salt
2 teaspoons freshly ground white pepper
1 teaspoon freshly ground black pepper
Juice of 1 lemon
2 cups dry white wine

(continued)

Dust the scallops with flour. Heat oil in large skillet over medium-high heat. Add scallops in four separate batches and cook until lightly browned.

In the same skillet, melt the butter. Add onions and cook until soft. Stir in mushrooms, shallots, garlic, salt, and pepper; cook until mushrooms are tender. Add scallops, lemon juice, and wine. Simmer 4 minutes, shaking pan occasionally.

Italian Vegetable & Seafood Casserole

Serves: 4

> 2 cups Creamy Potato Sauce
>   (page 16)
> 3 medium potatoes, scrubbed
> 2 cloves garlic, minced
> 1 large onion, chopped
> 1 green or yellow bell pepper,
>   cut into strips
> 14 1/2-ounce can stewed tomatoes, drained
>   (reserve liquid)
> 1 bay leaf
> 1 teaspoon dried basil leaves
> 1/4 teaspoon dried thyme leaves
> 1 cup fresh mushrooms, thickly sliced
> 2 small zucchini, cut into 1-inch chunks
> 6 teaspoons chopped fresh parsley,
>   divided
> 1 pound bay scallops, shrimp and/or firm-
>   fleshed fish such as swordfish, salmon,
>   or tuna

Prepare Creamy Potato Sauce; set aside. Slice one of the potatoes very thinly. In large skillet filled with 1 inch of boiling water, cook sliced potato until tender, about 5 minutes. Drain and reserve potato. Meanwhile, cut remaining 2 potatoes into 3/4-inch chunks. Wipe skillet dry.

In same pan combine potato chunks, garlic, onion, bell pepper, stewed tomato liquid, bay leaf, basil, and thyme. Bring to a boil, then reduce heat and simmer, covered, 10 minutes. Stir in mushrooms, zucchini, stewed tomatoes, and 4 teaspoons of the chopped parsley. Cover again and simmer for an additional 6 minutes. Remove and discard bay leaf. Preheat oven to 350°F.

Spoon mixture into a 3-quart shallow casserole dish. Stir in scallops, shrimp and/or fish, then the Creamy Potato Sauce. Arrange sliced potatoes near rim of dish. Loosely cover with aluminum foil and bake 20 minutes or until fish is tender and sauce is bubbly. Sprinkle remaining parsley on potato slices. Serve warm with crusty bread.

Greek-Style Baked Fish

Serves: 8

> 2 pounds fish fillets—cod, haddock, or
>   flounder
> Juice of 1 lemon
> Salt & pepper to taste
> 1/3 cup olive oil
> 6 onions, sliced

2 cloves garlic, chopped
1/2 cup chopped parsley
3 tomatoes, peeled and chopped
1/2 cup water, mixed with 1/2 teaspoon
    vinegar
1 teaspoon olive oil
3 tomatoes, peeled and sliced
1 lemon, thinly sliced

Sprinkle the fish with the lemon juice, and season with salt and pepper. In a heavy skillet, heat the olive oil for 1 minute. Add the onions and garlic and cook until translucent, about 5 minutes. Add the parsley.

Stir in the chopped tomato and cook for 5 more minutes. Add the water and vinegar mixture and continue to cook the vegetables for 5 minutes longer. Preheat oven to 350°F.

Grease a large baking dish with the olive oil and spoon half of the sauce into the dish. Place the fish in the sauce in a single layer. Place the tomato slices and lemon on top of the fish in an overlapping pattern. Pour the remaining sauce over the casserole. Bake the fish, uncovered, for 20 to 30 minutes, or until it flakes easily.

Flounder Amandine

Serves: 4

5 tablespoons butter, divided
1 tablespoon olive oil
1 pound flounder fillets
Flour for dredging
2 eggs, beaten

1/4 cup slivered almonds
1/4 cup white wine or vermouth
2 tablespoons fresh lemon juice

Melt 4 tablespoons butter with oil in a large skillet. Dip fillets in flour, then egg. Cook until golden (2 to 3 minutes per side). Remove from skillet and keep warm. Melt remaining tablespoon of butter, scraping pan. Add almonds; cook 1 minute. Add wine and lemon juice and simmer until thick. Pour over fish and serve.

Kedgeree

Though most Americans figure the only kind of fish served in Great Britain is the deep-fried dish known as fish and chips, the truth is that the dish known as kedgeree is popularly known as a classic. Kedgeree is a dish of flaked fish, boiled rice and eggs. Some Brits also prepare this light dish with smoked fish.

Swordfish Puttanesca

Serves: 4

½ cup + 2 tablespoons olive oil
4 cloves garlic
2 28-ounce cans plus 1 15-ounce can plum tomatoes, drained
Salt to taste
12 cloves garlic, sliced
1 cup sliced green olives, divided
8 tablespoons capers, rinsed and drained, divided
4 8-ounce swordfish steaks
½ cup coarsely chopped fresh parsley
Dried red pepper flakes to taste
Freshly ground black pepper to taste

Heat ½ cup oil in large heavy saucepan over medium heat. Add 4 garlic cloves and stir until lightly browned, about 3 minutes. Discard garlic. Add tomatoes. Season with salt. Increase heat and boil, crushing tomatoes with back of spoon until reduced to thick sauce consistency, about 8 minutes.

Spread half of tomato sauce in bottom of large heavy skillet. Top with half of sliced garlic, ¼ cup olives, and 2 tablespoons capers. Drizzle with remaining 2 tablespoons oil. Arrange swordfish atop sauce. Cover with remaining tomato sauce, garlic, olives, capers, and all of the parsley. Sprinkle with red pepper and black pepper.

Cover and simmer until fish is just opaque, about 15 minutes. Transfer fish to plates. Spoon sauce over fish and serve immediately.

Grilled Japanese Swordfish

Serves: 4

4 8-ounce swordfish steaks

Marinade:
½ cup tamari or good soy sauce
½ cup water
1 tablespoon sherry or Chinese rice wine
1 tablespoon grated ginger
½ cup minced scallions
2 cloves garlic, minced
2 teaspoons sesame oil
2 teaspoons cider vinegar
2 teaspoons sugar

Whisk all marinade ingredients together. Place swordfish steaks in a zippered plastic bag, pour in the marinade, seal, and refrigerate for several hours. Prepare the grill. Use a grilling rack or cover the grill with foil. Remove the swordfish from the marinade and grill until just cooked, a few minutes per side.

Tuna & Tomato "Pie"

Serves: 6

Butter
1 12-ounce can tuna, drained and flaked
1 tomato, seeded and chopped
⅓ cup shredded mozzarella cheese
1 cup milk
1 cup biscuit baking mix
2 eggs

1 teaspoon dried dill weed
Salt and pepper to taste

Preheat oven to 400°F. Butter a pie plate. Sprinkle the tuna, tomato, and cheese evenly in the pie plate. Blend all remaining ingredients in a blender on high speed for 15 seconds, or with a hand beater or wire whisk for 1 minute, until smooth. Pour mixture into the pie plate.

Bake for 30 to 35 minutes, or until a knife inserted in the center comes out clean. Allow to stand for 10 minutes before serving.

Sherried Tuna Noodle Casserole

Serves: 6

Butter
2 7-ounce cans chunk-style tuna, drained
*   and flaked*
1 10-ounce package frozen peas, thawed
1/2 pound mushrooms, sliced and sautéed
*   (optional)*
1/2 teaspoon garlic salt
1/4 teaspoon dill weed
1/4 teaspoon celery seeds
1/8 teaspoon pepper
2 10 1/4-ounce cans condensed cream of
*   mushroom soup*
1/4 cup milk
3 tablespoons dry sherry
3 cups cooked shell or bowtie pasta
3 slices bread
2 tablespoons melted butter

Preheat oven to 350°F. Lightly butter a shallow 2 1/2-quart casserole and arrange half the tuna in the bottom. Arrange the peas, mushrooms, garlic salt, dill weed, celery seeds, and pepper over the tuna.

Mix together soup, milk, and sherry; spoon half the soup mixture into casserole and top with all the noodles. Repeat layering, ending with soup mixture. Tear bread into coarse crumbs; you should have 1 1/4 cup. Combine bread crumbs and melted butter; sprinkle over top.

Bake, uncovered, for about 30 minutes or until top is bubbly and lightly browned.

Tuna Fish Sauce

Makes: About 4 cups

1 7-ounce can oil-packed tuna
Olive oil
1/4 cup finely chopped onions
1 large clove garlic, minced
1 tablespoon chopped fresh parsley
1 large can (about 2 cups) Italian tomato
*   purée*
1 6-ounce can Italian tomato paste mixed
*   with 1 can water*
1/2 teaspoon ground black pepper
1/4 teaspoon dry basil
1/4 teaspoon oregano

Drain the tuna over a measuring cup to collect the oil, and add enough olive oil to yield 1/4 cup. Heat the oil in a skillet. Add tuna, onions, garlic, and parsley. Stir and cook

(continued)

over low heat for 10 minutes. Add the tomato ingredients. Pulverize and add the seasonings, and simmer over low heat for 1 hour.

Creamy Tuna Corn Casserole

Serves: 4

1 egg, beaten
1 cup milk
1 15-ounce can cream-style corn
1 12-ounce can tuna, drained and flaked
1/2 cup fine soda cracker crumbs
1/4 cup chopped scallions
2 tablespoons butter, melted
1/2 cup coarse soda cracker crumbs
Salt and pepper to taste

Preheat oven to 350°F. Combine the egg and milk in a medium saucepan. Add the corn and heat over medium heat until hot and bubbly. Stir in tuna, fine cracker crumbs, scallions, salt, and pepper. Pour into a buttered 1-quart casserole dish. Toss the melted butter with the coarse cracker crumbs and sprinkle on casserole. Bake for 20 minutes.

Tuna & Spinach Casserole

Serves: 6

1 10-ounce package frozen chopped
*   spinach, thawed and squeezed dry*
6 slices bacon, cooked and crumbled
1/2 cup fine dry bread crumbs

1 cup sour cream
1 teaspoon salt
1/2 teaspoon pepper
Juice of one small lemon
1 12-ounce can tuna, drained and flaked
4 tablespoons grated Parmesan cheese

Preheat oven to 350°F. Butter an 8-inch square baking dish. In a bowl, combine all ingredients except 2 tablespoons of Parmesan cheese and mix well. Place in prepared dish, and sprinkle with remaining Parmesan cheese. Bake until lightly browned and hot, about 20 minutes.

Easy Seafood Casserole

Serves: 4

Butter
1 pound fresh sole fillets
1/4 pound small cooked shrimp
3 tablespoons fine dry bread crumbs
1/4 teaspoon pepper
2 tablespoons lemon juice
1/4 pound mushrooms, thinly sliced
2 tablespoons mayonnaise
2 tablespoons thinly sliced green onion
*   (including tops)*
1 clove garlic, minced
1 1/2 tablespoons butter, softened
1/4 cup dry vermouth (optional)

Generously butter a shallow 4 1/2-quart casserole or 9-inch-square baking dish. Preheat oven to 350°F.

Place half of the fish fillets in an even layer in pan. Sprinkle evenly with half the shrimp, bread crumbs, pepper, lemon juice, and sliced mushrooms. Repeat layers. Combine mayonnaise, green onion, garlic, and softened butter; dot over mushrooms. Drizzle evenly with vermouth, if desired.

Bake, covered, for 30 minutes or until fish flakes readily when prodded in thickest portion with a fork.

Baked Creamy Sole

Serves: 4

2 pounds fresh or frozen sole fillets
Butter
1 small onion, thinly sliced
³/₄ cup shredded carrot
1 10³/₄-ounce can condensed cream of
*   celery soup*
2 tablespoons dry white wine
1 tablespoon lemon juice
¹/₂ teaspoon marjoram leaves or thyme
*   leaves*
¹/₄ teaspoon garlic powder
¹/₄ cup grated Parmesan cheese
¹/₂ teaspoon ground nutmeg

Preheat oven to 450°F.

Arrange fish (overlap thin edges) in a buttered shallow 3-quart casserole or 9 x 13-inch baking dish. Mix separately the soup, wine, lemon juice, marjoram, and garlic powder. Top the fish with onion slices and sprinkle evenly with shredded carrot. Pour the soup, wine, lemon juice, marjoram, and garlic powder mixture over the fish. Sprinkle with Parmesan cheese. Dust lightly with nutmeg.

Bake, uncovered, for 15 to 20 minutes, or until fish flakes readily when prodded in thickest portion with a fork.

Plan Ahead

Save time by preparing casseroles ahead of time. Prepare the dish right up to the last step before popping it in the oven. You can store it up to 24 hours before you need to bake it. However, casseroles that use fish or seafood should be cooked immediately after preparation.

Shellfish

In America the two most popular shellfish are shrimp and scallops. They are usually served as a stand-alone entree: broiled, deep fried, or sautéed with garlic and butter. Tossed together with a bevy of other fresh ingredients and cooked in one pot, any of the following recipes will result in a dish that's able to stand up to any shellfish-based entrée any day.

Hot Shrimp Étouffée

Serves: 4

1/3 cup vegetable oil
1/4 cup flour
1 medium onion, chopped
2 cloves garlic, minced
2 stalks celery, diced
1 small bell pepper, diced
2 medium tomatoes, peeled and chopped
1 cup fish stock or clam juice
1/2 teaspoon basil
1/4 teaspoon thyme
1 bay leaf
4 teaspoons Louisiana hot sauce
1 pound shrimp, peeled
1/2 cup chopped scallions, including the greens
Freshly ground black pepper

To make the roux: Heat oil in a heavy skillet until hot. Gradually stir in the flour; stir constantly until the mixture turns brown. Be very careful you don't burn roux.

Sauté the onions, garlic, celery, and bell pepper in the roux for five minutes. Add the tomatoes, stock, basil, thyme, and bay leaf. Bring to a boil, stirring constantly. Reduce the heat and simmer for 15 minutes or until it thickens to a sauce. Add the hot sauce, shrimp, and scallions and simmer for an additional 5 minutes or until the shrimp are cooked. Remove the bay leaf, pepper to taste, and serve.

Shrimp in Indian Sauce

Serves: 4

1 1/2 pounds medium shrimp, shelled, cleaned, and deveined
2 tablespoons butter
1/2 cup finely chopped onion
1/4 teaspoon dried red pepper
Salt and pepper to taste
1/2 teaspoon cardamom
1/2 teaspoon ground cumin
Juice of 1 lime

1 cup sour cream
½ cup plain yogurt
¼ cup chopped fresh cilantro

Rinse the shrimp well and pat dry. Set aside. Heat the butter in a skillet and add the onion. Add the red pepper. Cook briefly and add the shrimp; salt and pepper to taste. Cook, stirring often, about 3 minutes. Add the cardamom and cumin and stir. Add the lime juice, sour cream, and yogurt. Stirring, bring gently to a boil. Sprinkle with cilantro and serve hot with saffron rice.

Cajun Shrimp

Serves: 8

2 tablespoons unsalted butter
2¼ cups chopped onions
1½ cups chopped green bell peppers
¾ cup chopped celery
3 cups chopped tomatoes
1 cup tomato sauce
3 tablespoons minced jalapeño pepper
2 bay leaves
2 cloves minced garlic
2¼ cups seafood stock
1½ teaspoons dark brown sugar
¾ teaspoon salt
2 pounds large shrimp, shelled and deveined
4 cups hot cooked rice
1½ teaspoons white pepper
1 teaspoon black pepper
2 tablespoons cayenne pepper

Melt the butter in a 4-quart saucepan over high heat. Add the onions, bell peppers, and celery; sauté about 2 minutes, stirring occasionally. Add the tomatoes, tomato sauce, jalapeños, bay leaves, black peppers, and garlic; stir well. Continue cooking about 3 minutes, stirring often and scraping the pan well. Stir in the stock, sugar, and salt and bring to a boil. Reduce heat and simmer about 20 minutes, stirring often and scraping the pan often. If the mixture scorches, pour mixture into a clean pot, leaving the scorched ingredients in the first pan.

Add the shrimp to the hot sauce and stir. Turn the heat up to high, cover pan, and bring mixture to a boil. Remove from heat. Let sit covered for 10 minutes.

Meanwhile, heat the serving plates in a 250°F oven. Stir, remove bay leaves, and serve immediately. To serve, mound ½ cup rice in the center of each heated serving plate; pour about ½ cup sauce around the rice and arrange about 8 shrimp on top of the sauce.

Easy Grilled Shrimp and Feta Pizza

Serves: 4

1 loaf frozen bread dough
24 medium-large shrimp, peeled and deveined
2 tablespoons olive oil
1 15-ounce can chunky pizza sauce
4 ounces feta cheese, crumbled

(continued)

In the morning, spray a cookie sheet with nonstick cooking spray. Place the frozen loaf on it and spray that. Cover loosely with a large piece of plastic wrap. Allow to sit at room temperature all day. It will defrost, then rise to double or triple its volume.

Adjust the grill so it is 4 inches above the coals. Light the grill. Skewer the shrimp on 4 long metal skewers and cook over the coals until cooked, a few minutes on each side. Remove from skewers and reserve. Meanwhile, punch the dough down, divide into two pieces and gently stretch into two rectangles on the cookie sheet. Carefully place each piece on the grill. It will quickly begin to rise. Rotate the pizzas so that the bottoms cook evenly. This will take just a couple of minutes.

Flip the pizzas over so the cooked side is up. Brush with the olive oil. Spoon on the pizza sauce, sprinkle with the feta cheese, and top with the cooked shrimp and any optional herbs and seasonings. Cover lightly with foil to help heat the toppings. Don't walk away or they could burn. Rotate the pizzas so the bottoms cook evenly. This should take just a couple of minutes. Serve immediately.

Shrimp Jambalaya

Serves: 8 to 10

2 tablespoons flour
3 tablespoons bacon fat

2 cups chopped, minced, or shredded lean ham
1 cup chopped onions
1 large clove garlic, minced
2 cups peeled, diced fresh tomatoes, or coarsely cut canned whole tomatoes
2 cups uncooked long-grain white rice
1 teaspoon salt
$\frac{1}{2}$ teaspoon thyme
Dash cayenne pepper
2 teaspoons chili powder
Dash Tabasco sauce
Boiling water
3 pounds shrimp, shelled and deveined

In a very large heavy skillet or Dutch oven stir the flour into the fat until it is brown. Add the ham, onions, and garlic and stir until the onions are limp. Add the tomatoes, rice, and seasonings, and stir. Pour in enough boiling water to moisten the mixture thoroughly. Add the shrimp, stir lightly to distribute, and cook, tightly covered, over low heat.

Raise the cover occasionally and add more boiling water as the rice absorbs the moisture. Continue cooking until the rice is tender.

Shrimp Creole

Serves: 8

1 cup chopped onions
1 cup diced green peppers
1 cup chopped celery
1 large clove garlic, minced

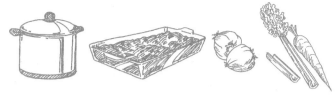

½ cup melted butter
3 tablespoons chopped parsley
½ teaspoon salt
½ teaspoon thyme
¼ teaspoon pepper
Few grains cayenne pepper
Dash Tabasco sauce
2 tablespoons flour
2 cups chopped fresh tomatoes
1 cup fish stock
3 pounds shrimp, shelled and deveined
4 cups hot cooked rice

Sauté the onions, green peppers, celery, and garlic in the hot butter over very low heat until the onions are limp. Add the parsley, seasonings, and flour. Stir to blend, and continue stirring over low heat for 2 minutes. Add the tomatoes and stock; stir. Add the shrimp, and simmer, covered, for 3 minutes.

Continue to simmer for 3 or 4 minutes longer. Serve with hot fluffy rice.

Haitian Seafood Casserole

Serves: 6

3 strips bacon, cut in ½-inch pieces
1 large onion, chopped
2 tablespoons olive oil
1 to 1½ pounds medium-size raw shrimp, shelled and deveined
2 cups uncooked white rice
1 10-ounce package lima beans

2 large tomatoes, cut in wedges
¼ cup + 2 tablespoons chopped parsley, divided
1½ teaspoons salt
1½ teaspoons vinegar
½ teaspoon Tabasco sauce
¼ teaspoon pepper
4 cups boiling water
2 tablespoons butter
Lime wedges

In a 5-quart pan over medium heat, cook bacon until limp. Stir in onion and cook until soft. Add oil and shrimp and cook, stirring, until shrimp turn pink.

Mix in rice and stir to coat with oil. Add limas, tomatoes, ¼ cup of the parsley, salt, vinegar, Tabasco, pepper, and boiling water. Bring mixture to a boil. Cover, reduce heat, and simmer for about 20 minutes or until rice has absorbed all the liquid.

Mix in butter, then spoon mixture into a serving dish. Garnish with remaining parsley and lime wedges.

Creole Succotash

Serves: 8

½ cup olive oil
1 large onion, chopped
3 sprigs parsley, chopped
1 medium bell pepper, diced
2 pounds okra, cut
1 16-ounce can chopped tomatoes
1 10-inch box frozen lima beans

(continued)

1 pound ham, cubed
2 pounds small shrimp
2 10-ounce cans corn
Salt and pepper to taste
Hot cooked rice

Heat oil in large saucepan. Sauté onions, parsley, and bell peppers. Add okra and fry over low heat. Add tomatoes, lima beans, and ham. Cook 20 minutes. Add the shrimp, corn, salt, and pepper, and cook another 20 minutes over medium heat. Add more water if mixture is too dry. Serve over rice.

Microwave Shrimp in Garlic & White Wine Sauce

Serves: 4

1 pound large shrimp
3 tablespoons sweet butter, cut into small
    pieces
2 cloves garlic, minced
$\frac{1}{2}$ cup dry white wine
2 teaspoons finely chopped fresh parsley
1 teaspoon fresh lemon juice
Salt and pepper to taste

Peel and devein the shrimp. Melt the butter in a 10-inch glass pie dish on high for 2 minutes. Stir in the garlic and microwave, uncovered, for 3 minutes, stirring once. Add the wine and microwave 5 minutes. Stir in the shrimp and parsley. Cover with microwavable plastic wrap and vent one side. Microwave for

1 minute. Stir and carefully move the partially cooked shrimp toward the center and the uncooked shrimp toward the outside edges. Microwave, covered and vented, 1 minute longer. Allow to stand covered for 1 minute. Drizzle with lemon juice and season with salt and pepper. Serve immediately.

Crab Imperial Stuffed Shrimp

Serves: 4

$\frac{1}{2}$ cup milk
$\frac{1}{2}$ tablespoon butter
1 tablespoon flour
1 egg, well beaten
$\frac{1}{2}$ teaspoon dry mustard
$\frac{1}{8}$ teaspoon cayenne pepper
$\frac{1}{4}$ teaspoon seasoned salt
$\frac{1}{4}$ teaspoon celery salt
$\frac{1}{4}$ teaspoon pepper
$\frac{1}{2}$ tablespoon lemon juice
$\frac{1}{4}$ teaspoon Worcestershire sauce
2 tablespoons mayonnaise
2 tablespoons chopped parsley
1 pound crabmeat (cartilage removed)
$1\frac{1}{2}$ pounds large shrimp (16 to 18
    to a pound)
$\frac{1}{2}$ cup dried bread crumbs
Paprika
Butter

In a small pot, heat the milk to the boiling point. In a separate pot, melt butter and stir in flour. Pour heated milk into flour and

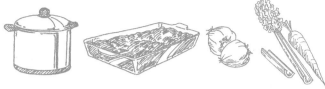

butter mixture, beating with a whisk until smooth and creamy. Cool. Add egg, seasonings, lemon juice, Worcestershire sauce, mayonnaise, and parsley. Add crabmeat and mix well, but gently.

Preheat oven to 500°F. Peel and devein the shrimp, leaving tail intact. Butterfly the shrimp by splitting them down the back almost, but not all the way through. Place split side up in well buttered baking pan. Spoon equal portions of crabmeat mixture into the shrimp cavity. Sprinkle with the bread crumbs and paprika. Dot with butter.

Bake for 2 1/2 minutes in oven on lower rack. Then broil for about 1 1/2 minutes about 5 inches from the heat until golden brown.

Oysters Poached in White Wine

Serves: 4

16 freshly shucked oysters
3/4 cup dry white wine
1/4 cup olive oil
2 tablespoons fresh lemon juice
1/4 teaspoon salt
1/4 teaspoon pepper
1/4 teaspoon dried thyme
1/4 teaspoon dried chervil
1 teaspoon chopped fresh parsley
1 clove garlic, crushed

Place all ingredients in an 8-quart stockpot that's not aluminum. Bring to a boil over moderate heat. Remove from heat and allow to cool to room temperature. Remove crushed garlic clove before serving.

Crab Surprise

Serves: 4

1/4 cup olive oil
3 tablespoons flour
2/3 cup chicken broth
2/3 cup light cream
1/4 cup ketchup
2 teaspoons Worcestershire sauce
1 teaspoon paprika
3 drops Tabasco sauce
1 tablespoon lemon juice
1 3/4 pounds shelled crab claws
3 cups cooked white rice

Heat the oil in a saucepan; add the flour and cook for 2 minutes over low heat. Whisk in the broth and cream and simmer until thick. Whisk in the ketchup, Worcestershire, paprika, Tabasco, and lemon juice; continue to simmer 2 more minutes. Add the crab claws; simmer for 10 minutes.

Place the rice on serving plates, cover with mixture, and serve.

Crab Imperial

Serves: 4

4 ounces (1 stick) butter
1/2 cup finely chopped green pepper
1/2 cup finely chopped red pepper

(continued)

1 cup finely chopped onion
4 tablespoons flour
3 cups half-and-half
1 teaspoon salt
$\frac{1}{2}$ cup finely chopped parsley
$\frac{1}{2}$ teaspoon cayenne pepper
1 pound crabmeat, shredded
Paprika

In a large skillet, melt the butter but do not allow to brown. Sauté onions, green pepper, and red pepper on low heat, about 2 minutes. Add flour and then half-and-half, blending with a whisk until smooth. Cook slowly until sauce becomes medium thick, about 8 to10 minutes.

Preheat oven to 350°F. Remove sauce from heat and add all remaining ingredients except crab and paprika. Fold in the crab gently and fill a lightly greased 2-quart casserole with mixture. Dust with paprika. Bake about 15 to 20 minutes.

Fish Fillets in Lobster Bisque

Serves: 4

2 pounds fish fillets: flounder, cod or
    haddock
1 or 2 tablespoons sherry (optional)
2 cans lobster bisque
2 tablespoons dry bread crumbs
2 tablespoons grated Cheddar, Swiss,
    Parmesan, or Romano cheese
2 tablespoons butter

Preheat oven to 400°F. Separate the fillets, brush them on both sides with sherry if desired, and arrange them in a shallow buttered casserole. Spread the bisque over the fillets, sprinkle with the combined crumbs and cheese, and dot with the butter. Bake for 10 minutes. Insert a meat thermometer in one of the fillets, reduce the heat to 375°F, and continue baking for 25 to 30 minutes longer, or until the thermometer reads 140°F.

French Country Mussels

Serves: 4

1 tablespoon olive oil
1 large onion, chopped
2 tablespoons minced garlic
1 16-ounce can peeled tomatoes, drained
$\frac{1}{2}$ cup fresh minced parsley
Black pepper to taste
1 cup dry white wine
4 pounds fresh mussels, cleaned, with
    beards removed

In an 8-quart pot, heat the oil, and cook the onion and garlic until browned. Add the tomatoes, breaking them up with a wooden spoon. Add the parsley and pepper. Increase the heat, and cook for about 2 minutes. Add the wine and cook for another 2 minutes.

Add the mussels, tossing them well to coat. Cover, and cook the mussels for 3 minutes, stirring occasionally, until the mussels have opened. Discard any mussels that did not open up. Serve immediately.

Chapter 5

*Pasta
Dishes*

Whether it's a hearty macaroni and cheese casserole or a simple supper of spaghetti and meat sauce, everybody likes pasta in many of its various incarnations.

Perhaps it's pasta's versatility—due to sauce, shape, or flavor—that makes it such a favorite. The following one-pot recipes show pasta in its finest clothes, both simple and complex, but always involving just one pot. Though in most cases the pasta needs to be precooked—which most often involves a large stockpot that requires a minimum of cleaning—the dishes in this chapter are still among the quickest and easiest around.

Chunky Pasta Sauce

Serves: 6

1 medium onion, coarsely chopped
3 cloves garlic, minced
1/2 pound mushrooms, sliced
1 green pepper, cut into 1-inch chunks,
    seeds reserved
1 stalk celery, cut into 1/2-inch slices
1 28-ounce can tomatoes, undrained
1 8-ounce can tomato sauce
1 6-ounce can tomato paste
1/2 cup red wine (or water)
1 teaspoon dried oregano
2 tablespoons dried sweet basil
    (or 41/4 cup chopped fresh basil)
2 teaspoons chopped fresh parsley
1/8 teaspoon crushed red pepper (optional)
Salt (optional)

In a nonstick skillet, heat onion and garlic in several tablespoons of water until tender.

Add mushrooms and continue cooking over low heat about 4 minutes. Add pepper, pepper seeds, and celery, and cook until barely tender. Add tomatoes with the juice. Whisk tomato sauce and paste together with wine or 1/2 cup water and add to the pan along with oregano, basil, parsley, pepper, and salt and heat for additional 15 minutes. Serve hot over hot pasta.

Easy No-Cook Pasta Sauce

Makes: Enough sauce for 1 pound of cooked pasta

21/2 cups fresh, ripe tomatoes, chopped
1/2 cup virgin olive oil
1 green bell pepper, seeded and chopped
11/2 cups cubed white cheese (Gouda,
    Provolone, or Monterey Jack)
4 cloves garlic, minced

1 tablespoon lemon juice
¼ cup fresh basil
½ teaspoon dried oregano
Salt and pepper to taste

In a large mixing bowl, stir together all ingredients. Chill up to 3 hours before serving.

Spaghetti Meat Sauce

Serves: 8

1 pound lean ground beef
1 large onion, chopped
1 clove garlic, minced
½ cup chopped celery
1 green pepper, diced
2 teaspoons salt
1 cup water
1 8-ounce can tomato sauce
⅛ teaspoon red pepper
1 teaspoon parsley flakes
½ teaspoon oregano
½ teaspoon sweet basil
¼ teaspoon thyme
2 teaspoons sugar
3 drops Tabasco sauce
1 18-ounce can tomato paste

Heat the pressure cooker and brown beef. Stir in remaining ingredients except tomato paste. Close cover securely. Place pressure regulator on vent pipe and cook 8 minutes with pressure regulator rocking slowly. Cool cooker at once. Stir in tomato paste and simmer, uncovered, to desired thickness. Serve sauce over long spaghetti.

Fast & Easy Spaghetti Sauce

Serves: 6

1 pound ground beef
½ cup chopped onion
½ cup chopped bell pepper
1 cup chopped celery
1 clove garlic minced
1 teaspoon Italian herb seasoning
1 16-ounce can stewed tomatoes
1 8-ounce can tomato paste
1 large can tomato sauce
3 cups water
1 package spaghetti sauce seasoning mix

Brown beef with onion, bell pepper, celery, and garlic. Drain well and put into a Crockpot with all other ingredients. Leave Crockpot on high until sauce comes to a boil and then turn it to low and simmer for 6 hours.

Serve hot over favorite noodles.

Make-Ahead Meat Pasta Sauce

Makes: 12 cups sauce

1 pound Italian sausage
2 tablespoons olive oil
1 large onion, chopped
4 cloves garlic, minced

(continued)

1 pound ground beef
3 28-ounce cans crushed tomatoes
1 12-ounce can tomato paste
2 cups water
4 bay leaves
4 teaspoons dried basil
2 teaspoons dried oregano
2 teaspoons salt

Remove sausage meat from casings and crumble. Heat oil in a large pot; add the sausage and cook until browned. Add onions, garlic, and beef, and continue cooking until the meat is no longer pink. Drain any excess fat. Press the crushed tomatoes through a food mill or cheesecloth to remove skins and seeds. Add remaining ingredients and simmer for 2 hours, stirring occasionally.

Madhouse Spaghetti

Serves: 8

Salt
2 pounds ground beef
2 medium onions, chopped
1 28-ounce can tomatoes
1 6-ounce can tomato paste
12 Spanish olives, sliced
1 pound cooked spaghetti
1/4 cup grated Parmesan cheese

Sprinkle Dutch oven with salt. Add beef and onions and cook until beef is browned. Pour off fat. Remove from heat and add tomatoes and liquid, chopping tomatoes as you

add them. Add tomato paste and sliced olives. Return mixture to heat. Bring to a boil and reduce to a simmer. Simmer for 45 to 60 minutes, stirring occasionally.

Add cooked spaghetti and mix well. Place in large serving bowl. Sprinkle with Parmesan cheese.

Summer Vegetable Spaghetti

Serves: 8

2 cups small yellow onions, cut in eighths
2 cups chopped, peeled fresh ripe
    tomatoes
1 cup thinly sliced yellow squash
1 cup thinly sliced zucchini
1 1/2 cups fresh green beans
2/3 cup water
2 tablespoons minced fresh parsley
1 clove garlic, minced
1/2 teaspoon chili powder
1/4 teaspoon salt
1/8 teaspoon freshly ground black pepper
6 ounces tomato paste
1 pound uncooked spaghetti
1/2 cup grated Parmesan cheese

Combine onions, tomatoes, yellow squash, zucchini, beans, water, parsley, garlic, chili powder, salt, and pepper in a large saucepan; cook for 10 minutes, then stir in tomato paste. Cover and cook gently for 15 minutes, stirring occasionally, until vegetables are tender. Cook

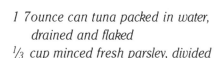

spaghetti in unsalted water according to package directions.

Spoon sauce over drained hot spaghetti and sprinkle Parmesan cheese over top.

Spaghetti Carbonara

Serves: 4

1 pound spaghetti, cooked and chilled
1/4 pound lean bacon
3 tablespoons heavy cream
1/2 cup grated Parmesan cheese
3 egg yolks
Chopped parsley for garnish
Freshly ground pepper (optional)

Cut bacon into short strips and fry in a large skillet until golden. Drain bacon and set aside. Place spaghetti in the skillet. Over low heat, mix in cream; add Parmesan cheese and mix; add the egg yolks and mix; add the bacon and mix. Garnish with a sprinkling of chopped parsley and season with a light sprinkling of freshly ground pepper, if desired.

Tuna Tomato Sauce

Serves: 4

1 tablespoon olive oil
2 large cloves garlic, minced
1 teaspoon anchovy paste
1 teaspoon hot red pepper flakes
2 cups tomato purée
1 teaspoon black pepper
1 7-ounce can tuna packed in water, drained and flaked
1/3 cup minced fresh parsley, divided

Heat the oil and garlic in a medium saucepan for a minute. Remove from heat, and add the anchovy paste and pepper flakes. Stir in the puréed tomatoes and black pepper, and bring to a boil. Reduce heat, and cook for 20 minutes, stirring occasionally. Stir in the tuna and half the parsley, and cook for another 10 minutes. Toss the sauce with hot pasta, and sprinkle on the rest of the parsley.

Ham and Green Noodle Casserole

Serves: 6

6 cups hot water
1 8-ounce package spinach linguine or noodles
1 10 3/4-ounce can Cheddar cheese soup
1 5-ounce can evaporated milk
1 teaspoon prepared mustard
1/4 teaspoon black pepper
1 cup diced cooked ham
1 4-ounce can mushroom pieces, drained
1/2 cup sliced ripe olives
1/2 cup peanuts

Place water in a 4-quart round casserole. Cover and microwave on high 6 minutes or until water boils. Add linguine; stir. Cover and microwave on high 4 minutes; stir. Cover

(continued)

again and microwave on high 4 minutes or until pasta tests done; drain.

Stir in soup, evaporated milk, mustard, and black pepper. Fold in ham, mushrooms, olives, and peanuts. Cover again. Microwave on high 6 to 8 minutes or until steaming hot, stirring midway through cooking.

Easy Microwave Lasagna

Serves: 6

> 1 8-ounce can tomato sauce
> 1 medium onion, chopped
> $1/4$ teaspoon basil leaves
> $1/4$ teaspoon salt (optional)
> $1/8$ teaspoon freshly ground pepper
> $1/4$ teaspoon oregano leaves
> 1 cup ricotta cheese
> $1/2$ cup shredded mozzarella cheese
> 1 teaspoon parsley
> 3 medium zucchini, about 9-inches long
> 1 large tomato, sliced
> 2 tablespoons grated Parmesan cheese

Combine tomato sauce, onion, basil, salt, pepper, and oregano in small mixing bowl; set aside. In medium bowl, combine ricotta, mozzarella, and parsley. Set aside.

Peel zucchini and cut off ends. Slice zucchini lengthwise into strips. Arrange strips in 8 x 8-inch baking dish. Cover with waxed paper.

Microwave on high for 6 to 8 minutes, or until fork tender, rearranging after half the time. Drain liquid; place zucchini on towels to absorb excess moisture; cool slightly. Layer 4 to 6 of the strips in the bottom of baking dish. Reserve 6 strips for second layer. Spread ricotta mixture over zucchini. Layer with sliced tomatoes.

Spread half of tomato sauce mixture over tomatoes; top with zucchini slices. Pour remaining sauce over zucchini and sprinkle with Parmesan. Reduce power to 50 percent (medium). Microwave uncovered 20 to 25 minutes or until zucchini is tender and mixture is hot in center. Let stand 5 minutes before serving.

Gorgonzola and Fresh Thyme Sauce for Pasta

Serves: 4

> $1 1/2$ cups heavy cream
> 6 ounces aged gorgonzola cheese, crumbled
> 1 teaspoon fresh thyme or $1/2$ teaspoon dried thyme
> 3 generous grates nutmeg or $1/8$ teaspoon ground nutmeg
> Salt
> White pepper
> 1 pound hot cooked pasta

Stir together cream, cheese, thyme, and nutmeg in a large skillet. Cook gently over medium heat until mixture reduces by one-fourth. Add salt and pepper to taste. Toss with pasta to coat well. Serve with extra nutmeg, if desired.

Eggplant and Tomatoes with Gemelli

Serves: 4

> 2 tablespoons olive oil
> ³/₄ cup onion, chopped
> 3 cloves garlic, minced
> ³/₄ pound eggplant, cut in ¹/₂ to 1-inch cubes
> 2 tablespoons balsamic vinegar
> ¹/₂ cup chicken broth
> 1 16-ounce can Italian plum tomatoes with juice
> 1 tablespoon tomato paste
> ¹/₂ teaspoon dried oregano
> 2 tablespoons chopped fresh basil
> Dash hot red pepper flakes
> Salt to taste
> 12 ounces gemelli pasta, cooked

In a large, deep skillet, heat oil over medium heat. Add onion and cook until softened. Add garlic and sauté briefly. Add eggplant, vinegar, and chicken broth. Cover and cook until eggplant is tender, about 10 minutes. Add tomatoes, breaking up with a wooden spoon, tomato paste, and oregano. Cook uncovered until the sauce becomes slightly thickened.

Stir in basil and red pepper flakes. Add salt to taste. Combine sauce with hot pasta and toss thoroughly.

Thawing Basics

One-pot dishes vary in the amount of time it will take to thaw them thoroughly. Assume it will take twice as long if a frozen one-pot dish is thawed in the refrigerator compared to room temperature. However, bacteria experts warn that frozen food should never be thawed at room temperature.

Greek Shrimp and Feta

Serves: 6

> 1 pound medium shrimp, cleaned and cooked
> 1 pound feta cheese, drained and coarsely crumbled
> 1 cup sliced scallions
> 1 tablespoon tomato sauce
> ¹/₂ cup olive oil
> ¹/₄ cup fresh lemon juice

(continued)

1 tablespoon chopped parsley
1 tablespoon chopped fresh basil
1 tablespoon chopped fresh dill
1/2 teaspoon salt
1/4 teaspoon pepper
1 1/2 pounds fettuccine, cooked and drained

Combine shrimp, feta cheese, and scallions in a large bowl. Add tomato sauce, olive oil, lemon juice, parsley, basil, dill, salt, and pepper; mix well. Cover and refrigerate 1 hour.

Toss shrimp mixture with hot noodles and serve immediately or refrigerate at least an hour and serve cold.

Crockpot Beef Fettuccine Alfredo

Serves: 4

1 1/2 pounds top round steak, 1 inch thick
1 10 3/4-ounce can condensed Cheddar cheese soup
1/4 cup dried minced onion
3 tablespoons tomato paste
1/2 teaspoon lemon pepper seasoning
2 cups small mushrooms, halved
9 ounces frozen Italian green beans
1/2 cup buttermilk
9 ounces fettuccine

Trim fat from steak. Cut into 1-inch pieces. Spray a pan with nonstick cooking spray, and heat over medium heat. Cook the steak, half at a time, until brown. Place meat in a 3 1/2 or 4-quart Crockpot. Combine soup, onion, tomato paste, and lemon pepper in a medium bowl. Pour mixture over meat. Add mushrooms. Cook on low setting for 8 to 10 hours (or high for 4 to 5 hours).

Turn heat to high. Add frozen green beans and buttermilk. Stir, cover, and cook for 30 minutes more. Meanwhile, cook fettuccine. Serve meat over fettuccine.

Fettuccine Alfredo with Chicken & Broccoli

Serves: 8

1 12-ounce package fettuccine
1 pound chicken tenders
1 1/4 cups chopped onion
2 1/2 cups sliced mushrooms
1 13 1/2-ounce can chicken broth
1 cup cream cheese, softened
1 20-ounce package frozen broccoli florets
1 teaspoon white pepper

Prepare fettuccine according to package directions; drain and keep warm. Lightly spray a large nonstick skillet with nonstick cooking spray and heat over medium-high heat. Add chicken tenders and cook until chicken is no longer pink and is cooked through; remove chicken from skillet and set aside.

Lightly respray skillet. Sauté onions until soft and transparent, about 5 minutes. Add mushrooms and continue cooking until mushrooms are tender. Stir in chicken broth and cream cheese; heat over medium-high heat until mixture thickens and almost comes to a boil.

Add chicken, broccoli, and pepper to skillet; cook over medium heat until heated through. Toss with fettuccine and serve immediately.

Fettuccine with Light Alfredo Sauce

Serves: 6

> 1 cup evaporated skim milk
> 1/2 cup grated Parmesan cheese
> 1/2 cup finely chopped fresh parsley
> 1 pound fettuccine, cooked
> 1/4 teaspoon white pepper
> Pinch of red pepper flakes (optional)

Heat the evaporated milk in a deep saucepan over medium heat. Simmer, but do not boil. Add Parmesan cheese and parsley. As soon as the cheese has melted and the sauce is thick and creamy, remove from heat and toss with pasta. Season to taste with white pepper and (optional) red pepper flakes. Serve immediately.

Hot Dill Pasta & Scallops

Serves: 4

> 1 pound fresh or frozen sea scallops
> 8 ounces packaged dried fettuccine or linguine
> 1 tablespoon butter
> 1 tablespoon olive oil
> 2 large carrots, thinly sliced
> 2 to 3 cloves garlic, minced
> 6 ounces sugar snap peas or pea pods
> 3 green onions, thinly sliced
> 1/2 cup dry white wine
> 1/3 cup water
> 1 tablespoon snipped fresh dill
> 1 teaspoon instant chicken bouillon granules
> 1/4 teaspoon crushed red pepper
> 2 tablespoons cornstarch
> 2 tablespoons cold water
> 1/4 cup grated Parmesan cheese
> Freshly ground black pepper

Thaw scallops, if frozen. Cut any large scallops in half; set aside. Cook fettuccine according to package directions; drain. Return fettuccine to pan; toss with butter. Cover to keep warm.

Meanwhile, pour oil into a wok or large skillet. Preheat over medium-high heat. Add carrots and garlic; stir-fry for 4 minutes. Add sugar snap peas and green onions; stir-fry for 2 to 3 minutes or until crisp. Remove vegetables from wok. Cool wok for 1 minute.

Carefully add wine, the 1/3 cup water, dill, bouillon granules, and crushed red pepper to wok. Bring to boiling. Add scallops; reduce heat. Simmer, uncovered, for 1 to 2 minutes or until scallops are opaque, stirring often.

Stir together cornstarch and 2 tablespoons cold water; add to wok. Cook and stir until mixture is thickened and bubbly. Return vegetables to wok; add pasta. Toss to mix; heat through. Transfer to dinner plates. Sprinkle with Parmesan cheese and cracked black pepper.

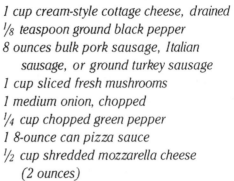

Pasta with Prosciutto and Walnuts

Serves: 4

3 cloves minced garlic
1/4 cup olive oil
1/4 pound thinly sliced prosciutto, chopped
1 cup chopped walnuts
1/2 cup chopped fresh parsley
1/4 cup chopped fresh basil
1 7-ounce jar roasted red peppers, chopped
1/2 cup pitted, chopped Kalamata olives
1 pound linguine, cooked al dente, and well drained

In a large heavy skillet, sauté the minced garlic in olive oil. When the garlic starts to turn brown, add the chopped prosciutto and sauté until crisp. Add the walnuts and sauté until they are toasty brown. Add the parsley, basil, red peppers, and olives.

Add the linguine to the sauce and stir well. Heat over a low flame until pasta is heated through.

Sausage Linguine Tart

Serves: 4

5 ounces packaged dried spaghetti
1 beaten egg
1/3 cup grated Parmesan cheese
1 tablespoon butter, cut up
1 beaten egg
1 cup cream-style cottage cheese, drained
1/8 teaspoon ground black pepper
8 ounces bulk pork sausage, Italian sausage, or ground turkey sausage
1 cup sliced fresh mushrooms
1 medium onion, chopped
1/4 cup chopped green pepper
1 8-ounce can pizza sauce
1/2 cup shredded mozzarella cheese (2 ounces)

Cook spaghetti according to package directions. Drain spaghetti; rinse with cold water. Drain again. For the spaghetti crust, combine 1 egg, Parmesan cheese, and butter in a medium mixing bowl. Add spaghetti; toss to coat. Press the spaghetti mixture against the bottom and sides of a well-greased 9-inch pie plate to form an even crust. Preheat oven to 350°F.

Combine 1 egg, cottage cheese, and black pepper in a small mixing bowl. Spread over the spaghetti crust; set aside. Cook the sausage, mushrooms, onion, and green pepper in a large skillet until the meat is brown and vegetables are tender. Drain off fat. Stir in pizza sauce. Cook until heated through. Spoon meat mixture into spaghetti crust. Cover loosely with foil.

Bake for 20 minutes. Remove foil; sprinkle with mozzarella cheese. Bake, uncovered, about 5 minutes more or until cheese melts. Let stand for 5 minutes before serving. Cut into wedges.

Linguine Fra Diavolo

Serves: 4

2 tablespoons olive oil
3 cloves garlic, minced
1 pound tomatoes, chopped
1 cup finely chopped fresh basil
Salt and pepper to taste
$\frac{1}{4}$ pound scallops
$\frac{1}{4}$ pound shrimp
$\frac{1}{4}$ pound haddock
8 mussels
8 ounces linguine, cooked

Heat the oil in a large skillet for 1 to 2 minutes. Add garlic and sauté for 5 minutes. Add the tomatoes, basil, salt, and pepper. Cook for 2 minutes. Add the scallops, shrimp, haddock, and mussels. Cook for 3 minutes. Toss with the hot pasta.

Linguine with White Clam Sauce #1

Serves: 6

3 cloves garlic, minced
1 tablespoon olive oil
1 10-ounce can minced clams, drained
  with juice reserved
1 teaspoon hot red pepper flakes
1 teaspoon oregano
1 teaspoon basil
2 tablespoons chopped fresh parsley
$\frac{1}{2}$ cup white wine
1 pound linguine, cooked

Sauté the garlic in olive oil in a large skillet for 3 minutes. Add the clams, hot red pepper flakes, oregano, basil, parsley, wine, and clam juice. Cook over medium heat for 15 minutes. Serve over hot linguine.

Linguine with White Clam Sauce #2

Serves: 4

$\frac{1}{2}$ pound linguine
$\frac{1}{4}$ cup olive oil
4 cloves garlic, minced
2 tablespoons flour
2 tablespoons white vermouth
2 6$\frac{1}{2}$-ounce cans clams, juice reserved
$\frac{1}{4}$ cup chopped fresh parsley
Salt and pepper to taste

Cook linguine according to package directions and drain. In a large skillet, heat oil and sauté garlic until lightly golden, not burned. Add flour, vermouth, and juice from the clams and stir, bringing to a boil. Add clams and parsley and simmer a few minutes. Season with salt and pepper. Toss with drained cooked pasta and serve immediately.

Linguine Stir-Fry with Asparagus and Garlic

Serves: 4

2 tablespoons olive oil, divided
1 pound skinless, boneless chicken breasts,
    cut into slivers
1 pound asparagus, trimmed and cut into
    1-inch pieces on a diagonal
2 red bell peppers, diced
4 cloves garlic, minced
1/4 cup teriyaki sauce
1 cup salt-reduced chicken broth, defatted
1 pound linguine, cooked

In a wok or large, deep skillet, heat
1 tablespoon olive oil over high heat. Add
chicken and stir-fry until firm, about 4
minutes. Remove the chicken and set aside.
Add the second tablespoon oil to the pan.
Add asparagus and red pepper and stir-fry
until crisp-tender. Add the garlic and stir-fry
for 30 seconds. Stir in the teriyaki sauce and
the chicken broth.

Return chicken to the skillet and heat
through. Add pasta and toss with chicken and
sauce. Transfer to a warm platter and serve.

Linguine with Mushroom and Garlic Cream Sauce

Serves: 2

3 tablespoons Butter
8 ounces fresh mushrooms, sliced

3 medium cloves garlic, minced
1/2 teaspoon dried rosemary, crumbled
Freshly ground pepper
1/2 cup heavy cream
Salt
1 4-ounce package dried linguine
2 ounces Bel Paese cheese, cut into
    small cubes
Chopped fresh parsley

Melt butter in large heavy skillet over
medium-low heat. Add mushrooms,
garlic, rosemary, and generous amount of
pepper. Cook until mushrooms exude
their juices, stirring occasionally, about
5 minutes. Add cream and simmer until
sauce thickens slightly, about 3 minutes.
Season with salt.

Meanwhile, cook linguine in large pot of
boiling salted water. Drain well. Add pasta
and cheese to sauce and stir until cheese
melts. Sprinkle with parsley and serve.

Italian-Style Pistachio Pasta

Serves: 4

1 tablespoon butter or margarine
1 yellow onion, cut into thin wedges
1/4 cup finely diced green bell peppers
1/4 cup finely diced yellow bell peppers
1/4 cup finely diced red bell peppers
2 tablespoons minced garlic
1/4 pound prosciutto, sliced 1/8-inch thick,
    then diced

1 cup natural pistachios,
*   coarsely chopped*
1 1/2 teaspoons crumbled rosemary
3 tablespoons olive oil
4 cups hot cooked penne pasta

Melt butter in skillet. Add onion and sauté until nearly tender. Add bell peppers, garlic, prosciutto, pistachios, rosemary, and olive oil. Continue cooking and stirring until hot and sautéed. Spoon over hot pasta.

Tomato Pasta

Serves: 8

2 tablespoons butter
1 onion, minced
6 cloves garlic
4 28-ounce cans Italian-style
*   tomatoes*
3 beef bouillon cubes
2 teaspoons salt or to taste
5 small dried red hot chilies or 3 slices
*   bacon*
2 tablespoons olive oil
2 pounds dry macaroni
1/2 cup grated Parmesan cheese

Melt butter in a skillet; add onion and whole garlic cloves. Sauté until onion is golden. Add tomatoes with liquid and simmer over low heat 1 1/2 hours, or until sauce is thick. Add bouillon cubes; season to taste with salt once cubes dissolve. Add

chilies and/or bacon, if using, and simmer 30 minutes longer.

When ready to serve, remove garlic cloves and chilies. Stir in oil. Meanwhile, cook macaroni until tender but firm; drain. Pour tomato sauce over macaroni and add cheese. Toss with fork and spoon until sauce and cheese are well distributed.

Preventing Boil-Over

A lump of butter or a few teaspoons of cooking oil added to water when boiling rice, noodles, macaroni, or spaghetti will prevent the liquid from boiling over.

Chicken and Seafood Pasta

Serves: 3

*1 whole boneless, skinless chicken breast,
    split*
2 tablespoons olive oil, divided
¼ cup flour
¼ pound jumbo shrimp
¼ pound scallops
4 cloves garlic, minced
1 cup chicken broth
1 teaspoon basil
1 teaspoon oregano
Salt and pepper to taste
10 sundried tomatoes
1 cup fresh spinach, trimmed and washed
½ pound radiatore pasta, cooked

Cut and pound chicken to create thin cutlets. In a skillet, bring 1 tablespoon oil to high heat. Cook the chicken for 5 minutes, turning once. Remove from pan and set aside. Lightly flour shrimp and scallops. Sauté the shrimp and scallops for 3 to 4 minutes; remove from the pan and set aside. To the same pan, add the remaining tablespoon of olive oil and the garlic; heat until garlic is browned.

Add the chicken, shrimp, scallops, and chicken broth. Add the basil, oregano and salt and pepper to taste. Add the sun-dried tomatoes and the spinach. Cook for 1 minute and remove from heat. Put the cooked pasta in a large serving bowl and add the chicken and seafood mixture on top.

Bow Ties with Sausage, Tomatoes, and Cream

Serves: 4

2 tablespoons olive oil
*1 pound sweet Italian sausage, casings
    removed, crumbled*
½ teaspoon dried red pepper flakes
½ cup diced onions
3 cloves garlic, minced
*1 28-ounce can Italian plum tomatoes,
    drained and coarsely chopped*
1½ cups whipping cream
½ teaspoon salt
12 ounces bow-tie pasta, cooked
3 tablespoons minced fresh parsley
Grated Parmesan cheese

Heat oil in large heavy skillet over medium heat. Add sausage and pepper flakes. Cook until sausage is no longer pink, stirring frequently, about 7 minutes. Add onion and garlic to skillet and cook until onion is tender and sausage is light brown, stirring occasionally, about 7 minutes. Add tomatoes, cream, and salt. Simmer until mixture thickens slightly, about 4 minutes. Add parsley.

Toss with hot pasta and top with Parmesan cheese and serve.

Crockpot Stuffed Shells

Serves: 6

1 pound lean ground beef
1 onion, chopped

1 clove garlic, minced
2 cups shredded mozzarella cheese
$^1\!/_2$ cup seasoned bread crumbs
1 tablespoon parsley flakes
1 egg, beaten
18 jumbo pasta shells, cooked and drained
2 15$^1\!/_2$-ounce jars meatless
    spaghetti sauce
$^1\!/_2$ cup grated Parmesan cheese

Brown ground beef, onion, and garlic in a skillet; drain. Add cheese, bread crumbs, parsley, and egg. Gently stuff shells with beef mixture; set aside. Pour 1 jar of sauce into Crockpot. Arrange stuffed shells in sauce. Top with the other jar of sauce and Parmesan cheese. Cover and cook on low 5 to 7 hours.

Shells Stuffed with Crab

Serves: 8 to 10

1$^1\!/_2$ pounds crab meat
24 ounces cream cheese
$^3\!/_4$ cup grated Parmesan cheese
1 teaspoon minced garlic
$^1\!/_4$ cup chopped shallots
Freshly ground pepper to taste
$^1\!/_3$ cup chopped fresh tarragon or
    1 tablespoon dried tarragon
$^1\!/_2$ teaspoon red pepper flakes
8 ounces large pasta shells
2 tomatoes, peeled, seeded,
    and chopped
Grated Parmesan cheese for garnish

Cream Sauce:
4 cups heavy cream
2 teaspoons minced garlic
2 tablespoons chopped shallots
Salt and pepper to taste

Blend the first 8 ingredients in a bowl; adjust the seasonings. Cook the pasta shells according to the instructions on the package.

Combine the cream sauce ingredients in a saucepan and heat until the mixture is reduced by half. Pour the reduced cream sauce into a shallow baking dish that will hold the shells in one layer. Preheat oven to 400°F.

Stuff the shells with the crabmeat mixture, arrange them on top of the sauce, and bake, covered, for 15 to 20 minutes. Remove from the oven and top with the chopped tomato and Parmesan cheese.

Shells with Green, Red & Yellow Peppers

Serves: 4

3 tablespoons butter
1 tablespoon olive oil
1 cup chopped onion
1 cup diced green peppers ($^1\!/_2$-inch cubes)
1 cup diced red peppers ($^1\!/_2$-inch cubes)
1 cup diced yellow peppers ($^1\!/_2$-inch cubes)
Salt
Freshly ground black pepper
$^2\!/_3$ cup heavy cream
1 pound shell pasta, cooked
2 tablespoons parsley
$^1\!/_2$ cup freshly grated Parmesan cheese

(continued)

In a large skillet melt the butter and oil. Add the chopped onion and turn heat to medium. Sauté until onion turns pale gold. Add all diced peppers. Turn up heat to medium-high and cook until tender, turning them from time to time. Add salt and generous grindings of pepper; stir well. Add cream and turn up heat to high. Cook until cream is reduced by half.

Add the pasta and mix well. Sprinkle with parsley and grated cheese; toss again and serve at once.

Shells with Spinach and Chick Peas

Serves: 4

2 tablespoons virgin olive oil
1 small onion, finely chopped
1 clove garlic, minced
Pinch red pepper flakes
1 carrot, diced
2 tablespoons chopped parsley
Salt
2 teaspoons tomato paste
1 15-ounce can chickpeas
1 bunch spinach leaves, chopped
1 cup water
$\frac{1}{2}$ pound medium-sized pasta shells, cooked
Freshly ground pepper
Olive oil
Freshly grated Parmesan cheese

Heat olive oil in large skillet and add onion, garlic, pepper flakes, carrot, and

parsley. Sauté for 2 minutes. Season with salt and add tomato paste, chickpeas, spinach, and water. Reduce the heat and simmer.

Add the shells to the pan. Toss well and season generously with pepper. Drizzle olive oil and freshly grated cheese over the top.

Rigatoni alla Fontina

Serves: 4

1 pound rigatoni
1 tablespoon salt
6 tablespoons sweet butter, divided
$\frac{1}{2}$ pound sliced fontina cheese
$\frac{1}{2}$ teaspoon nutmeg
1 cup grated Parmesan cheese, divided
$\frac{1}{2}$ teaspoon black pepper

Preheat oven to 400°F. Cook the rigatoni in 5 to 6 quarts salted boiling water until just before they're done (they will finish cooking in the oven). Drain well and place in a large bowl. Add 4 tablespoons of the butter, $\frac{1}{2}$ cup of the Parmesan and all of the nutmeg. Mix well until all the pasta is coated.

In a buttered baking dish, make a layer of the pasta and a layer of the fontina cheese; sprinkle with some Parmesan, and repeat the process until the pasta is used up, ending with a layer of the fontina on top. Sprinkle with Parmesan and black pepper and dot with the remaining butter. Bake for 15 minutes, or until the cheese is melted.

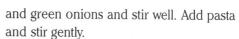

Stovetop Greek Rotelli

Serves: 4

> 2 1/2 cups marinara sauce
> 1 1/2 pounds large shrimp, peeled and
>   deveined
> 8 ounces feta cheese, crumbled
> 1 pound rotelli pasta

Bring marinara sauce to a simmer in a medium saucepan. Add shrimp and simmer until cooked. Meanwhile, cook pasta until al dente. Drain and place in a large serving bowl. Toss with feta. Add the sauce and shrimp and toss again.

Rotini Salad Alfredo

Serves: 8

> 2 cups plain nonfat yogurt
> 1 cup reduced-fat mayonnaise
> 1 cup grated Parmesan cheese
> 1 tablespoon dried basil leaves
>   or dill
> 2 cloves garlic, minced
> 1 teaspoon salt
> 1/2 teaspoon white pepper
> 4 large red bell peppers, chopped
> 3 cups blanched peas
> 1/2 cup chopped green onions
> 1 pound rotini, cooked and chilled

In a large bowl, blend the yogurt, mayonnaise, Parmesan cheese, basil or dill, garlic, salt, and pepper. Add the bell peppers, peas, and green onions and stir well. Add pasta and stir gently.

Cover and refrigerate, at least 2 hours.

Spinach & Mushroom Casserole

Serves: 6

> 1 package frozen chopped spinach, thawed
>   and squeezed dry
> 1 can condensed cream of mushroom
>   soup
> 1 clove garlic, minced
> 1/2 teaspoon dried tarragon
> 1/2 teaspoon marjoram
> salt and pepper to taste
> 4 cups cooked egg noodles
> 1 pound sweet Italian sausage, cooked,
>   drained, and chopped
> 1 large onion, coarsely chopped
> 1 egg
> 1 15-ounce container ricotta cheese
> 1 tomato, seeded and chopped
> Chopped parsley

Preheat oven to 375°F.

Spread noodles in buttered 3-quart flat casserole. Combine spinach, cream of mushroom soup, garlic, and seasonings in a small bowl; spread evenly over noodles. Distribute chopped sausage over the spinach mixture and sprinkle with chopped onion. Blend egg into ricotta and spread over all.

(continued)

Bake 25 to 30 minutes or until golden, then allow to cool slightly. Top with garnish of tomato and parsley.

Lasagna Rollups

Serves: 4

> 8 no-boil lasagna noodles or regular packaged dried lasagna noodles
> 1 small eggplant, peeled
> 12 ounces ground turkey
> 1 stalk celery, sliced
> 2½ cups meatless spaghetti sauce, divided
> ½ teaspoon dried Italian seasoning, crushed
> ¼ teaspoon garlic powder
> Fresh parsley, oregano, and chives (optional)

Soak no-boil lasagna noodles in warm water for 10 minutes. Or, cook regular lasagna noodles according to package directions. Drain well.

Cut the eggplant into 12 inch-thick slices crosswise starting from the bottom of the eggplant. Then cut the slices in half. Set aside. Chop the remaining eggplant; you should have about 1 cup.

Cook chopped eggplant, turkey, and celery in a large skillet about 5 minutes or until turkey is no longer pink and eggplant is tender. Drain well. Stir in 1 cup of the spaghetti sauce, the Italian seasoning, and garlic powder.

Preheat oven to 375°F. Spread ½ cup of the spaghetti sauce in a 1½- to 2-quart au gratin dish or baking dish. Spread about ¼ cup of the turkey mixture on each noodle. Roll up noodles starting from one of the short ends. Place rolls, seam side down, in the dish. Place halved eggplant slices around edge of the dish, rounded edge up, overlapping slightly. Spoon remaining spaghetti sauce over rolls.

Bake, covered, about 35 minutes or until filling is heated through and pasta is tender. Garnish with fresh parsley, oregano, and chives, if desired.

Chinese Pork Rice Sticks

Serves: 4

> 3 ounces rice sticks (cellophane rice noodles)
> 1 pound lean ground pork or beef
> 2 tablespoons soy sauce
> 1 teaspoon sesame oil
> 1 tablespoon peanut oil
> 1 teaspoon chili oil
> 2 medium carrots, thinly sliced (1 cup)
> 4 green onions, cut into 1-inch pieces
> 2 stalks celery, thinly bias sliced (1 cup)
> 2 cloves garlic, minced
> 2 teaspoons grated gingerroot
> ½ cup chicken broth

Place rice sticks in a medium mixing bowl. Add enough warm water to cover; let stand for 15 minutes. Drain well. Cut rice

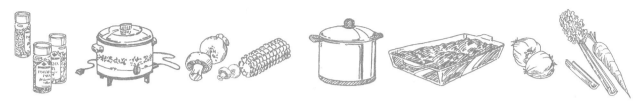

sticks into 2- to 3-inch lengths. Set aside. Combine ground pork, soy sauce, and sesame oil in another medium mixing bowl; mix well. Let meat mixture stand for 20 minutes.

Pour the three oils into a wok or large skillet. Preheat over medium-high heat. Add carrots and green onions; stir-fry for 2 minutes. Add the celery; stir-fry for 2 minutes or until vegetables are crisp-tender. Remove the vegetables from wok.

Add half of the meat mixture, the garlic, and gingerroot to wok; stir-fry 2 to 3 minutes or until meat is no longer pink, breaking meat into small pieces. Remove meat mixture from wok. Repeat with remaining meat. Drain off fat. Wipe out wok with paper towels.

Return all meat to wok. Add soaked rice sticks and cooked vegetables; stir-fry for 1 minute. Add chicken broth. Cook and stir about 1 minute or until heated through. Serve immediately.

Spanish Noodles

Serves: 4

2 slices bacon
1/2 cup chopped onion
1 pound ground beef
1 28-ounce can tomatoes, cut up
1/2 cup chopped green pepper
1/4 cup chili sauce
1 teaspoon salt
Pepper
3 cups uncooked egg noodles

In a large skillet, cook bacon until crisp; remove from skillet and drain on paper toweling. Crumble and set aside. Add onion to bacon drippings in skillet; cook until tender but not brown. Add the meat; cook until browned. Drain fat.

Stir in tomatoes, green pepper, chili sauce, salt, and a dash of pepper; add uncooked noodles. Cook, covered, over low heat for 30 minutes or until noodles are tender, stirring frequently. Stir in the bacon.

Cooking Pasta for Salad

When preparing pasta noodles for a cold pasta salad, it's possible to save time by cooking a batch of pasta ahead. Once they're cooked, rinse immediately under cold water and drain thoroughly, patting with paper towels to absorb the excess moisture. Then place in a large plastic bag and store in the refrigerator. The pasta will keep for up to three days.

Crazy Ziti

Serves: 4

5 to 6 cloves garlic, minced
1 teaspoon red pepper flakes
3 tablespoons olive oil
3 tomatoes, chopped
1/4 cup dry vermouth
1/4 cup whole Kalamata olives
1 7-ounce can Italian tuna, packed
  in olive oil
1 tablespoon capers
Chopped fresh parsley
Chopped fresh oregano
1 pound ziti pasta, cooked and rinsed

In a large heavy skillet sauté the garlic and red pepper flakes in olive oil.

When the garlic is just about brown, add the tomatoes, vermouth, olives, tuna, capers, parsley, and oregano, and cook over a high flame until the sauce comes together, about 10 minutes.

Add the pasta to the tomato mixture and reheat over a low flame. Stir the sauce and pasta until well blended. Cook for a few minutes to let the pasta absorb the sauce and to make it piping hot.

Quickie Pasta Bake

Serves: 6

1 tablespoon olive oil
1 onion, chopped
2 cloves garlic, minced

1 28-ounce can tomatoes, crushed
1 teaspoon oregano
Salt and pepper to taste
1 pound Pasta; ziti or rotini, cooked and
  drained
2 cups grated cheese, any type

Preheat oven to 350°F. Heat oil in a heavy, large ovenproof skillet. Add onion and garlic; sauté till soft (about 5 minutes). Add tomatoes, oregano, salt, and pepper. Cook till heated through, about 5 minutes. Add the cooked pasta and 1/2 cup grated cheese to the mixture. Sprinkle remaining cheese on top.

Bake 15 to 20 minutes or until cheese on top is bubbly.

Seafood Pasta Salad

Serves: 4

2 cups cooked pasta, tri-colored spirals
1 cup shrimp, cooked, or tuna
1 green pepper, diced
1/4 cup sliced carrots
1/2 cup sliced zucchini
1/3 cup Worcestershire sauce
1/3 cup mayonnaise
Salt and pepper to taste

In a mixing bowl, combine pasta, shrimp or tuna, green pepper, carrots, and zucchini. Add Worcestershire sauce, mayonnaise, salt, and pepper and toss lightly to combine. Refrigerate at least 30 minutes before serving.

Chapter 6

Dishes with Rice or Other Grains

Like pasta, rice is a wonderful vehicle for anything that's added to it, from chicken and vegetables to soy sauce and butter. And it stands up particularly well in rice casseroles and stir-fries that are first frozen before being served.

Many of the rice recipes in *The Everything One-Pot Cookbook* contain a little bit of everything: vegetables, spices or other flavorings, meat, and cheese or other dairy products. Feel free to add and subtract from the recipes as you see fit. Create your own one-pot book; you only have an infinite number of variations to choose from.

Poor Man's Paella

Serves: 8

2 tablespoons vegetable oil
1 ½ pounds smoked Polish or Italian
    sausage
1 large bell pepper, chopped
1 large onion, chopped
1 clove garlic, minced
Small bay leaf, crushed
2 teaspoons paprika
½ teaspoon salt
½ teaspoon seasoned pepper
2 cups uncooked long-grain rice
1 20-ounce can tomatoes
1 10½-ounce can chicken broth
¼ cup red wine
Water

In a paella pan, heavy Dutch oven, or ovenproof sauté pan, heat oil and brown sausage, which has been cut into 4-inch lengths. Remove; drain on paper towels.

Add pepper, onion, garlic, and bay leaf to drippings in pan and sauté, stirring, over medium heat until onion is golden. Add paprika, salt, seasoned pepper, and rice to pan and cook, stirring, until rice is lightly browned, about 8 to 10 minutes. Preheat oven to 350°F.

Drain tomatoes and put tomato liquid into a 1-quart measuring cup. Add chicken broth, wine, and enough water to make 1 quart of liquid. Mix well and add with tomatoes to pan. Bring to a boil, then remove from heat.

Arrange sausage pieces on top, cover and bake for 1 hour. Serve directly from the pan.

Sweet Sausage Risotto

Serves: 8

1 pound sweet Italian sausage
3 onions, chopped
3 ribs celery, chopped
1 green pepper, seeded and chopped
1 1/2 cups uncooked long-grain rice
1/3 cup grated Parmesan cheese
3 cups hot water, in which 3 beef bouillon
*   cubes have been dissolved*

In a 3-quart stockpot, fry the sausage until crisp, crumbling with a fork so it cooks evenly. Remove and place on paper towels to drain. Set aside. Preheat oven to 350°F.

In the same pot, sauté the onion, celery, and pepper until the onion is translucent. Add the rice, stirring to coat thoroughly. Add the sausage and the cheese, and, using two forks, toss the mixture lightly. Add the bouillon mixture. Bake, covered, for 45 minutes, or until the rice is tender and the liquid is absorbed.

Creamy Roasted Corn Risotto

Serves: 2

3 tablespoons olive oil
1 cup uncooked risotto rice
4 cups hot chicken broth
1/2 cup milk
1/2 cup dry white wine
1/3 pound cream cheese, cut into 1/2-inch cubes
3 ears of corn, cooked, and corn cut off
*   each ear*

4 fresh scallions, thinly cut on the bias
Salt, pepper, and nutmeg to taste

In a large heavy skillet, lightly brown the rice in the oil.

Add the hot chicken broth, milk, and wine, 1/2 cup at a time, stirring until absorbed. It will take about 30 minutes for the rice to cook fully.

Add the cheese and heat until the cheese starts to melt. Stir the corn kernels into the risotto. Remove from heat. Add the scallions, and stir to mix well. Add the salt, pepper, and nutmeg.

About Risotto

Although it sounds rather exotic, risotto is a simple Italian rice dish that is a cornerstone of a meal that doesn't include pasta. Risotto is made when you add a hot broth to uncooked rice in increments while cooking it in a saucepan over low heat. You must stir the rice continually, and wait until the rice has absorbed all of the broth before adding more. Risotto is typically creamy and served in a puddle of broth. The average cooking time is about 25 minutes.

Stovetop Paella

Serves: 5

1 6½-ounce package rice pilaf mix
3 tablespoons butter
1 teaspoon Cajun seasoning
1 teaspoon finely chopped fresh garlic
½ pound (8 ounces) boneless, skinless chicken breast tenders
1 medium onion, cut into eighths
2 9-ounce package frozen peas
½ pound (8 ounces) cooked medium shrimp

Cook rice mix according to package directions. Meanwhile, in a 12-inch skillet, melt butter until sizzling. Stir in seasoning and garlic. Add chicken and onion. Cook 7 to 9 minutes over medium-high heat, stirring occasionally, until chicken is no longer pink.

Add peas, shrimp, and cooked rice mix. Continue cooking, stirring occasionally, until peas and shrimp are heated through, 4 to 5 minutes.

Lemony Bulgur Garbanzo Pilaf

Serves: 8

1 cup medium-grind bulgur
2 cups vegetable stock or bouillon
1 teaspoon ground cumin or more to taste, divided
1 tablespoon olive oil
1 small onion, chopped

1 small green bell pepper, chopped
3 large cloves garlic, minced
2 cups cooked chickpeas (1 cup dried) or 1 14-ounce can, drained
⅓ cup fresh lemon juice
1 cup chopped fresh parsley
Salt and freshly ground pepper to taste

Place the bulgur in a bowl. Bring the stock to a boil, add half the cumin, and pour the stock over the bulgur. Stir once and let sit for 10 to 15 minutes, until most of the liquid has been absorbed and the bulgur is fluffy.

Heat the olive oil in a large heavy-bottomed skillet or Dutch oven over medium heat. Add the onion, green pepper, and half the garlic. Sauté, stirring, until the onion is translucent, about 3 to 5 minutes. Add the remaining garlic and cumin. Sauté for about 30 seconds. Stir in the bulgur and chickpeas. Stir together for a few minutes. Then add the lemon juice and parsley. Combine well, add salt and pepper, and serve hot.

Risotto with Vegetables

Serves: 8

2 tablespoons butter, divided
1 Spanish onion, chopped
1 cup white rice, uncooked
4 cups chicken broth
1 cup green beans
1 cup snow peas
1 cup zucchini, chopped
⅓ cup minced fresh parsley

¹/₄ cup grated Parmesan cheese
Salt and pepper to taste

Melt half of the butter in large skillet over medium heat; cook the onions until softened. Add rice and stir to coat. Add 2 cups of the chicken broth, ¹/₂ cup at a time, stirring until it's absorbed before adding the next ¹/₂ cup, about 2 minutes for each addition. Add the green beans, snow peas, and zucchini; cook for 2 minutes. Add the remaining broth, again ¹/₂ cup at a time, as before. This time, it should take up to 15 minutes until the rice is cooked. Add the parsley, Parmesan, remaining tablespoon of butter, and salt and pepper.

Couscous with Yogurt and Fruit

Serves: 4

1 cup milk
1 tablespoon butter
¹/₄ teaspoon salt
²/₃ cup quick-cooking couscous
¹/₂ cup vanilla yogurt
2 tablespoons sugar
¹/₂ cup diced fresh fruit or berries
Sugar

In medium saucepan, combine milk, butter, and salt and bring to a boil. Stir in couscous. Cover. Remove from heat and let stand 5 minutes. Fluff couscous with fork to separate. Stir in yogurt and sugar, and fold in fruit. Sprinkle with sugar.

Cheesy Tuna, Rice & Peas

Serves: 4

1 ¹/₂ cups hot water
1 package chicken bouillon
1 10-ounce package frozen baby peas
1 can condensed Cheddar cheese soup
1 6-ounce can tuna, drained and flaked
1 ¹/₂ cups instant rice

In a medium saucepan mix the water and bouillon until dissolved. Add peas and bring to boil. Add soup and stir until smooth. Add tuna and bring to boil again. Stir in rice, cover, remove from heat, and let stand 5 minutes.

Bangkok Fried Rice

Serves: 8

¹/₄ cup + 1 tablespoon vegetable oil
5 cloves garlic
³/₄ cup peeled and finely slivered shallots
4 quarter-sized slices of fresh ginger, cut into fine slivers
1 fresh hot green chili, seeded and cut into fine slivers
6 cups cooked, unsalted, cold white rice
1 cup mung bean sprouts, washed and drained
1 large egg
1 ¹/₂ teaspoons salt or to taste
2 tablespoons minced fresh cilantro

(continued)

Sauce:

6 tablespoons mashed red bean curd
1 tablespoon very finely grated fresh ginger
2 tablespoons very finely minced fresh hot green chilies
2 tablespoons very finely minced peeled shallots
½ cup fresh lime or lemon juice
Fresh mint sprigs for garnish
12 cucumber sticks (3" x ⅓" x ⅓") for garnish

Heat the oil in a wok or a heavy skillet over a medium flame. When hot, add the garlic. Stir and cook for 1 minute. Add the shallots. Stir-fry for another 2 minutes. Add the ginger and the chili. Stir-fry another minute. Add the cooked rice and mung bean sprouts. Stir-fry for 2 minutes.

Make a hole in the center of the rice and break the egg into it.

Stir the egg, first in its hole and then, when it sets a bit, mix it up with the rice. Add the salt. Stir-fry the rice for 10 minutes or until it has heated through. Stir in the minced cilantro.

Mix all the ingredients for the sauce in a bowl.

To serve, make a mound of the rice on a large platter. Garnish with the mint and cucumber. Pass along the sauce on the side.

Chinese Vegetable Fried Rice

Serves: 4

1 tablespoon peanut oil
2 cups sliced zucchini
1 cup minced celery
4 cups cold cooked rice
1 red pepper, diced
2 eggs, lightly beaten
2 cups bean sprouts
1 cup oyster sauce
1 Spanish onion, chopped

A Grain of Rice

If you like your cooked rice to have every grain separate from the rest, add a few drops of lemon juice to the pot of simmering rice. The acid in the juice will help keep the grains separate as they cook.

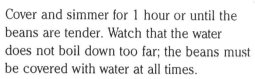

In a large skillet, heat oil over medium-high heat. Stir-fry the zucchini and celery for 2 minutes. Add the rice and stir-fry for another minute. Add the red pepper and stir-fry for another minute. Add the eggs and stir 30 seconds. Add the bean sprouts and stir-fry for another minute or until eggs are set. Add the oyster sauce and stir. Sprinkle with chopped onion.

Garlicky Red Beans and Rice

Serves: 4

> 1 pound red beans, soaked overnight
> 1 medium onion, chopped
> 1 bunch green onions, chopped
> 7 cloves garlic, chopped
> ½ cup parsley
> 1 rib celery, chopped
> ½ cup ketchup
> 1 bell pepper, seeded and chopped
> 1 tablespoon Worcestershire sauce
> 2 tablespoons Tabasco sauce
> 2 bay leaves
> 1 teaspoon thyme
> Salt and pepper to taste
> 1 pound smoked sausage cut into 1-inch pieces
> 1 pound pickled pork, rinsed and cut into cubes
> 4 cups cooked white rice

Drain the beans. Put them in a large heavy pot and add 3 quarts of fresh water.

Cover and simmer for 1 hour or until the beans are tender. Watch that the water does not boil down too far; the beans must be covered with water at all times.

Add the rest of the ingredients, except for the rice. Add more water to cover if needed. Simmer for 1 to 1½ hours or until the liquid has thickened. Serve over rice.

Sausage, Red Beans, and Rice

Serves: 8

> 1 pound red kidney beans
> 1 meaty ham bone
> 2 large onions, chopped
> 1 bell pepper, chopped
> 2 ribs celery, chopped
> 2 cloves garlic, finely chopped
> Salt and pepper to taste
> Pinch of sugar
> 1 bay leaf (optional)
> 2 pounds Owen's spicy sausage links
> ¼ cup chopped parsley
> 4 cups cooked white rice

Soak beans overnight; rinse. Cover with water and cook with ham bone (fat trimmed off), onion, bell pepper, celery, garlic, salt, pepper, sugar, and bay leaf.

While beans are cooking, boil sausage in skillet. Drain, fry until crisp, and set aside. Cook beans until fork tender, about 1 to 2 hours; then add fried sausage. Just before serving, remove bay leaf and add parsley. Serve over rice. Freezes well.

Caribbean Beans and Rice

Serves: 6

> 1 large pimiento or roasted red pepper cut
> in short, thin strips
> ½ green pepper cut in short, thin strips
> 2 cloves garlic, finely chopped
> 1½ teaspoons olive oil
> 2 16-ounce cans black beans, drained and
> rinsed
> 2 tablespoons white vinegar
> 5 to 10 dashes hot pepper sauce
> 3 cups cooked white rice (1 cup raw)
> 3 tablespoons finely chopped fresh cilantro
> Salt and pepper to taste

Sauté pimiento, green pepper, and garlic in oil in large sauté pan 2 minutes. Add black beans, vinegar, and hot pepper sauce. When hot, reduce heat to low, cover, and simmer 5 minutes. Stir in rice and cilantro. Taste and adjust seasonings. Serve with additional hot pepper sauce.

Salsa Black Beans and Rice

Serves: 6

> ½ cup diced onion
> 1 strip of bacon
> 2 cloves garlic, minced
> 2 16-ounce cans black beans
> ¼ cup of more prepared picante sauce
> 4 heaping tablespoons of prepared picante
> sauce

> Salt and pepper to taste
> 4 cups cooked white rice

Sauté the onions in oil or nonstick spray until slightly translucent. Cut the bacon strip into 1-inch pieces. Add the garlic and bacon to the onions and sauté until the bacon is somewhat cooked but still limp. Stir in the beans. Stir in picante sauce. Simmer for about 10 minutes. Keep covered and stir occasionally. You may want to try to mash up some of the beans with a spoon. Add salt and pepper to taste. This mixture should be slightly soupy. Serve over rice in a bowl.

Brazilian Paella

Serves: 6

> ½ pound sausage, rolled into small balls
> 2 3-pound broiler-fryer chickens, cut into
> serving pieces
> Salt and pepper to taste
> 2 large onions, chopped
> 1½ cups uncooked long-grain rice
> 1 1-pound can tomatoes, drained and
> chopped (reserve the liquid)
> 3 chicken bouillon cubes

In an ovenproof casserole, fry the sausage balls until they are well browned and crisp; set them aside on paper towels. In the same pot, season the chicken with salt and pepper, and then brown the chicken for 10 minutes. Remove the chicken from the pot and set it aside. Preheat oven to 350°F.

Discard all but 3 tablespoons of the fat. In the same pot, cook the onion until translucent. Add the rice, stirring to coat each grain. Stir in the tomatoes. Return the sausage balls and chicken pieces to the pot and spoon the rice mixture over them.

To this liquid, add enough hot water to make 3 cups. Add the bouillon cubes and stir until dissolved. Pour the mixture over the casserole. Bake, covered, for an hour, or until the chicken and rice are tender and the liquid is absorbed.

Herbed Rice Pilaf

Serves: 4

> 1 yellow onion, chopped
> 2 ribs celery, chopped
> 1 clove garlic, minced
> 1 teaspoon dried thyme
> 1 tablespoon olive oil
> 1 bay leaf
> 2½ cups water
> 1 cup uncooked long-grain rice
> Thyme sprig for garnish

In a medium saucepan, sauté onion, celery, garlic, and thyme in oil for 5 minutes or until onions are translucent. Add bay leaf and water. Bring to a boil; add rice. Cover and simmer for 20 minutes or until all water is absorbed and rice is tender. Remove bay leaf. Spoon into a serving bowl. Garnish with a sprig of thyme.

Making Non-Stick Pans

There's no need to buy special nonstick pots and pans. Just use a bit of vinegar before you cook in a new pan the first time. Pour enough vinegar into the pan to cover the bottom of the pan, and then bring it to a boil. Wipe out the pan. Let cool and wash the pan.

Authentic Beijing Stir-Fry

Serves: 4

> 12 dried shiitake mushrooms
> 12 ounces skinless, boneless chicken breasts or thighs
> ½ cup chicken broth
> 2 tablespoons soy sauce
> 2 tablespoons dry sherry
> 2 teaspoons cornstarch

(continued)

¼ to ½ teaspoon chili oil or chili paste

3 tablespoons peanut oil or cooking oil

1 medium carrot, thinly sliced

3 medium stalks celery, cut into thin diagonal slices

1 medium red or green sweet pepper, cut into lengthwise strips

2 green onions, cut into 2-inch lengths

½ of a medium bok choy, coarsely chopped (4 cups)

1½ cups pea pods, strings removed and cut in diagonal halves

1 tablespoon grated gingerroot

2 cloves garlic, minced

1 14-ounce can baby corn, drained

3 cups hot cooked rice

Place dried mushrooms in a small bowl. Add boiling water to cover. Let soak for 30 minutes. Drain; trim and discard the stems. Cut caps into halves. Set aside.

Meanwhile, rinse chicken and pat dry with paper towels. Cut chicken into thin, bite-size strips; set aside. For sauce, stir together chicken broth, soy sauce, sherry, cornstarch, and chili oil; set aside.

Pour half of the peanut oil into a wok or large skillet. Preheat over medium-high heat. Add carrot; stir-fry for 1 minute. Add celery; stir-fry for 1 minute. Add red or green pepper and onions; stir-fry for 1 to 2 minutes or until crisp-tender. Remove from wok. Add bok choy to wok; stir-fry for 2 minutes. Add soaked mushrooms and pea pods; stir-fry

for 1 to 2 minutes or until crisp. Remove from wok.

Add remaining oil to the wok. Add chicken, gingerroot, and garlic; stir-fry for 4 to 5 minutes or until chicken is no longer pink. Push chicken from center of wok. Stir sauce; add to center of wok. Cook and stir until thickened and bubbly. Return all of the cooked vegetables to wok. Add corn. Stir to coat all ingredients. Cook and stir about 1 minute or until heated through. Serve immediately over rice.

Brown Rice Curry with Vegetables and Shrimp

Serves: 4

1 tablespoon olive oil

1 large onion, sliced

3 cloves garlic, minced

1 tablespoon curry powder

½ teaspoon cinnamon

½ teaspoon salt (optional)

1½ cups water

2 large carrots, sliced

2 large potatoes, peeled and cubed

1 large zucchini, sliced

1 16-ounce can tomatoes, with juice, chopped

1 pound shrimp, cleaned and deveined

4 cups hot cooked brown rice

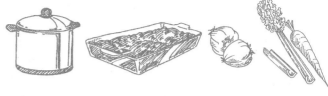

Heat the oil in a large skillet, and sauté the onion and garlic until translucent. Add the curry powder, cinnamon, salt, and water. Bring to a boil. Add the carrots and potatoes. Reduce the heat, cover, and cook for 10 minutes. Add the zucchini, tomatoes with their juice, and shrimp. Cover again, and cook for another 10 minutes. Serve over cooked rice.

Pear Brown Rice

Serves: 8

> 3 tablespoons lemon juice
> 2 teaspoons finely chopped garlic
> $1/4$ teaspoon ground ginger
> $1/4$ teaspoon freshly ground black pepper
> $3 1/2$ cups cooked brown rice
> $1/2$ cup sliced green onions
> $1/2$ cup grated carrots
> $1/2$ cup thinly sliced celery
> 3 tablespoons olive oil
> 2 fresh Bartlett pears, diced

In a medium bowl, combine the lemon juice, garlic, ginger, and black pepper. Mix in the rice, onions, carrots, celery, and olive oil. Gently fold in pears. Chill.

Spinach, Rice & Vegetable Skillet

Serves: 6

> 2 tablespoons olive oil
> 1 bunch parsley, finely chopped

> 1 large yellow onion, finely chopped
> 1 tablespoon finely chopped garlic
> 3 cups water
> 2 tablespoons tomato paste
> 1 cup chopped tomatoes
> $1/8$ teaspoon salt
> $1/8$ teaspoon pepper
> 2 bunches spinach, stems removed, chopped
> 1 cup uncooked white rice

Heat oil over medium-high heat in a large saucepan. Add the parsley, onions, and garlic. Sauté for 3 to 4 minutes, or until the onions are translucent. Add water to the pan and bring to a boil.

Add the tomato paste, chopped tomatoes, salt, and pepper. Mix thoroughly to combine. Add the spinach and rice. Simmer for 30 minutes on low heat, or until the rice is done.

Pineapple Fried Rice

Serves: 6

> 1 large ripe pineapple
> $2 1/2$ tablespoons vegetable oil
> $2 1/2$ teaspoons finely minced garlic
> $1/2$ cup finely diced yellow onion
> $1/2$ cup diced firm tofu or tempeh
> 2 teaspoons grated or finely minced fresh ginger
> $1/3$ cup ($1 1/2$ ounces) finely sliced long beans or green beans
> $1/3$ cup sliced canned straw mushrooms

(continued)

$\frac{1}{4}$ red bell pepper, diced
1 mild fresh red chili, seeded and
    chopped
2 teaspoons tomato paste
1$\frac{1}{2}$ teaspoons mashed yellow bean sauce
    or fermented tofu and its brine
8 cups cooked white rice
Superfine white sugar, to taste
Light soy sauce, to taste
2 tablespoons shredded coconut, toasted,
    for garnish

Cut the pineapple in half lengthwise, cutting straight through the crown. Using a sharp knife, remove the flesh from the skins. Cut the flesh into $\frac{1}{2}$-inch cubes. You will need 1$\frac{1}{2}$ cups for this recipe.

Heat the oil in a wok or large skillet over high heat. Add the garlic and fry, stirring constantly, for 30 seconds. Add the onion and diced tofu or tempeh, and stir-fry until lightly golden, about 3$\frac{1}{2}$ minutes. Add the ginger, beans, mushrooms, bell pepper, chili, tomato paste, and yellow bean sauce or fermented tofu. Stir over high heat for about 2 minutes, then add the rice and continue stirring, tossing and turning, until well mixed.

Stir the 1$\frac{1}{2}$ cups diced pineapple into the rice and vegetable mixture, and add the sugar and soy sauce. Cook a little longer until heated through. Garnish with the toasted coconut. Serve at once.

Green Veggie Casserole

Serves: 4

4 cups cooked rice
$\frac{1}{4}$ cup butter, softened
2 teaspoons lemon juice
$\frac{3}{4}$ cup slivered or sliced almonds
1 clove garlic, minced
1 medium onion, chopped
$\frac{3}{4}$ teaspoon salt
1 10-ounce package frozen spinach, thawed
$\frac{3}{4}$ cup chopped green onions
$\frac{3}{4}$ cup finely minced parsley
1 egg
1 cup milk

Preheat oven to 350°F. In a greased shallow 3-quart casserole or 9 x 13-inch baking dish, combine rice, butter, lemon juice, almonds, garlic, onion, salt, spinach, green onions, and parsley.

Beat together egg and milk, and add to rice mixture; toss gently. Bake, uncovered, for 30 minutes or until custard is set. Stir lightly before serving.

Yucatan Rice

Serves: 6

1 tablespoon butter
1 small onion, chopped
$\frac{3}{4}$ cup chicken broth
1$\frac{1}{2}$ teaspoons chili powder
$\frac{1}{4}$ teaspoon ground cinnamon
$\frac{1}{4}$ teaspoon ground cumin

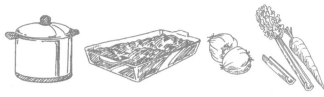

¼ teaspoon oregano leaves
¾ teaspoon salt
4 cups cooked rice
1 2¼-ounce can sliced ripe olives, drained
1 small green pepper, seeded and chopped
1 avocado for garnish
2 tablespoons lemon juice
2 medium-size tomatoes, cut in wedges, for garnish

In an ovenproof 2-quart saucepan over medium heat, melt the butter. Add onion and cook until soft. Stir in broth, chili powder, cinnamon, cumin, oregano, and salt. Reduce heat and simmer, uncovered, for about 5 minutes. Stir in the rice, olives, and green pepper.

Preheat oven to 375°F. Bake, covered, for about 25 minutes or until heated through.

Meanwhile, peel, pit, and slice avocado; sprinkle with 1 tablespoon of the lemon juice. When the casserole is done, stir the remaining 1 tablespoon lemon juice into the rice mixture. Garnish with avocado slices and tomato wedges.

Scallion Tabouleh

Serves: 4

1 cup bulgur
2 cups boiling water
½ cup chopped fresh parsley
⅔ cup raisins
1 cup chopped scallions
⅓ cup fresh lime juice

3 tablespoons olive oil
Salt and pepper to taste

In a medium bowl, mix together the bulgur and boiling water. Allow it to stand for up to an hour until tender. Strain the bulgur through a colander to remove excess moisture. Place the bulgur in a serving bowl and add the parsley, raisins, and scallions. Toss to mix well. In a small bowl, stir together the lime juice, oil, salt, and pepper. Add to the bulgur salad and serve.

Thawing Frozen One-Pot Dishes

One of the best ways to quickly thaw one-pot meals that have been frozen is to place the container into warm or even simmering water. First loosen the top, and then check it every five minutes or so to determine the status of the frozen food.

Chapter 7

*Soups,
Stews, and
Chowders*

Of course, soups, stews, and chowders are the original one-pot delights. People *expect* them to be prepared and served in only one pot.

At the same time, they probably don't expect them to be as flavorful and as easy to prepare as the recipes included in The Everything One-Pot Cookbook. The following recipes make copious use of beans, garlic, and hearty stocks, which can only result in tasty and easy to prepare dishes that have people coming back for seconds, if not thirds.

Soups

Undoubtedly, soups are the most common form of one-pot cooking in America today. Unfortunately, many people shy away from creating soups from scratch because opening a can is so much easier. The good news is that the following recipes are so delicious, and most require just a *little* more effort to create than opening a can. The end result is worth it!

Tortilla Soup

Serves: 6

1 small onion, chopped
4 or 5 fresh green chili peppers, roasted, peeled, deveined, and chopped
2 cloves garlic, crushed
1 tablespoon olive oil
1 cup fresh tomatoes, peeled and chopped
1 10.5-ounce can beef broth
1 10.5-ounce can chicken broth
1 1/2 cups water

1 1/2 cups tomato juice
1 teaspoon ground cumin
1 teaspoon chili powder
1 teaspoon salt
1/8 teaspoon pepper
2 teaspoons Worcestershire sauce
1 tablespoon bottled steak sauce
3 corn tortillas, cut in 1/2-inch strips
1/4 cup shredded Cheddar cheese

Sauté onion, chilies and garlic in oil until soft. Add tomatoes, broth, water, tomato juice, cumin, chili powder, salt, pepper,

Worcestershire, and steak sauce. Bring soup to a boil; reduce heat and simmer, covered, 1 hour.

Add tortillas and cheese and simmer 10 minutes longer.

Crockpot French Onion Soup

Serves: 6

4 large yellow onions, thinly sliced
1/4 cup butter
3 cups rich beef stock
1 cup dry white wine
1/4 cup medium dry sherry
1 teaspoon Worcestershire sauce
1 clove garlic, minced
6 slices French bread, buttered
1/4 cup grated Romano or Parmesan
  cheese

In a large frying pan, slowly sauté the onions in butter until limp and glazed. Transfer to Crockpot. Add beef stock, white wine, sherry, Worcestershire, and garlic. Cover. Cook on low 6 to 8 hours.

Place buttered French bread on a baking sheet. Sprinkle with cheese. Place under preheated broiler until lightly toasted. To serve, ladle soup into bowl. Float a slice of toasted French bread on top.

Macaroni and Cheese Soup

Serves: 6

1 cup uncooked elbow macaroni
1/4 cup butter
1/2 cup finely chopped carrots
1/2 cup finely chopped celery
1 small onion, finely chopped
6 ounces American cheese, shredded
2 tablespoons chicken flavored bouillon
  granules
1/2 teaspoon ground white pepper
2 tablespoons cornstarch
2 tablespoons water
1 8-ounce can whole kernel corn, drained
1/2 cup frozen peas
1 cup milk

Cook macaroni per package directions, omitting salt; drain. Rinse in cold water; drain and set aside.

Melt butter in a large skillet over medium-high heat; add carrots, celery, and onion, and cook, stirring constantly, 5 to 7 minutes or until tender. Remove vegetable mixture from heat; set aside.

Combine milk and cheese in a heavy Dutch oven. Cook over medium heat, stirring often, until cheese melts. Stir in the bouillon granules and pepper.

Combine cornstarch and water, stirring well; stir into the milk mixture. Cook over medium heat, stirring constantly, until mixture

(continued)

thickens and comes to a boil. Boil 1 minute, stirring constantly.

Stir in macaroni, vegetable mixture, corn, and peas; cook over low heat, stirring constantly, until thoroughly heated.

Vegetarian Barley-Vegetable Soup

Serves: 12

2 medium onions, peeled and diced
2 large carrots, scraped and diced
2 stalks celery, chopped
3 tablespoons butter
1 1 pound, 12-ounce can chopped
   tomatoes
8 cups water
1 teaspoon dried basil
$\frac{1}{2}$ teaspoon dried thyme
2 teaspoons salt
$\frac{1}{4}$ teaspoon pepper
1 cup pearl barley
2 cups frozen green beans or peas
1 tablespoon chopped fresh dill

Sauté onions, carrots, and celery in heated butter in a large kettle for 5 minutes. Add tomatoes, water, basil, thyme, salt, and pepper. Bring to a boil. Stir in barley and reduce heat. Cook slowly, covered, 1 $\frac{1}{2}$ hours, until barley is tender.

Stir in beans or peas during last 10 minutes of cooking. Remove from heat and stir in dill.

Yogurt and Cucumber Soup with Mint and Dill

Serves: 6

3 cups low-fat yogurt
2 cups low-fat (1%) milk
1 large cucumber, peeled, seeded, and
   coarsely grated
2 medium cloves garlic, put through a
   garlic press
2 tablespoons olive oil
2 tablespoons plus 1 teaspoon finely
   chopped fresh dill weed, divided
1 tablespoon finely chopped fresh mint
2 tablespoons fresh lemon juice
$\frac{1}{4}$ to $\frac{1}{2}$ teaspoon salt
Freshly ground black pepper to taste
4 drops hot pepper sauce
6 paper-thin slices cucumber with skin for
   garnish

Put the yogurt into a cheesecloth-lined strainer and let drip over a bowl 2 hours at room temperature, or overnight in refrigerator. Discard the water and place yogurt in a bowl.

Whisk the milk into the drained yogurt until smooth. Stir in the cucumber, garlic, olive oil, 2 tablespoons dill, mint, lemon juice, salt, pepper, and hot pepper sauce. Refrigerate 1 to 2 hours, until ice cold.

Garnish each serving with a little of the remaining teaspoon dill and a slice of cucumber.

Artichoke Hearts Soup

Serves: 8

> *4 large artichokes or 6 smaller ones,*
>   *cleaned*
> *Juice of 2 small lemons*
> *1 gallon water*
> *1 tablespoon salt*
> *3 medium-large taro roots*
> *1 medium leek*
> *3 stems of celery leaves (Chinese celery)*
> *1 tablespoon garlic powder*
> *1 teaspoon marjoram*
> *3 tablespoons whipping cream (not*
>   *whipped) or yogurt*

To prepare the artichokes, remove the outer leaves and the stem. Cut the rest of the leaves straight, about $1\frac{1}{2}$ inches from the stem, with a sharp knife. Continue to remove the outer leaves as long as they come off easily. Cut the artichokes in half and then into quarters. With a sharp small knife remove the inner thistles and hair. Cut each quarter into a few small bite-size pieces. Throw the cleaned pieces into clean water with the juice of one lemon in the water to prevent the artichokes from becoming black.

When all the artichokes are cleaned and cut, bring 1 gallon of water in a large pot to boil. Add the salt and the artichoke pieces, after rinsing them off. Simmer for 20 minutes or until all artichoke hearts are well cooked. While the artichokes are cooking, peel, clean, and cut the taro roots into $\frac{1}{2}$-inch cubes.

Puréeing Soups

Though it technically does add another pot to your one-pot technique, puréeing a soup in a blender or food processor adds an elegant creamy touch to the soup course, whether used as an appetizer or the main course. Go slow and purée the soup in stages, since a couple of seconds too long can result in a soupy mess.

Soak in fresh water and set aside. Chop up the leek and the celery leaves. When the artichokes are cooked, remove from the cooking water and set aside.

Add the taro root, celery, and leeks to the water. Bring to a boil and simmer for another 15 to 20 minutes until the taro roots are soft. With a hand-held blender, blend the root vegetables with the cooking water until puréed. Adjust the flavor: Add water if the soup is too salty, or add salt if needed.

(continued)

Return the artichoke hearts to the pot. Add garlic powder, marjoram, and the juice of 1 lemon. Bring to a light boil and simmer for 3 more minutes. Add the whipping cream to the soup just before turning off the heat.

Mushroom Vegetable Barley Soup

Serves: 10

1 pound fresh mushrooms
4 celery stalks
5 medium carrots
3 tablespoons olive oil
2 cups chopped onion
1 1/2 tablespoons minced garlic
1/2 teaspoon ground thyme
1/2 bay leaf
1/2 cup dry barley
96 ounces canned chicken broth
1/4 teaspoon nutmeg
Salt and pepper to taste
2 tablespoons fresh parsley

Clean the mushrooms with a damp towel (don't wash in water); quarter the mushrooms. Cut celery and carrots into 1/2-inch pieces. Place oil in a large pot. Add chopped onions; cook over low heat for about 10 minutes until wilted. Add garlic, thyme, and bay leaf. Add mushrooms and cook for 20 minutes over medium heat, stirring.

Add the barley, celery, carrots, and broth. Season with nutmeg and salt and pepper to taste. Bring to a boil; reduce heat to medium low and simmer 25 to 30 minutes or until barley and vegetables are tender. Skim off any foam that rises to the top. Remove bay leaf. Stir in the parsley just before serving piping hot.

Farmer's Fresh Tomato Soup

Serves: 6

1/4 cup + 2 tablespoons olive oil
2 medium onions, coarsely chopped
3 cloves garlic, minced
2 ribs celery, coarsely chopped
3 pounds plum tomatoes, washed, stemmed, and coarsely chopped
Salt to taste
1 pinch sugar (optional)
3 pieces day-old Italian bread, crusts removed
4 cups hot meat broth
1/2 cup fresh basil leaves, torn in strips
2 tablespoons chopped fresh parsley
2 tablespoons chopped fresh marjoram
6 teaspoons olive oil
6 small fresh marjoram sprigs for garnish

Heat the oil, onions, garlic, and celery in a soup pot over medium-low heat, stirring occasionally, until golden (about 20 minutes). Add the tomatoes and salt; cook, partially covered, until the tomatoes are softened, about 20 minutes. If necessary, add a pinch of sugar to balance the acidity of the tomatoes.

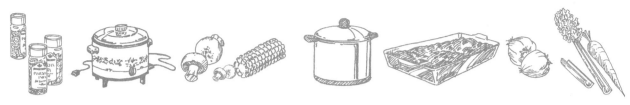

Put the bread in a small bowl and add 1 cup of hot broth to soften. Mash the bread well with a wooden spoon. Add the softened bread and remaining 3 cups broth to the pot, stirring well to completely dissolve the bread. Simmer for about 30 minutes.

Add the herbs during the last 5 minutes of cooking. Pass the soup through the fine blade of a food mill or purée in a food processor and strain.

Put the soup back in the soup pot and correct the seasoning. Simmer for 10 minutes. Ladle into heated soup bowls and pour 1 teaspoon of olive oil over each serving. Garnish with sprigs of fresh marjoram.

Winter Potato & Vegetable Soup

Serves: 6

1 clove garlic, minced
1 large onion, chopped
1 tablespoon butter
6 cups chicken broth
3 medium russet potatoes, peeled and
    diced
2 medium carrots, sliced
2 medium celery stalks, minced
1 zucchini, sliced
1 teaspoon dill
1 bunch fresh parsley, minced
Salt and pepper to taste
2 tablespoons cornstarch mixed into
    2 tablespoons cold water

Sauté the garlic and the onion in the butter in a sauté pan until the onion is soft. Add the broth, potatoes, carrots, celery, and zucchini. Bring the soup to a boil; reduce the heat and cook until the potatoes are tender, about 20 minutes. Add the dill, parsley, salt, pepper, and cornstarch/water mixture. Continue to cook until the soup is slightly thickened.

Freezing Soups

To serve a soup after it's been stored in the freezer, release it into a saucepan over low heat. As it thaws, cook diced potatoes and pasta, allowing a cupful of each for 4 servings. If the soup has thickened during freezer storage, add a little boiling stock, consommé, or bouillon.

Although it's best to freeze soup without potatoes, which may become mushy during storage, or pasta, which may absorb too much liquid, any pasta cooked al dente (firm) freezes like a charm when stored by itself. You can freeze it—with or without sauce—for use in soups, or to be served again as a side dish.

Georgian Potato Soup

Serves: 6

1 1/4 cups heavy cream
1/2 cup cottage cheese
2 1/2 tablespoons flour
1/4 teaspoon cumin
2 teaspoons dry mustard
1/2 teaspoon white pepper
1 tablespoon dried hot pepper flakes
2 teaspoons salt
1 teaspoon dried, crushed dill
1 tablespoon fresh chopped parsley
6 cups diced potatoes (1/2-inch chunks)
1/2 cup finely chopped onions
1/4 cup chopped scallions
1 clove garlic, minced
3 carrots, julienned
1/4 cup apple juice
1 cup apple sauce
3 cups chicken stock or vegetable stock
1/3 cup raisins
1/3 cup chopped dried apricots

Mix 1 cup of the cream, the cottage cheese, and the flour in a mixing bowl. Beat until smooth, then blend in the remaining cream. This can be done by hand, with a hand mixer, or in a blender. Set aside in refrigerator. Mix all of the spices together and divide into two equal portions.

Heat a large, heavy pot on high for 3 to 4 minutes. Add the vegetables except for 2 cups of the diced potatoes, plus one of the spice portions. Stir and cook over high heat for 4 to 6 minutes, scraping the crusts that form on the bottom of the pot. Add the apple juice and then the apple sauce. Stir and cook for 2 to 3 minutes, then add the stock and the other spice portion. Cook while stirring for 12 minutes.

Remove and either rice the mixture or purée it in a blender until it is smooth. Return soup to the pot; add the 2 cups of diced potatoes, and bring to a boil. Reduce heat to low, stir well, cover, and cook for 15 minutes. Add more stock if more liquid is needed. Blend in the cream mixture and raisins and apricots and continue to cook, stirring as you do, for 3 to 4 minutes.

German Potato Soup

Serves: 6

1 medium onion, sliced
1/4 cup butter
3 medium leeks (white part only)
2 pounds (about 6 medium) potatoes
1 ham bone, any size
1/4 teaspoon dried thyme leaves
6 cups chicken or beef stock or water
1/2 pint heavy cream
Salt and white pepper to taste
Croutons

Brown onions in butter in a saucepan to a light golden color. Clean leeks well and slice. Peel potatoes and slice. Add leeks, potatoes, ham bone, thyme, and stock (or water) to

onion. Cover and simmer until potatoes are very soft.

Remove ham bone; discard. Cool potato/leek mixture slightly. Purée in a food processor or blender and return to pot. Add cream and cook a few minutes longer. Season with salt and pepper to taste. Serve with croutons.

Lima Bean Soup

Serves: 8

1 pound frozen lima beans
3½ cups sliced carrots
3 tablespoons olive oil
5 green onions, finely chopped
5 cups chopped mushrooms
1 teaspoon basil
1 teaspoon black pepper
¼ teaspoon cayenne pepper
¾ cup soy sauce
1 cup milk

Cook lima beans in water according to package instructions. Steam carrots till tender. Drain, reserving cooking water.

Heat oil in a skillet and sauté green onions and mushrooms until tender. Add spices and sauté for one more minute.

Combine all ingredients except milk, along with 1 cup of bean and carrot water. Using a blender, blend in batches till smooth. Pour mixture into a large soup pot. Add milk. Cook slowly for 15 to 20 minutes.

Nigerian Peanut Soup

Serves: 2

2 cups water
2 2-ounce packets instant chicken broth and seasoning mix
1½ small dried green chili peppers, finely chopped
¼ cup diced green bell pepper
¼ cup diced onion
3 tablespoons chunky-style peanut butter

Heat water in 1-quart saucepan; dissolve broth mix in water. Add chili peppers and bring mixture to a boil. Stir in bell pepper and onion and return to a boil. Reduce heat to low, cover, and simmer until vegetables are tender, about 10 minutes.

Reduce heat to lowest possible temperature; add peanut butter and cook, stirring constantly, until peanut butter is melted and mixture is well blended.

Rich Tomato Bisque

Serves: 8

4 tablespoons butter
2 onions, chopped
2 cloves garlic, minced
1 28-ounce can whole tomatoes
1 46-ounce can tomato juice
2 bay leaves
1 8-ounce package cream cheese
2 cups half-and-half
Salt and pepper to taste
Croutons for garnish

(continued)

Melt the butter in a medium saucepan; add onions and garlic and sauté over medium heat until soft. Add the undrained tomatoes, tomato juice, and bay leaves. Simmer 20 minutes, stirring occasionally, chopping the tomatoes with the side of the spoon.

Remove from heat and let cool slightly. Purée the solids with some of the liquid in a blender or food processor, along with the cream cheese. Return to the saucepan. Add the half-and-half and season to taste with salt and pepper. May be served hot or cold. Garnish with your favorite croutons.

Shaker Bean Soup

Serves: 12

> 1 pound dried white navy beans
> Water
> 1 ham bone (or 2 ham hocks)
> 1 large onion, chopped
> 3 celery stalks, diced
> 2 carrots, shredded
> Salt and pepper to taste
> $\frac{1}{2}$ teaspoon thyme, dried
> 1 28-ounce can tomatoes in purée
> 2 tablespoons brown sugar
> $1\frac{1}{2}$ cups spinach leaves, finely shredded

Sort and rinse beans. Place in soup kettle or Dutch oven. Cover with water and bring to a boil. Boil 2 minutes. Remove from heat. Let stand 1 hour.

Drain beans and discard liquid. In the same kettle, place ham bone or hocks, 3 quarts of water and beans. Bring to a boil; reduce heat and simmer, covered, $1\frac{1}{2}$ hours or until meat easily falls from the bone.

Remove bones from broth and, when cool enough to handle, trim meat. Discard bones. Add ham, onion, celery, carrots, salt, pepper, and thyme. Simmer, covered, 1 hour or until beans are tender.

Add tomatoes and brown sugar. Cook for 10 minutes. Just before serving, add spinach.

Hot and Sour Chinese Soup

Serves: 6

> 3 cups chicken broth
> 1 tablespoon soy sauce
> 4 dried Chinese mushrooms, soaked for 15 minutes in boiling water, cut into strips
> 1 6-ounce can bamboo shoots, drained
> $\frac{1}{4}$ pound lean pork, cut into strips
> 1 cake tofu, cut into strips
> 1 teaspoon white pepper
> 2 tablespoons lemon juice
> 3 tablespoons cornstarch mixed with 3 tablespoons cold water
> 1 egg, lightly beaten
> 1 tablespoon sesame oil
> 2 stalks scallions, chopped

In a soup pot, mix together the broth, soy sauce, mushrooms, bamboo shoots, and pork. Bring to a boil; reduce the heat, and simmer for 5 minutes. Add the tofu, pepper, and

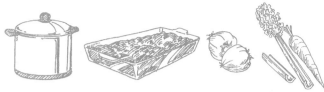

lemon juice. Bring to a boil, and add the cornstarch and water mixture. Cook the soup, stirring constantly, until it thickens slightly. Stir the egg into the broth. Remove the pot from the heat; stir in the sesame oil and sprinkle with scallions.

Lime-Chicken Soup

Serves: 6

$\frac{1}{2}$ pound boneless, skinless chicken breast
1 quart chicken broth
Juice of 2 limes
1 teaspoon oregano
1 teaspoon basil
1 jalapeño pepper, minced
1 bay leaf
Salt and pepper to taste
1 tomato, chopped
1 red onion, chopped
1 tablespoon minced cilantro
4 ounces Monterey Jack cheese, cubed
2 corn tortillas, cut in strips, for garnish
4 lime slices for garnish
4 cilantro sprigs for garnish

Poach chicken breasts in water; when cool, shred. Combine broth, lime juice, oregano, basil, jalapeño, bay leaf, salt, and pepper in a soup pot. Bring to a boil. Simmer for 15 minutes. Add the chicken, tomatoes, red onion, and cilantro. Return to a boil. Simmer for 5 minutes. Ladle the soup into a large bowl. Add the cheese cubes. Garnish with tortillas, lime slices, and cilantro.

Pappa con Pomodoro Soup

Serves: 6

1 tablespoon olive oil
$1\frac{1}{2}$ tablespoons puréed garlic
1 tablespoon chopped fresh sage
4 cups chicken stock
$1\frac{1}{2}$ pounds ripe tomatoes
1 pinch salt
1 pinch black pepper
9 ounces stale coarse bread, cut in $\frac{1}{2}$-inch cubes

Heat olive oil in saucepan. Add garlic and sage; sauté lightly. Add chicken stock and tomatoes. (If using fresh tomatoes, peel, seed, and dice before adding.) Bring to a boil; reduce heat. Add salt, pepper, and bread. Simmer until thick. Serve hot or chilled.

Italian Minestrone Soup Coca-Cola

Serves: 12

$2\frac{1}{2}$ pound blade chuck roast
$2\frac{1}{2}$ quarts water
2 teaspoons salt
1 small onion
$\frac{1}{2}$ cup celery leaves
1 bay leaf
2 slices bacon, diced
$\frac{1}{4}$ cup diced onion
$\frac{1}{4}$ cup chopped parsley
1 clove garlic, minced

(continued)

½ cup dry elbow macaroni
1 6-ounce can tomato paste
1 cup cola
1 tablespoon olive oil
1 tablespoon Worcestershire sauce
1½ cups cooked kidney beans
1 tablespoon Italian seasoning
½ cup chopped fresh green beans
1 teaspoon salt
½ cup diced celery
¼ teaspoon black pepper
½ cup green peas
½ cup thinly sliced zucchini
½ cup thinly sliced carrots
Grated Parmesan cheese (optional)

In a large pan, combine the meat, water, salt, small onion, celery leaves, and bay leaf. Cover and simmer about 2½ hours until the meat is tender.

Remove the meat. Strain the broth (should measure 2 quarts). Add ice cubes to the broth to harden and remove the fat. Discard the fat.

Finely dice the meat, discarding any fat and bones (should be about 2 cups meat). In a 5- to 6-quart kettle or Dutch oven, combine the beef broth and the meat. Place over low heat while preparing the rest of the ingredients.

Pan-fry the bacon until crisp. Add the bacon and the drippings and all the remaining ingredients, except Parmesan cheese, to the broth. Cover and simmer about 30 minutes, until the vegetables and macaroni are tender. Serve sprinkled with Parmesan cheese, if desired.

Peanut Butter Soup

Serves: 4

2 tablespoons minced onion
3 tablespoons butter
1 tablespoon flour
1 cup peanut butter
4 cups chicken broth
Salt and pepper to taste
1 cup whipping cream
1 tablespoon Madeira wine

Cook onion in butter until soft in 2-quart saucepan. Add flour and cook, stirring, until smooth. Stir in peanut butter; add chicken broth. Season to taste with salt and pepper. Cook, stirring, over low heat until thickened and smooth. Add cream. Just before serving, add Madeira.

Chili-Beef-Potato Soup

Serves: 4

½ pound ground beef
½ cup chopped onion
½ cup chopped celery
1 16-ounce can tomatoes, cut up
2 cups peeled and diced potatoes
1 10½-ounce can condensed beef broth
1⅓ cups water
1 teaspoon chili powder

½ teaspoon salt
½ teaspoon Worcestershire sauce
1 cup cooked or leftover peas

Brown meat in saucepan. Drain off fat. Add onion and celery and cook until vegetables are tender-crisp. Stir in tomatoes, potatoes, beef broth, water, chili powder, salt, and Worcestershire sauce. Cover and cook until potatoes are tender, about 15 minutes. Stir in peas; heat through.

Very Quick Sausage & Vegetable Soup

Serves: 4

1 14½-ounce can beef broth
1 14½-ounce can Italian stewed tomatoes
1½ cups water
2 cups frozen hash brown potatoes
1 10-ounce package frozen mixed vegetables
8 ounces smoked sausage, sliced
⅛ teaspoon pepper
2 tablespoons grated Parmesan cheese

Combine beef broth, undrained stewed tomatoes, and water in a large saucepan. Bring to a boil. Stir in hash brown potatoes, mixed vegetables, sausage, and pepper. Return to boiling. Reduce heat and simmer, covered, for 5 to 10 minutes. Ladle into soup bowls and sprinkle with Parmesan cheese.

Stock Smarts, Part 1

If you plan to make a large amount of stock at once, pour it into bread pans when cool before popping it into the freezer. When the stock has frozen through, dip the pans into lukewarm water until the stock cubes loosen. Then pop into plastic bags and freeze.

Cheeseburger Soup

Serves: 6

1½ tablespoons olive oil
1 large onion, chopped
2 ribs celery, chopped
1 green pepper, chopped
1 pound lean ground beef
3 packets beef bouillon
3 tablespoons flour
4 cups milk
8 ounces grated Cheddar cheese

(continued)

Heat oil in a soup pot. Sauté onion, celery, and green pepper until tender. Add the meat and brown. Mix in the beef bouillon and flour. Slowly add the milk, stirring constantly; do not boil. Add the cheese. Stir until melted and serve immediately.

Curry Powder

Makes: About ½ cup

3 tablespoons coriander seeds
2 tablespoons cumin seeds
2 tablespoons turmeric
1 tablespoon mustard seeds
2½ teaspoons fennel seeds
8 pods cardamom seeds
8 whole cloves
1½ teaspoons ground ginger
1½ teaspoons black peppercorns
¼ teaspoon freshly grated nutmeg
¼ teaspoon cayenne pepper

Preheat oven to 250°F.

In a bowl, combine all the ingredients. Spread mixture out on a jelly roll pan and toast in the oven for 20 minutes.

Let cool to room temperature. Pulverize the spice mixture in batches with an electric spice or coffee grinder and strain it through a sieve into a bowl. The curry powder will keep six months in a tightly sealed jar in a cool dark place.

Chinese Curried Corn Soup with Chicken

Serves: 4

4 cups chicken stock
1 12-ounce can corn kernels, drained
1 tablespoon rice wine vinegar or sake
1 tablespoon curry powder
1 teaspoon salt
1 teaspoon sugar
½ pound boneless chicken breasts
1 egg white
1 teaspoon cornstarch
1 whole egg
1 teaspoon sesame oil
2 tablespoons chopped scallions for garnish

Bring the stock to a boil in a large pot and add the corn. Simmer for 10 minutes, uncovered, and then add the rice wine, curry powder, salt, and sugar. Simmer for another 5 minutes. While the stock is cooking, use a sharp knife or cleaver to slice the chicken breasts into fine shreds about 3 inches long. Mix the chicken shreds together with the egg white, 1 teaspoon cornstarch, and salt in a small bowl and set aside. In another small bowl beat the whole egg and sesame oil together and set aside. Bring a small pot of water to a boil. Quickly blanch the chicken shreds in it until they just turn white (this should take about 20 seconds). Remove them with a slotted spoon and drain them in a colander or sieve. Add the blanched chicken

202

shreds to the simmering soup. Slowly pour in the egg and sesame oil mixture in a steady stream, stirring all the time. Transfer the soup to a tureen, garnish with the scallions and serve.

Tomato Noodle Soup Curry-Style

Serves: 8

1 onion, finely chopped
2 cloves garlic, finely minced
1 tablespoon curry powder
2 28-ounce cans plum tomatoes
4 cups chicken broth, divided
1/4 teaspoon cinnamon
Salt to taste
4 cups cooked egg noodles

Spray a heavy soup pot with nonstick cooking spray. Add onion and cook over low heat for 5 minutes. Add garlic and curry powder and cook for a few more minutes, stirring constantly. Chop tomatoes and add to pot with their liquid. Add 2 cups chicken broth, cinnamon, and salt. Simmer over medium-low heat, partially covered, for 25 minutes.

Remove from heat and cool slightly. Purée soup in a blender in small batches and return to the pot. Add remaining 2 cups chicken broth. Adjust seasonings and heat through until piping hot. Divide the cooked noodles among 8 soup bowls. Ladle hot soup into bowls.

Straciatella a la Romana, or Raggedy Cheesy Egg Soup

Serves: 4

3 eggs
3 tablespoon freshly grated Parmesan cheese
6 cups chicken stock

Beat the eggs until frothy and stir in the cheese. Bring the broth to a gentle boil, pour in the egg mixture, and stir gently until eggs are set.

Minestrone with Meatballs

Serves: 6

24 cooked meatballs
1 15-ounce can navy or other white beans, drained
1 package beef bouillon
1 tablespoon dried minced onion
1 teaspoon basil
1 bay leaf
4 cups water
1 cup ditali, orzo, or other pasta
1 16-ounce can tomatoes, cut up (undrained)
1 10-ounce package frozen mixed vegetables, thawed
1 teaspoon sugar
Grated Parmesan cheese

(continued)

In a 4-quart saucepan combine meatballs, beans, bouillon, onion, basil, bay leaf, and water; bring to a boil. Add pasta and cook for 15 minutes. Add undrained tomatoes, vegetables, and sugar and heat through. Serve in individual bowls, topped with grated Parmesan cheese.

Crockpot Chicken Broth

Makes: About 6 cups of chicken and 3+ cups double-strength chicken stock

1 onion, sliced
1 carrot, sliced
1 celery rib, sliced
1 large chicken, 3$\frac{1}{2}$ pounds
$\frac{1}{2}$ cup chicken broth or water

Place sliced vegetables in a Crockpot. Sit whole chicken on top, neck up. If you wish you may season with herbs, pepper, etc., but this is not necessary. Pour broth over chicken, cover, and cook on low 8 or 9 hours.

Remove chicken from pot and let cool until easy to handle. Meanwhile, strain stock and skim fat. This stock is double strength, so mix with equal parts water for use. Remove chicken from bones and cut into pieces sized appropriately for your recipe.

Thai Shrimp-Chicken Soup

Serves: 6

2 whole chicken breasts, halved
6 cups water
1 small onion, peeled and chopped
1 bay leaf
2 sprigs parsley
$\frac{1}{2}$ teaspoon thyme
1 teaspoon salt
$\frac{1}{8}$ teaspoon freshly ground pepper
1 clove garlic, crushed
2 teaspoons ground coriander
1$\frac{1}{2}$ teaspoons chili powder
1 tablespoon soy sauce
$\frac{1}{2}$ pound small shrimp, shelled and deveined
2 cups sliced mushrooms
6 scallions, with tops, sliced
$\frac{1}{3}$ cup chopped fresh cilantro or parsley
3 cups hot cooked rice

Remove skin from chicken breasts. Carefully cut meat from bones and pull out the pieces of cartilage. Cut meat into strips and set aside. Put bones in large saucepan. Add water, onion, bay leaf, parsley, thyme, salt, and pepper. Bring to a boil. Reduce heat and cook slowly, covered, 1 hour.

Strain broth into a saucepan. Combine garlic, coriander, chili powder, and soy sauce. Stir into broth. Bring to a boil. Add chicken, shrimp, and mushrooms. Cook slowly, covered, about 5 minutes, until the shrimp

turns pink and the chicken is tender. Stir in scallions and fresh cilantro or parsley. Remove and discard bay leaf.

Serve over rice.

Lemon Chicken and Okra Soup

Serves: 4

1 broiler chicken, (2½ pounds)
Juice of 2 lemons
6 cups chicken broth or water
1 large onion, peeled and chopped
3 medium tomatoes, peeled and chopped
1 6-ounce can tomato paste
2 cups sliced okra (or 1 15-ounce can, drained)
⅓ cup uncooked long-grain rice
2 teaspoons salt
¼ teaspoon pepper
½ teaspoon ground red pepper
1 teaspoon ground turmeric

Cut up chicken into individual pieces. Rub lemon juice over chicken pieces. Put in a large kettle with chicken broth or water. Bring to a boil. Reduce heat and cook slowly, covered, for 12 to 15 minutes.

Add remaining ingredients and continue to cook slowly about 30 minutes, until chicken and rice are tender. Remove chicken pieces, skin, and debone. Cut meat into small pieces and return to kettle.

London Fish Soup

Serves: 6

3 pounds haddock or cod
2 large onions, peeled
1 clove garlic, crushed
3 tablespoons butter
6 medium potatoes, peeled and quartered
10 cups water
2 bay leaves
1 teaspoon dried thyme
½ teaspoon dried marjoram
4 sprigs parsley
2 teaspoons salt
½ teaspoon pepper
6 inch-thick slices crusty French bread

Cut fish into 2-inch chunks. Sauté onions and garlic in hot butter in a large kettle until tender. Add potatoes, water, bay leaves, thyme, marjoram, parsley, salt, and pepper. Bring to a boil. Add fish and reduce heat to moderate. Cook, covered, about 25 minutes, until fish and potatoes are tender.

Remove and discard bay leaves. Put slices of bread in 6 wide soup plates. Ladle soup over bread.

Hungarian Soup

Serves: 10

4 medium onions, peeled and chopped
2 cloves garlic, crushed
½ cup olive oil
3 tablespoons paprika

(continued)

205

3 pounds lean beef chuck, cut into
   1-inch cubes
2 large tomatoes, peeled and chopped
2 teaspoons caraway seeds
1 1/2 teaspoons dried marjoram
1 teaspoon minced lemon peel
8 cups water
2 teaspoons salt
1/2 teaspoon pepper
4 medium potatoes, peeled and cubed

Sauté onions and garlic in heated oil in a large kettle until tender. Stir in paprika; cook 1 minute. Brown beef cubes, several at a time, on all sides. Add tomatoes, caraway seeds, marjoram, lemon peel, water, salt, and pepper. Bring to a boil. Reduce heat and cook slowly, covered, 45 minutes.

Add the potatoes and continue to cook about 20 minutes longer, until potatoes are tender.

Albuquerque Meatablespoonall Soup

Serves: 8

3/4 pound ground beef
3/4 pound ground pork
1/3 cup uncooked long-grain rice
1 egg, slightly beaten
1 teaspoon dried oregano
1 teaspoon salt (or to taste)
1/4 teaspoon pepper (or to taste)
1 medium onion, peeled and minced
1 clove garlic, crushed

2 tablespoons olive oil
1/2 cup tomato paste
10 cups beef bouillon
1/2 cup chopped fresh cilantro or parsley

Combine beef, pork, rice, egg, oregano, salt, and pepper in a large bowl. Shape into small balls about the size of golf balls.

Sauté onion and garlic in heated oil in a large kettle until tender. Mix in tomato paste. Add bouillon; season with salt and pepper. Bring to a boil. Add meatballs and reduce heat. Cook slowly, covered, about 30 minutes, until meatballs are cooked. Stir in cilantro or parsley.

Frankfurter Lentil Soup

Serves: 8

2 medium onions, peeled and chopped
1 clove garlic, crushed
2 medium carrots, scraped and chopped
2 stalks celery, minced
2 tablespoons olive oil
8 cups water
2 cups lentils, rinsed and drained
1 bay leaf
1 1/2 teaspoons salt
1/4 teaspoon pepper
1 pound frankfurters, sliced thickly
2 tablespoons cider vinegar

Sauté onions, garlic, carrots, and celery in heated oil in a large kettle for 5 minutes. Add water, lentils, bay leaf, salt, and pepper. Bring

to a boil. Reduce heat and cook slowly, covered, about 30 minutes, until lentils are just tender. Add frankfurters and cook another 10 minutes. Remove from heat and stir in vinegar. Remove and discard bay leaf.

Scandinavian Pork & Pea Soup

Serves: 8

1 pound yellow split peas, rinsed
2 pounds lean bacon
3 medium carrots, scraped
1 celery stalk, minced
4 medium leeks
2 medium onions, peeled and halved
1/2 teaspoon dried thyme
1 1/2 teaspoons salt
1/4 teaspoon freshly ground black pepper
1 pound pork sausage links, cooked and drained

Soak peas in cold water according to package directions. Put peas in a large kettle with 6 cups water. Cook slowly, covered, for about 1 1/2 hours, until tender.

Meanwhile, put bacon, carrots, celery root, leeks, onions, thyme, salt, and pepper in another kettle. Cover with water. Cook slowly, covered, 40 minutes until vegetables and bacon are tender. Take out bacon; slice and keep warm. Remove vegetables and add to cooked split peas; add some of the broth in which the vegetables were cooked if desired to thin the soup.

Reheat, if necessary. Ladle soup, including vegetables, into wide soup plates and serve sliced bacon and the cooked sausage links separately on a platter.

Pepper Pot Soup

Serves: 8

1/4 pound salt pork
1 1/2 pounds short rib of beef, cut into 3-inch pieces
1 1/2 pounds stew beef, cut into 2-inch cubes
12 cups water
1/2 teaspoon dried thyme
1 1/2 teaspoons salt
1/4 teaspoon pepper
1 large onion, peeled and diced
2 cloves garlic, crushed
2 scallions
2 tablespoons olive oil
1 large green pepper, cut into strips
10 ounces fresh spinach, washed and trimmed
10 ounces fresh kale, washed and trimmed
1 15 1/2-ounce can okra, drained
4 medium sweet potatoes, peeled and cubed
1 large tomato, peeled and cubed

Place the salt pork and short rib pieces in a large kettle; brown ribs on all sides. Add the stew beef and brown on all sides.

Add water and slowly bring just to a boil. Skim. Add thyme, salt, and pepper. Reduce

(continued)

heat and simmer, covered, 1 hour, occasionally removing any scum that rises to the top.

While meat is simmering, sauté onion, garlic, and scallions in heated oil in a skillet until tender. Add green pepper and sauté 1 minute. Remove from heat and set aside.

After meat has cooked 1 hour, add sautéed vegetables and remaining ingredients to the kettle. Continue to cook slowly, covered, about 30 minutes, until vegetables and meat are cooked. Remove from heat and cool slightly. Take out short ribs and cut off and discard any fat. Cube meat and return to kettle. Reheat, if necessary.

Hearty Ground Turkey & Vegetable Soup

Serves: 4

1 pound ground turkey
1 small onion, chopped
1 small green pepper, chopped
1 16-ounce can green beans
1 16-ounce can diced potatoes
1 16-ounce can stewed tomatoes
1 can tomato soup
Salt and pepper to taste

Brown turkey in a Dutch oven until cooked through. Add chopped onion and chopped green pepper. Mix in green beans, diced potatoes, stewed tomatoes, and the tomato soup. Heat until warmed through, about 15 minutes. Add salt and pepper to taste.

Hearty Barley Lamb Soup

Serves: 6

3 tablespoons butter
2½ pounds lean stewing lamb, trimmed of excess fat and cut into 1inch cubes
Salt and pepper to taste
2 onions, sliced
1 cup medium-sized pearl barley
3 ribs celery, chopped, with their leaves
3 cups coarsely chopped parsley
1 bay leaf
1½ teaspoons salt
¼ teaspoon freshly ground black pepper
6 cups water

In a heavy kettle, heat the butter until brown. Brown the lamb for about 7 minutes, and season with salt and pepper. Remove the meat. Drain and discard all but 3 tablespoons of the fat.

In the fat, cook the onion until translucent. Put the meat back in the pot and add the barley, celery, parsley, seasonings, and water. Bring to a boil, reduce the heat, and simmer, covered, for 2 hours, or until it is very tender.

Spicy Sausage and Bean Soup

Serves: 6

1 pound dried navy or pea beans
8 cups hot water
2 tablespoons salt

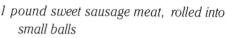

1 pound sweet sausage meat, rolled into
  small balls
6 slices bacon, diced
3 onions, chopped
2 cloves garlic, chopped
¼ teaspoon cayenne pepper
2 teaspoons chili powder
1 teaspoon ground cumin
1 6-ounce can tomato paste
Grated rind and juice of 1 lemon
2 or 3 ripe bananas, peeled and sliced

In a large stockpot, cover the beans with the water and add the salt. Bring to a rolling boil; boil for 5 minutes. Remove from the heat and let stand, covered, for 1 hour.

In a skillet, cook the sausage balls until golden. Drain on absorbent paper and add balls to the beans. In the remaining fat, fry the bacon until crisp. Drain on paper towels and add to the beans. Discard all but 3 tablespoons of the fat. In the same pot, sauté the onion and garlic until translucent. Add the mixture to the beans. Simmer, covered, for 1 hour, or until the beans are tender.

Add cayenne, chili powder, cumin, tomato paste, and lemon rind and juice, and continue simmering, covered, for ½ hour. Add the banana and cook for 5 more minutes, or long enough to heat the banana through.

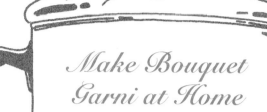

Make Bouquet Garni at Home

It's easy to make your own bouquet garni. Tie a little fresh thyme and parsley plus a bay leaf or two in a square of cheesecloth. Be sure to use 100-percent cotton cheesecloth, and remember to remove the cheesecloth bundle before serving. Or if you like, look for bouquet garni seasoning in the herb and spice section of your supermarket.

Kansas City Steak & Vegetable Soup

Serves: 4

2 4-ounce cubed beef steaks
¼ teaspoon garlic salt
⅛ teaspoon pepper
1 tablespoon olive oil
⅓ cup butter
1 medium onion, chopped
1 medium carrot, chopped

(continued)

1 stalk celery, chopped
⅓ cup frozen baby lima beans
½ cup all-purpose flour
4 cups water
1 24-ounce can tomatoes, cut up
⅓ cup frozen whole kernel corn
⅓ cup frozen peas
1 tablespoon snipped fresh basil or
*   1 teaspoon crushed dried basil*
2 teaspoons instant beef bouillon granules
2 teaspoons Worcestershire sauce

Sprinkle steaks with garlic salt and pepper. Heat oil in a Dutch oven. Cook steaks in hot oil about 3 minutes or until done, turning once. Remove steaks from pan and cut into cubes; set aside. Drain off fat.

Melt butter in the same pan. Cook and stir onion, carrot, celery, and lima beans in hot butter until onion is tender. Stir in flour. Stir water into flour mixture all at once. Cook and stir until thickened and bubbly.

Stir in undrained tomatoes, corn, peas, basil, bouillon granules, and Worcestershire sauce. Stir in cubed meat. Return to boiling; reduce heat. Simmer, covered, about 5 minutes or until heated through.

Chicken Tortellini Soup

Serves: 6

1 tablespoon olive oil
1 medium onion, chopped
1 minced clove garlic
6 cups chicken broth

1 9-ounce package refrigerated fresh
*   cheese tortellini, or dried tortellini*
2 cups frozen mixed vegetables
2 cups chopped cooked chicken
1 teaspoon bouquet garni seasoning or
*   fines herbes*
¼ teaspoon pepper
Grated Parmesan or Romano cheese
*   (optional)*

Heat oil in a Dutch oven. Cook onion and garlic in hot oil for 2 minutes. Stir in chicken broth, tortellini, vegetables, chicken, bouquet garni seasoning, and pepper. Bring to boiling; reduce heat. Simmer, uncovered, for 5 to 10 minutes for fresh tortellini or 15 to 20 minutes for dried tortellini, or until pasta is tender.

Spoon into soup bowls. Sprinkle each serving with Parmesan cheese, if desired.

Hearty Winter Chicken & Noodle Soup

Serves: 6

3 chicken drumstick-thigh pieces (about
*   2 pounds)*
4 cups water
½ cup chopped celery leaves
2 tablespoons snipped parsley
1 teaspoon salt
1 teaspoon dried thyme, crushed
¼ teaspoon pepper
1 bay leaf
4 medium carrots, sliced
3 medium onions, chopped

2 stalks celery, sliced
3 cups packaged dried wide noodles
2 cups milk, divided
1 cup frozen peas
2 tablespoons all-purpose flour

Skin chicken. Rinse chicken; pat dry with paper towels. Place chicken, water, celery leaves, parsley, salt, thyme, pepper, and bay leaf in a large Dutch oven. Bring to boiling; reduce heat. Simmer, covered, for 30 minutes.

Add the carrots, onions, and sliced celery. Simmer, covered, about 30 minutes more or until chicken is tender and no longer pink. Remove from heat. Remove chicken; cool slightly. Discard the bay leaf. Remove chicken from bones; discard bones. Chop chicken and set aside.

Heat vegetable mixture to boiling. Add noodles; cook for 5 minutes. Stir in 1 ½ cups of the milk and the peas. Combine remaining milk and the flour in a screw-top jar. Cover and shake until smooth. Stir into noodle mixture. Cook and stir until thickened and bubbly. Stir in chicken. Cook for 1 to 2 minutes more or until heated through.

Minestrone

Serves: 12

1 cup dried red kidney beans, soaked
    overnight
1 cup dried chickpeas, soaked overnight
4 quarts boiling water with 1 tablespoon
    salt
¼ cup olive oil

1 cup chopped onions
1 cup chopped celery
2 cloves garlic, minced
2 cups shredded cabbage
1 cup diced carrots
2 cups chopped fresh tomatoes or canned
    Italian tomatoes
¾ cup chopped fresh parsley
½ teaspoon basil
½ teaspoon oregano
½ teaspoon pepper
1 large potato, diced
1 cup dried pasta, elbow macaroni, or
    radiatore

Wash the beans and chickpeas, picking them over for defects, and add them slowly to the boiling salted water in a large soup pot. When the boil resumes, reduce the heat and simmer until tender. This may take more than an hour.

Heat the olive oil in a skillet, and sauté the onions, celery, and garlic for 5 minutes, stirring. Add these to the soup pot along with the cabbage, carrots, and tomatoes. Turn up the heat, and cook at a fairly rapid boil for 10 minutes. Reduce the heat to a steady simmer, and stir in the parsley and seasonings.

To serve, scoop 6 cupfuls of the soup to a smaller pot over very low heat. Boil the potato rapidly in lightly salted water for 10 minutes. At the same time, cook the pasta according to package directions. Drain both and stir them into the soup. Serve in large soup plates and pass a bowlful of grated Romano or Parmesan cheese.

1 teaspoon red chili powder
1 pinch cayenne pepper
1 tablespoon tomato paste
1 10-ounce can pinto beans
3 quarts chicken stock
Salt and pepper to taste
4 teaspoons sour cream

Heat the butter in a large saucepan over medium heat until it melts. Add the onions, green bell peppers, tomatoes, and garlic. Cover the pan with a lid and simmer the ingredients for 4 minutes.

Add the cilantro, red chili powder, cayenne pepper, and tomato paste. Stir the ingredients together and simmer them for 3 minutes.

Add the pinto beans, chicken stock, salt, and pepper. Bring to a boil and cook vigorously for 4 minutes, or until the beans are heated through. Garnish the soup with a dollop of sour cream.

Chilled Shrimp and Cucumber Soup

Serves: 4 to 6

8 large cucumbers (about 2 pounds),
   peeled and coarsely chopped
1/4 cup red wine vinegar
1 tablespoon sugar
1 teaspoon salt
1 pound raw shrimp, the smallest you can
   find, peeled and deveined
2 tablespoons sweet butter

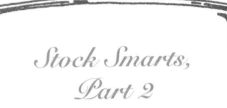

Stock Smarts, Part 2

To make vegetable stock, keep a coffee can with a lid in the freezer. Whenever you cook vegetables in liquid, add the liquid to the coffee can. Thaw at least partially before you use it.

Pinto Bean Soup

Serves: 4

4 tablespoons butter
1/4 cup finely chopped onions
2 tablespoons finely chopped green bell
   peppers
2 tomatoes, finely chopped
1 teaspoon finely chopped garlic
1 teaspoon finely chopped fresh cilantro

¼ cup dry white vermouth
Salt and freshly ground black pepper to taste
1½ cups cold buttermilk
¾ cup chopped fresh dill (or more to
taste), plus additional dill for garnish

Toss chopped cucumbers with the vinegar, sugar and salt; let stand for 30 minutes. Rinse the shrimp and pat them dry. Melt the butter in a small skillet. Add shrimp, raise the heat, and toss until they turn pink, 2 to 3 minutes. Remove shrimp with a slotted spoon and reserve. Add vermouth to the skillet and boil until it is reduced to a few teaspoonfuls. Pour over the shrimp and season with salt and pepper.

Drain the cucumbers and transfer them to a food processor fitted with a steel blade. Process briefly, then add the buttermilk and continue to process until smooth. Add fresh dill to taste and process briefly, about 1 second.

Pour the soup into a bowl, add the shrimp and their liquid, and refrigerate, covered, until very cold. Garnish with additional chopped dill and serve in chilled bowls.

Hearty Veal Stock

Makes: At least 2 quarts of stock

8 pounds veal bones
One quartered calf's foot (from the butcher)
2 large yellow onions, sliced
2 cups chopped carrots
4 stalks celery, minced
1 tablespoon peppercorns
At least 2 quarts water

Place the veal bones and the calf's foot into a large 8-quart stockpot with enough water to cover. Bring to a boil, then reduce heat. Simmer for 15 minutes. Add the onions, carrots, celery, and peppercorns. Add a few more cups of water and bring to another boil. Reduce heat, and cook at a slow simmer for about 5 hours, stirring occasionally. Remove the bones and strain the stock through a very fine sieve. The stock is now ready to use or freeze.

Pumpkin and Coconut Cream Soup

Serves: 8

6 cups (1¾ pounds) peeled and cubed
fresh pumpkin
2 cups water
½-inch piece fresh ginger, peeled
1 tablespoon chopped lemongrass
2 scallions, white parts only, finely sliced
2 cups coconut cream
1⅓ teaspoons salt
¼ teaspoon white pepper
Freshly squeezed lime or lemon juice to
taste
Very finely shredded zest of 1 small fresh
lime for garnish

In a large saucepan, combine the pumpkin, stock or water, ginger, and lemongrass. Cover, bring to a boil, reduce the heat to medium-low, and simmer until the pumpkin is very tender, about 12 minutes. Add the scallions and cook briefly.

(continued)

Transfer the contents of the saucepan to a blender or food processor and process until the soup is partially puréed. Pour in half of the coconut cream and process until smooth.

Return the purée to the saucepan. Add half of the remaining coconut cream. Season with salt and pepper, and heat through without allowing the soup to boil. Taste and adjust the seasoning; squeeze in lime or lemon juice.

Ladle the soup into bowls. Add the remaining coconut cream to each bowl, forming a swirl on each serving, and garnish with the lime zest.

Pea Soup

Serves: 4

> 2 10-ounce packages frozen peas
> 2 cups water
> 2 14$\frac{1}{2}$-ounce cans chicken broth
> Juice of 1 lemon
> 1 small onion, chopped
> 1 clove garlic
> Salt and pepper to taste
> Small handful mint leaves, chopped
> $\frac{1}{4}$ cup plain low-fat yogurt

Cook the peas in 2 cups of boiling water for just a few minutes. Drain, reserving water for use later in the recipe.

Purée the peas in a food processor. Mix 2 cups of the cooking water, broth, and lemon juice in a saucepan. Add the puréed peas and bring to a simmer. Add garlic, onion, salt and pepper. Turn off heat. Add the mint to the soup. Serve with a dollop of yogurt.

Turkey Leftover Soup

Serves: 8

> 6 cups chicken broth
> $\frac{1}{4}$ cup white rice, uncooked
> $\frac{1}{4}$ cup wild rice, uncooked
> 1 cup green onions, chopped fine
> $\frac{1}{2}$ cup butter
> $\frac{3}{4}$ cup all-purpose flour
> $\frac{1}{2}$ teaspoon salt
> $\frac{1}{4}$ teaspoon pepper
> 2 cups milk
> 1$\frac{1}{2}$ cups cubed cooked turkey
> 8 slices bacon, cooked crisp and crumbled
> 3 tablespoons dry sherry (optional)

In a large saucepan combine chicken broth, rice, and onions. Bring to a boil; reduce heat and simmer 40 minutes.

In a medium saucepan or skillet melt butter. Stir in the flour, salt, and pepper; cook 1 minute, stirring until smooth and bubbly. Slowly stir in the milk and cook until slightly thickened.

Slowly stir the milk mixture into the rice mixture. Add remaining ingredients and heat gently; do not boil.

Split Pea Soup

Serves: 6

1 pound dried green split peas
2 tablespoons olive oil
1 medium onion, minced
2 carrots, peeled and diced
2 celery stalks, diced
2 cloves garlic, minced
1/2 teaspoon thyme
1 teaspoon black pepper
1 teaspoon Worcestershire sauce
1/2 teaspoon Tabasco sauce
2 bay leaves
2 whole cloves
2 pounds ham hocks
1 pound baking potatoes, peeled and diced
Salt and pepper to taste

Rinse the split peas then soak in enough water to cover overnight. Heat the oil in a soup pot over medium heat. Add the onions, carrots, celery, garlic, thyme, pepper, Worcestershire, and Tabasco. Sauté over medium heat for five minutes. Add the split peas along with their soaking liquid, bay leaves, cloves, ham hocks, and potatoes to the vegetables and bring to a boil. Skim off any foam that appears on the surface. Reduce the heat and simmer gently for 2 hours. Remove the ham hocks and allow to cool. Cut the meat into small cubes and add to the pot. Add salt and pepper to taste.

Cioppino

Serves: 8

3 tablespoons olive oil
1 large Spanish onion, chopped
1 large green pepper, chopped
2 cloves garlic, minced
2 cups canned clam juice
1 cup fresh tomatoes, coarsely chopped
1/2 cup dry white wine
2 tablespoons minced fresh parsley
1 bay leaf
Salt and pepper
4 soft shell crabs
12 mussels
12 clams
12 large shrimp, shelled and deveined
1 pound cod, cubed

Heat the olive oil in a soup pot over moderate heat for 1 minute. Add the onions, green peppers, and garlic. Sauté for 5 minutes until the onions are translucent. Stir in the clam juice, tomatoes, wine, parsley, and bay leaf. Bring to a boil, reduce the heat, and cover. Simmer for 30 minutes.

Add salt and pepper to taste, and remove the bay leaf. Add the crabs, mussels, clams, shrimp, and fish and stir gently. Bring to a boil, reduce the heat to low, and cook for 5 to 10 minutes. Discard any mussels or clams that remain closed.

Cooking Dried Beans

Soak dried beans in two to three times as much water as beans. Remove any beans that float and any other debris. Soak overnight and bring to boil in the same water the next day. Reduce heat and simmer until beans are tender.

If you have forgotten to soak beans overnight, cover beans with cold water, bring to boil and simmer for 2 minutes. Turn off heat and let stand, tightly covered, for 1 hour before cooking until tender but not mushy. To see if the beans are done, blow on a few of your cooked beans in a spoon. If the skins burst, they are cooked.

Blue Cheese Soup

Serves: 8

2 tablespoons butter
½ cup finely chopped onion
½ cup finely chopped celery
½ cup finely chopped carrot
1 teaspoon minced garlic
⅓ cup flour
2 teaspoons cornstarch
3 cups chicken stock
½ pound Stilton cheese, crumbled
½ pound Cheddar cheese, crumbled
⅛ teaspoon baking soda
1 cup cream, heavy or light, as desired
⅓ cup dry white wine (optional)
Salt to taste
Dash of cayenne pepper
¼ teaspoon freshly ground black pepper
1 bay leaf
¼ cup chopped fresh parsley for garnish

Melt the butter, and add the onion, celery, carrot, and garlic in a stockpot. Cook until tender, about 8 minutes.

Stir in the flour and cornstarch, cooking until bubbly, about 2 minutes. Add the stock, the two cheeses, baking soda, cream, and wine. Stir and blend until smooth and thickened. Add salt, cayenne, pepper, and bay leaf. Bring to a slow boil and let simmer 8 to 10 minutes.

Remove the bay leaf. Test for consistency. May be thinned with a little milk or wine if too thick. Garnish with the parsley and serve.

Amish Chicken and Corn Soup

Serves: 8

½ stewing hen or fowl
2 quarts chicken stock or broth
¼ cup coarsely chopped onion
½ cup coarsely chopped carrots
½ cup coarsely chopped celery
1 teaspoon saffron threads
    (optional)
¾ cup corn kernels, fresh or frozen
½ cup finely chopped celery
1 tablespoon fresh chopped parsley
1 cup cooked egg noodles

In a large stockpot, combine stewing hen with chicken stock, onions, carrots, celery coarsely chopped, and saffron threads. Bring the stock to a simmer. Simmer for about 1 hour, skimming the surface as necessary.

Remove and reserve the stewing hen until cool enough to handle; then pick the meat from the bones. Cut into neat little pieces. Strain the saffron broth through a fine sieve.

Note: The soup can be made through this step in advance. Simply refrigerate broth and diced chicken meat for 2 to 3 days, or freeze the broth and the chicken meat in separate containers. Be sure to label and date them. To use, defrost, remove congealed fat, return the broth to a full boil, and add the diced meat. Continue with recipe.

Add the corn, finely chopped celery, parsley, and cooked noodles to the broth. Return the soup to a simmer and serve immediately.

Beer Soup

Serves: 4

1½ tablespoons all-purpose flour
3½ tablespoons butter
1 l2-ounce bottle beer
1 small piece of cinnamon
Sugar to taste
2 egg yolks
½ cup milk
Toasted white French bread

In a large stockpot, brown the flour in the butter, then add beer. Add cinnamon and sugar and bring to a boil. Whisk together the egg yolks and milk and stir into the hot (but no longer boiling) beer. Strain, and serve with toasted slices of bread.

Buddhist Monk's Soup

Serves: 8

1 quart water
1 pound pumpkin or butternut squash,
*   peeled and cut into large chunks*
1 sweet potato, peeled and cut into large
*   chunks*
1/2 cup raw peanuts, shelled and skinned,
*   soaked 30 minutes, drained, and*
*   roughly chopped*
1/3 cup dried mung beans, soaked 30
*   minutes and drained*
3 tablespoons vegetable oil
1 square tofu
1 quart unsweetened coconut milk
Salt
1/2-ounce package cellophane noodles,
*   soaked 20 minutes, drained and cut*
*   into 1-inch sections*

In a large stockpot, boil the water and drop in the pumpkin/squash, sweet potato, peanuts, and mung beans. Cook on medium heat for 35 minutes. Meanwhile, heat the oil in a frying pan and cook the bean curd until light brown on both sides. Slice lengthwise into 1/4-inch strips and set aside.

After the 35 minutes, check the mung beans for softness. If they're soft, add the coconut milk and a touch of salt. Bring to a boil and add the cellophane noodles and fried bean curd.

Chinese Chicken Corn Soup

Serves: 6

3 cups chicken broth
1 8 1/4-ounce can creamed corn
1 cup diced, cooked, and skinned
*   chicken*
1 tablespoon cornstarch
2 tablespoons cold water
2 egg whites
2 tablespoons finely minced fresh parsley

Combine chicken broth, corn, and chicken pieces in a large saucepan. Bring mixture to a boil over medium heat, stirring occasionally. Blend cornstarch with cold water and add to soup. Continue cooking, uncovered, for 3 minutes.

Beat egg whites until foamy; stir into soup. Reduce heat to a simmer and cook until foamy. Ladle soup into individual bowls and garnish with parsley. Serve hot.

Crockpot Country Chicken Rice Soup

Serves: 6

3 onions, chopped
4 stalks celery, sliced
Salt and pepper to taste
1 teaspoon basil
1/2 teaspoon thyme

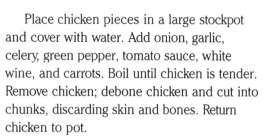

¹/₂ teaspoon sage
1 20-ounce package frozen peas
2¹/₂ pounds chicken pieces
5¹/₂ cups water
³/₄ cups raw converted rice

Place all ingredients except rice in slow cooker in order listed. Cover and cook 1 hour on high; reduce heat to low and cook an additional 8 to 9 hours. One hour before serving, remove chicken and cool slightly. Remove meat from bones and return meat to slow cooker. Add rice. Cover and cook an additional hour on high.

Drunken Chicken Soup

Serves: 6

1 chicken, cut into pieces
1 large onion, diced
2 cloves garlic, minced
2 stalks celery, sliced
¹/₂ green pepper, diced
1 6-ounce can tomato sauce
³/₄ cup white wine
4 carrots, sliced
4 potatoes, diced
Salt and pepper to taste

Place chicken pieces in a large stockpot and cover with water. Add onion, garlic, celery, green pepper, tomato sauce, white wine, and carrots. Boil until chicken is tender. Remove chicken; debone chicken and cut into chunks, discarding skin and bones. Return chicken to pot.

Add potatoes and salt and pepper to taste. Cook until potatoes are tender. Serve with garlic bread.

Stock Smarts, Part 3

To make a quick and easy thick vegetable stock, place 1 cup of water into a food processor. Add 1 cup of minced raw vegetables, and purée until it reaches the consistency you desire. Freeze for future use or cook immediately.

Stews

Americans have long been brainwashed into assuming that stew means beef, and that's a shame, as you'll see from the following recipes. Open up your eyes, try a few of the recipes that use such unorthodox ingredients as chicken, pork, even shrimp, and you'll be well on the way to broadening your horizons.

Gone-All-Day Stew

Serves: 6

1 10¾-ounce can tomato soup
1 cup water
¼ cup flour
2 pounds beef chuck, cut into 1-inch cubes
3 medium carrots, cut diagonally in 1-inch pieces
6 medium yellow onions, quartered
4 medium potatoes, peeled and cut into 1 ½-inch cubes
½ cup celery chunks
2 beef bouillon cubes
1 tablespoon Italian herb seasoning
1 bay leaf
Pepper to taste

Mix together soup, water, and flour until smooth. Combine with remaining ingredients in a covered roasting pan. Bake for 4 to 5 hours at 275°F. When ready to serve adjust seasonings to taste and discard bay leaf.

Sloppy Joe Stew

Serves: 4

1 tablespoon olive oil
1 pound ground beef
½ cup chopped onions
½ teaspoon salt
Dash of pepper
1½ cups canned tomatoes
2 large potatoes, peeled and sliced
1 cup fresh sliced carrots
½ cup chopped celery

Heat the oil in a large, heavy skillet over low heat. Add the hamburger, and cook the meat until it browns. Drain the fat. Add the onions, salt, and pepper and stir. Add all the remaining ingredients. Stir, cover the skillet, and bring to a boil. Reduce the heat, and simmer until the potatoes are tender.

Carolyn's Southwestern Chicken Stew

Serves: 6

3 pounds chicken pieces, skin and fat
　　removed
¹/₄ cup flour
¹/₄ cup olive oil
1 tablespoon flour
2 tablespoons minced garlic
3 14-ounce cans chicken broth
1 14-ounce can whole tomatoes
1 6-ounce can tomato paste
16 pearl onions
1¹/₂ teaspoons seasoned salt
1¹/₂ teaspoons ground cumin
4 sprigs oregano
4 sprigs thyme
1 bay leaf
¹/₄ teaspoon red pepper flakes, crushed
8 ounces kielbasa or smoked turkey
　　sausage
2 cups new potatoes, cut in chunks
2 cups carrots, cut into chunks
2 cups zucchini, cut into chunks
2 cups yellow squash, cut into chunks
1 8-ounce can whole kernel corn
Chopped cilantro

In a bag, coat chicken with ¹/₄ cup flour.
Brown chicken in Dutch oven in hot oil;
remove and set aside. Drain drippings, except
1 teaspoon, from pot. Sauté 1 tablespoon
flour and garlic in drippings 30 seconds. Stir
in next 10 ingredients starting with chicken
broth and ending with red pepper flakes.
Bring to a boil; reduce heat and simmer,
uncovered, 20 minutes.

Add chicken and kielbasa; cover and
simmer 20 minutes longer.

Skim excess fat. Add vegetables. Simmer,
covered, 30 minutes longer. Sprinkle with
cilantro before serving.

Beef Stew Basics, Part 1

When selecting the meat for a beef
stew one-pot recipe, try to choose the
biggest pieces you can. Smaller
pieces tend to shrink more and dry
out more than larger pieces, which
retain their juiciness.

Brunswick Stew

Serves: 8

2 2½ pound whole chickens
2 quarts water
1 tablespoon salt
1½ cups ketchup, divided
2 tablespoons light brown sugar
1½ teaspoons dry mustard
1½ teaspoons grated fresh ginger
½ lemon, sliced
1 clove garlic, minced
1 tablespoon butter or margarine
¼ cup white vinegar
3 tablespoons vegetable oil
1 tablespoon Worcestershire sauce
¾ teaspoon hot sauce
½ teaspoon pepper
2 28-ounce cans diced tomatoes
2 15¼-ounce cans whole kernel corn, undrained
2 14¾-ounce cans creamed-style corn
1 large onion, chopped
¼ cup firmly packed light brown sugar
1 tablespoon salt and pepper

Bring first 3 ingredients to boil in a large heavy stockpot; cover, reduce heat, and simmer 45 minutes or until chicken is tender. Drain chicken, reserving 1 quart broth in pot; skin, bone and shred chicken, and return to pot. Cook ½ cup ketchup and next 11 ingredients (stopping with pepper) in a small saucepan over medium heat, stirring occasionally (10 minutes). Stir ketchup mixture, remaining 1 cup ketchup, tomatoes and all remaining ingredients into chicken and broth; simmer, stirring often, 4 hours or until thickened.

Montana Stew

Serves: 8

2½ pounds beef cubes
2 tablespoons all-purpose flour
1 tablespoon paprika
1 teaspoon chili powder
2 teaspoons salt
3 tablespoons lard
2 medium onions, sliced
1 clove garlic, minced
1 28-ounce can tomatoes
3 tablespoons chili powder
1 tablespoon cinnamon
1 teaspoon ground cloves
½ teaspoon crushed red pepper
2 large potatoes, cubed
2 cups chopped carrots

In a shallow dish, coat beef in a mixture of flour, paprika, 1 teaspoon chili powder, and salt. Place the lard in a large Dutch oven and brown the beef. Add onion and garlic and cook until soft. Then add tomatoes, chili powder, cinnamon, cloves, and peppers. Cover and simmer 2 hours.

Add potatoes and carrots and cook until vegetables are done, about 45 minutes.

Tomato-Seafood Stew

Serves: 6

$\frac{1}{2}$ pound shrimp, shelled and deveined
1 cup chopped onion
2 garlic cloves, minced
1 tablespoon olive oil
1 16-ounce can tomatoes, chopped
1 8-ounce can tomato sauce
1 potato, peeled and chopped
1 medium green pepper, chopped
1 celery stalk, chopped
1 medium carrot, shredded
1 teaspoon dried thyme, crushed
$\frac{1}{4}$ teaspoon pepper
4 dashes hot sauce
1 20-ounce can whole baby clams, drained
2 tablespoons snipped parsley

Cut shrimp in half lengthwise. In a large saucepan cook onion and garlic in oil till tender. Stir in undrained tomatoes, tomato sauce, potato, green pepper, celery, carrot, thyme, pepper, and hot pepper sauce. Bring to boiling; reduce heat. Cover and simmer 20 to 25 minutes or till vegetables are tender.

Add the shrimp, clams, and parsley. Bring to boiling; reduce heat. Cover and simmer 1 to 2 minutes more or till shrimp turns pink.

Scandinavian Beef and Vegetable Stew

Serves: 8

3 pounds beef marrow bones

3 quarts water
3 pounds stewing beef, trimmed of excess
    fat and cut into bite-size pieces
2 bay leaves
3 cloves
1 teaspoon rosemary
2 teaspoons salt
$\frac{1}{2}$ teaspoon freshly ground black pepper
6 carrots, scraped and cut into $\frac{1}{2}$-inch
    slices
1 medium-sized cabbage, cut into eighths
1 onion, chopped
$\frac{1}{4}$ cup cider vinegar
1 tablespoon brown sugar
1 tablespoon flour mixed with 3
    tablespoons cold water
Salt and pepper to taste

In a soup kettle, boil the beef bones in the water for $1\frac{1}{2}$ hours. Remove and discard the bones; reserve the marrow.

To the broth, add the beef and seasonings. Simmer the meat, covered, for 2 hours, or until it is tender.

Remove and reserve the meat. Drain the broth, then chill it and skim off the fat. Return the meat to the kettle, along with the reserved marrow. Add the broth, reserving about 1 cup. Bring the mixture to a boil. Add the carrots and cabbage and cook, covered, for 20 minutes, or until just tender.

Remove the meat and vegetables from the broth. Arrange in a serving dish and cover to keep warm. Simmer the onion in the broth for 5 minutes. Add the vinegar, sugar, and flour

(continued)

mixture, stirring constantly until the sauce is thickened and smooth. Add salt and pepper. Pour the sauce over the meat and vegetables.

French Chicken & Pork Stew

Serves: 4

>1 pork shoulder chop (about ⅓ pound), boned and cut into ¾-inch cubes
>1 broiler-fryer chicken (3 to 3¾ pounds), cut in pieces
>8 to 10 small white onions, peeled
>½ pound small mushrooms
>14-ounce can beef broth
>¼ cup wine
>2 tablespoons Dijon mustard
>2 tablespoons chopped parsley
>1 teaspoon cornstarch blended with 1 teaspoon water

In a 12-inch frying pan over medium heat, cook pork in its own fat until well browned and crisp. Remove pork with a slotted spoon and set aside.

To the pan drippings, add the chicken and onions. Cook, turning pieces occasionally for about 20 minutes or until chicken and onions are well browned. Lift meat and vegetables from pan and set aside.

Add the mushrooms and cook until soft; remove from pan and add to chicken.

Add the broth to the pan and bring to a boil, scraping brown pieces free from pan, until reduced to about 1 cup. Return chicken, onions, and mushrooms to pan. Add wine and mustard; bring to a boil. Cover, reduce heat, and simmer for about 30 minutes or until chicken thighs near bone are no longer pink when slashed. Stir in reserved pork and parsley; bring to a simmer again.

With a slotted spoon, lift meats and vegetables from pan and transfer to a warm serving platter. Stir cornstarch mixture into pan juices and quickly bring to a boil. Pour over chicken and vegetables.

Hearty Quick (or Slow) Tomato Stew

Serves: 6

>32 ounces tomato juice
>1 14½-ounce can Italian stewed tomatoes
>2 cups water
>2 medium potatoes, unpeeled, chopped
>1 15-ounce can garbanzo beans, washed
>1 15-ounce can kidney beans, drained
>1 cup lentils, rinsed
>1 large onion, chopped
>1 cup diced red pepper, seeded
>1 cup diced green pepper, seeded
>1 10-ounce package chopped frozen spinach
>2 carrots, julienned in 1-inch pieces
>2 tablespoons dried parsley
>2 tablespoons chili powder
>2 teaspoons dried basil
>2 teaspoons garlic powder
>1 teaspoon ground cumin

Topping:

$1/2$ *cup sour cream*
$1/2$ *cup yogurt*
$1/4$ *cup chopped chives*

Quick method: Combine all ingredients except toppings in a large Dutch oven. Bring to a boil, reduce heat, and simmer for 30 minutes or until lentils are tender.

Slow method: Combine all ingredients except toppings in a slow cooker. Set on low and cook for about 6 hours.

Mix the topping ingredients together in a small bowl. Garnish each serving with a dollop of the topping.

African Pork & Peanut Stew

Serves: 4

2 *tablespoons peanut oil, divided*
2 *pounds boneless pork butt, cut into*
    1-inch cubes
1 *onion, chopped*
2 *cloves garlic, minced*
$1/2$ *teaspoon curry powder*
$1/2$ *teaspoon ground coriander*
$1/2$ *teaspoon ground cumin*
$1/2$ *to 1 teaspoon crushed red pepper flakes*
$1/2$ *teaspoon ground ginger*
$1/4$ *teaspoon cinnamon*
1 *bay leaf*
1 *teaspoon salt*
2 *cups chicken broth*

1 *tablespoon tomato paste*
$1/2$ *cup chunky peanut butter*
2 *plum tomatoes, seeded and chopped*
1 *green bell pepper, cut into 1-inch pieces*
$1/4$ *cup cilantro, chopped*
$1/2$ *cup saltless peanuts, shelled*

In a large heavy pot, heat 1 tablespoon of the oil on high. When hot, add the pork cubes and brown on all sides. Add the onion to the pork and cook until soft. Stir in the garlic, curry powder, coriander, cumin, and crushed red pepper. Cook 1 minute. Add the ginger, cinnamon, bay leaf, salt, chicken broth, and tomato paste. Bring the liquid to a boil, then cover and simmer on low 45 minutes.

Add the peanut butter and stir well to blend. Cook the stew another 3 minutes, uncovered, for the flavors to blend. Stir in the chopped tomato and bell pepper. Simmer for 2 or 3 more minutes, just until the vegetables soften but still retain their shape. Before serving, taste to correct the seasonings; you may wish to add a final splash of lemon juice to refresh the flavors. Serve with the chopped cilantro and peanuts on top. If desired, pass additional red pepper flakes on the side.

Polish Stew

Serves: 8

1 *pound Polish sausage, cut in $1/2$-inch*
    pieces
3 *tablespoons oil*
$1 1/2$ *pounds beef, cubed*

(continued)

2 onions, sliced
2 cups sliced mushrooms
1 1-pound can sauerkraut
1 cup white wine
1 8-ounce can tomato sauce
2 teaspoons soy sauce
1 teaspoon caraway seeds
¼ teaspoon vegetable seasoning

In a heavy ovenproof skillet, sauté the sausage for 15 minutes. Remove and set aside. Add oil to sausage drippings; brown beef in oil for 15 minutes. Preheat oven to 375°F.

Remove beef from skillet and set aside. Add the onion and sauté; remove and set aside. Add the mushrooms and sauté with sauerkraut and wine. Add tomato sauce, soy sauce, caraway seeds, and vegetable seasoning. Return the sausage, beef, and onion to the skillet, mixing well. Cover and bake for 2 to 2½ hours. Stir casserole every 30 minutes.

New Hampshire Goulash

Serves: 6

3 pounds stew meat, cut in 1-inch cubes
3 tablespoons oil
3 cups chopped onions
1 cup chopped green peppers
1 clove garlic, minced
1 16-ounce can tomato sauce
1 tablespoon chili powder
½ teaspoon soy sauce

2 5-ounce cans mushrooms
1 tablespoon paprika
3 tablespoons brown sugar
¼ teaspoon pepper
1½ cups sour cream (optional)
Hot egg noodles, buttered, or rice

In a large heavy skillet, brown meat well on all sides in oil in large pan. Mix in onions, peppers, garlic, tomato sauce, soy sauce, mushrooms, paprika, brown sugar, and pepper. Stir thoroughly. Cover and cook slowly until beef cubes are tender, about 2½ to 3 hours.

If desired stir in sour cream just before serving. Serve on hot buttered noodles or rice.

Grandma's Beef Stew

Serves: 8

⅓ cup flour
1 teaspoon salt
¼ teaspoon freshly ground pepper
4 tablespoons shortening
2 pounds stewing beef, cut into cubes
4 cups boiling water
1 tablespoon lemon juice
1 tablespoon Worcestershire sauce
1 teaspoon sugar
1 large onion, sliced
2 bay leaves
¼ teaspoon allspice
12 small carrots, trimmed and scraped
12 small white onions, trimmed
8 small new potatoes, peeled

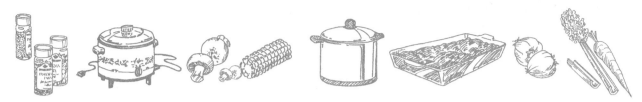

Mix the flour, salt, and pepper and roll the beef cubes in the mixture. Shake off excess.

Melt the shortening over high heat in a Dutch oven or heavy-bottomed pot with a cover. When the fat is very hot, add the beef, about 5 or 6 pieces at a time so as not to crowd them; brown on all sides, and remove. When the last batch of meat is a dark, rich color, return all the meat to the pot and add the boiling water. Stir and add the lemon juice, Worcestershire sauce, sugar, onion, bay leaves, and allspice. Reduce the heat, cover, and simmer for $1\frac{1}{2}$ to 2 hours, or until the meat is tender.

Add the carrots, onions, and potatoes and cook another 20 to 25 minutes or until they can be pierced easily with a fork.

Oniony Beef Stew

Serves: 4

1 $2\frac{1}{2}$-pound boneless chuck roast
3 cups chopped onion
1 clove garlic, crushed
1 tablespoon vegetable oil
1 8-ounce can tomato sauce
$1\frac{1}{2}$ teaspoons caraway seeds
$1\frac{1}{2}$ teaspoons salt
1 teaspoon dill seeds
$\frac{1}{4}$ teaspoon pepper
$1\frac{1}{2}$ teaspoons Worcestershire sauce
2 tablespoons brown sugar (optional)
1 cup sour cream
1 pound hot cooked noodles

Trim roast, and cut into 1-inch cubes. Sauté beef cubes, onion, and garlic in hot oil in a Dutch oven until beef is browned. Add tomato sauce and next 6 ingredients. Reduce heat and simmer, stirring occasionally, 1 hour and 30 minutes or until tender.

Stir in sour cream; cook, stirring often, just until thoroughly heated (do not boil). Serve over hot cooked noodles.

Beef Stew Basics, Part 2

The best cuts of beef for stew meat are chuck, flank, or brisket. You can use more expensive cuts, but the slow cooking of a stew tenderizes even the toughest meat.

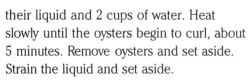

Hearty Smoked Sausage Stew

Serves: 8

1 pound dried red kidney beans
1 46-ounce can chicken broth
2 cups water
1 pound smoked sausage, sliced
1 cup barley
2 bay leaves
½ teaspoon garlic powder
1 teaspoon thyme

The night before, rinse beans, place in a large bowl with plenty of water to cover, and soak overnight.

Drain and rinse beans. Put all ingredients in a large Crockpot, stir, cover, and cook on low for 8 hours.

Coastal Oyster Stew

Serves: 4

1 pint shucked oysters, with their liquid
2 cups water
½ cup diced onions
½ cup diced celery
6 tablespoons sweet butter
1½ cups heavy cream
2 tablespoon chopped fresh parsley
1 tablespoon chopped fresh chervil
Freshly ground pepper

Pick through the oysters, removing any bits of shell. Place in a small saucepan with their liquid and 2 cups of water. Heat slowly until the oysters begin to curl, about 5 minutes. Remove oysters and set aside. Strain the liquid and set aside.

Slowly simmer the onion and celery in butter in a soup pot until tender, about 6 minutes. Add the oyster liquid and heavy cream. Heat almost to the boiling point and simmer for 10 minutes. Add oysters, parsley, and chervil. Season to taste with pepper. Simmer 1 minute more. Serve with crackers.

Cuban Chicken Stew

Serves: 4

2 tablespoons butter
3 pounds chicken, cut into bite-size pieces
1 cup finely diced onions
1 clove garlic, minced
1 teaspoon cayenne pepper
2 teaspoons paprika
1 cup chicken stock
3 cups milk
2 large yuccas, peeled and diced into
*   1-inch thick cubes*
4 ears yellow corn, shucked, sliced into
*   1-inch thick wheels*
Juice of 1 lime

Melt the butter in a 6-quart pot over medium heat. Cook chicken pieces in the butter until no longer pink.

Remove chicken with slotted spoon and place in a bowl. Put onion, garlic, cayenne, and paprika in pot and cook while stirring

until onion is translucent and colored with the paprika. Add stock, milk, yucca, corn, and chicken to the pot. Bring almost to a boil then reduce heat, cover, and simmer, stirring every now and then, for about 1 hour, or until yucca is tender. Remove from heat and stir in lime juice.

Potato & Garbanzo Stew

Serves: 4

1 tablespoon olive oil
1 Spanish onion, chopped
2 cloves garlic, minced
1 teaspoon paprika
3 fresh tomatoes, coarsely chopped, divided
1/3 cup chopped fresh basil
1 teaspoon oregano
2 large russet potatoes, diced
1 cup chicken broth or water
1 19-ounce can garbanzo beans, drained
1/4 cup basil, chopped
Salt and pepper to taste
1/2 cup chopped fresh parsley for garnish

In a large heavy saucepan, heat the oil over medium heat. Add the onion and cook about 5 minutes. Add the garlic, paprika, 2 tomatoes, and oregano. Reduce heat and cook, stirring occasionally, for 5 minutes. Add the potatoes and broth. Cover and bring to a boil. Keep at a boil for 5 minutes, stirring occasionally.

Add the garbanzo beans. Reduce the heat and cook for 5 minutes until potatoes are done. Add the remaining tomato, basil, and salt and pepper; heat for 3 minutes. Garnish with parsley and serve.

Tomato-Seafood Stew

Serves: 6

1/2 pound shrimp, shelled
1 cup chopped onion
2 cloves garlic, minced
1 tablespoon olive oil
1 16-ounce can tomatoes, chopped
1 8-ounce can tomato sauce
1 potato, peeled and chopped
1 medium green pepper, chopped
1 celery stalk, chopped
1 medium carrot, shredded
1 teaspoon dried thyme, crushed
1/4 teaspoon pepper
4 dashes bottled hot sauce
1 20-ounce can whole baby clams, drained
2 tablespoons snipped parsley

Thaw shrimp if frozen; halve lengthwise. In a large saucepan cook onion and garlic in oil till tender. Stir in undrained tomatoes, tomato sauce, potato, green pepper, celery, carrot, thyme, pepper, and hot pepper sauce. Bring to boiling; reduce heat. Cover and simmer 20 to 25 minutes or till vegetables are tender.

Stir in shrimp, clams, and parsley. Bring to boiling; reduce heat. Cover and simmer 1 to 2 minutes more or till shrimp turns pink. Spoon into serving bowls.

Low-Fat Stew Broth

A stew by definition is meat and vegetables simmered slowly in broth. If you want to make the broth you use low-fat, follow these steps:

1. Place a lamb shank, or beef bone, or chicken carcass in a large soup pot with enough water to cover. Add 1 bay leaf and 1 chopped onion.
2. Bring to a boil, lower hear and simmer uncovered for 1 hour.
3. Cover and place in the refrigerator overnight. The next day skim off the fat that has solidified on top. Store in the refrigerator for up to a week.

Daube of Beef

Serves: 6

5 shallots, sliced thin
4 cloves garlic, minced
2 medium carrots, sliced ¼-inch thick
⅓ cup baked ham, chopped

1 slice orange peel, ½" x 3"
1 bay leaf
3 pounds boneless lean beef chuck, cut in 1½-inch cubes
¼ cup flour
¼ teaspoon whole black peppercorns
¼ teaspoon dry thyme
⅛ teaspoon ground cloves
1/2 teaspoon dry sage
2 tablespoons balsamic vinegar
¾ cup dry white wine or beef broth
¼ cup brandy
2 tablespoons flour
2 tablespoons butter or margarine
Salt to taste
Chopped parsley

In slow cooker, combine shallots, garlic, carrots, ham, orange peel, and bay leaf. Coat beef cubes with flour; add to cooker. Sprinkle with peppercorns, thyme, cloves, and sage. Drizzle with vinegar; pour in wine and brandy. Cover; cook on low until beef is very tender.

Remove and discard bay leaf and orange peel. Blend flour and butter together, then add to pot. Increase cooker heat to high. Cover and cook, stirring 2 to 3 times, until sauce is thickened (about 20 minutes). Season to taste and sprinkle with parsley.

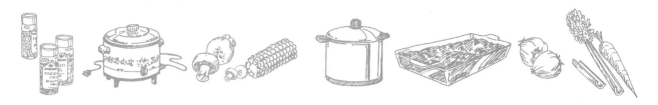

Chowders

You don't have to live in New England to appreciate a good chowder, traditionally defined to include any soup that uses a milk or cream base. Of course, clam chowder is the best known in this class, but as you'll see from the various chowder recipes, you can use a variety of other ingredients to make a chowder as good as one from the shores of Cape Cod.

Baked Fish Chowder

Serves: 8

3 large potatoes, peeled and thinly sliced
4 large onions, thinly sliced
2 pounds cod or haddock fillets, cut into bite-size pieces
2 tablespoons unsalted butter
Salt and pepper to taste
½ teaspoon celery seed
6 cups low-fat milk
¼ cup chopped fresh parsley

Preheat oven to 350°F. Grease a large casserole or baking dish with butter.

Arrange half of the potatoes in the dish; then add half of the onions. Dot the onion layer with butter and season with salt, pepper, and celery seed. Arrange the fish on top of the onions in a single layer, and season with salt and pepper. Add the remaining potato, then onion. Dot the onion layer with butter and season with salt and pepper. Pour the milk over the fish and vegetable mixture. Bake

dish, uncovered, for 1 hour, or until the fish flakes easily and the potatoes are tender. Garnish the chowder with the parsley.

Bar Harbor Fish Chowder

Serves: 6

¼ pound salt pork, diced
4 cups diced potatoes
3 medium onions, peeled and sliced
2 teaspoons salt, divided
3 pounds white fleshed fish, like flounder, haddock, or cod
2 cups scalded milk
1 tablespoon butter
¼ teaspoon freshly ground black pepper

Fry the salt pork in a heavy kettle and then remove. Set aside. Add the potatoes, onions, and ½ teaspoon salt. Cover with hot water and cook over medium heat, covered, 15 minutes, or until potatoes are just tender.

Meanwhile, cut fish into large chunks and put into another saucepan. Add boiling water

(continued)

to cover and 1 1/2 teaspoons salt. Cook slowly, covered, until fish is fork tender, about 15 minutes. Remove from heat. Strain and reserve liquid. Remove any bones from fish. Add fish and strained liquid to potato-onion mixture. Pour in milk and heat through, about 5 minutes. Mix in butter and pepper. Serve at once.

Harvest Time Corn Chowder

Serves: 6

> 4 slices bacon, chopped
> 1 large onion, chopped
> 3 medium potatoes, peeled and cubed
> 2 1/2 cups water, divided
> 1 teaspoon salt
> 1/4 teaspoon pepper
> 2 15-ounce cans whole corn kernels, undrained
> 1 8-ounce can evaporated milk
> 1/4 cup flour
> Paprika for garnish

Cook bacon until crisp in a large heavy saucepan or Dutch oven. Add onion and sauté until soft. Add potatoes, 2 cups water, salt, and pepper. Cover and simmer for 15 minutes or until potatoes are tender.

Stir in corn (with liquid) and evaporated milk. Heat to bubbling. Blend flour with remaining 1/2 cup water. Stir into chowder. Cook over medium heat, stirring constantly, until mixture thickens and bubbles, about

3 minutes. Ladle into soup bowls and sprinkle with paprika.

Potato and Corn Chowder

Serves: 4

> 4 Idaho potatoes, diced
> 1 Spanish onion, chopped
> 3 cloves garlic, minced
> 1 red pepper, diced
> 1 teaspoon cumin
> 1 teaspoon basil
> 1 teaspoon salt
> 1/2 teaspoon black pepper
> 1 4-ounce can diced green chilies
> 1 10-ounce package frozen corn, thawed
> 2 cups milk

Place the potatoes in a pot with 2 cups water. Bring to a boil; reduce heat, cover, and cook for 20 minutes. Heat another 1/2 cup water in a large pot and cook the onion, garlic, and red pepper for 5 minutes. Add the cumin, basil, salt, and pepper and cook for 5 more minutes. Meanwhile, mash the potatoes in their cooking water and add the onion mixture, along with the chilies, corn, and milk. Stir to blend. Heat for 5 more minutes.

Turkey Chowder

Serves: 6

> 2 tablespoons butter
> 1 large onion, thinly sliced
> 1 green pepper, chopped

2 cups chicken broth
3 medium carrots, sliced
3 medium potatoes, peeled and diced
2 celery stalks, thinly sliced
1 teaspoon salt
3 cups cooked, diced turkey
1 17ounce can corn kernels
½ teaspoon thyme
Black pepper to taste
3 cups milk
¼ cup finely chopped fresh parsley

Melt the butter in a large frying pan, and sauté the onion and pepper for 10 minutes. Stir in the broth and carrots. Bring to a boil; reduce the heat, cover, and cook for 5 minutes. Add the potatoes, celery, and salt. Cover and simmer for 10 minutes or until the potatoes and carrots are tender. Add the turkey, corn, thyme, pepper, and milk. Heat thoroughly. Sprinkle with chopped parsley and serve.

Hot Dog Corn Chowder

Serves: 8

4 tablespoons butter
3 onions, sliced
3 ribs celery, chopped, with their leaves
3 medium-sized potatoes, peeled and diced
3 cups water
6 hot dogs, cut into ¼-inch rounds
1 bay leaf
3 whole cloves
1 teaspoon thyme
1½ teaspoons salt

½ teaspoon pepper
1 10-ounce package frozen whole-kernel corn, thawed to room temperature
1 1-pound can cream-style corn
3 tablespoons flour
1 cup cold milk
2 cups hot milk
1 10-ounce package frozen peas, thawed to room temperature

In a large stockpot, heat the butter and in it cook the onion and celery until translucent. Add the potatoes; cook and stir over medium heat for 5 minutes.

Add the water, hot dogs, and seasonings to the vegetable mixture. Bring to a boil, reduce the heat, and simmer for 20 minutes, or until the potatoes are tender.

Add the frozen and canned corn and cook, stirring, for 5 minutes. Stir the flour and cold milk together until smooth. Add this mixture to the soup, stirring constantly. Add the hot milk and the peas, and continue to stir. Cook the chowder for 5 minutes longer.

Tuna Chowder

Serves: 6

2 tablespoons butter
3 stalks celery, chopped
1 large onion, chopped
1 large potato, diced
3 tablespoons flour
3 cups milk
2 6½-ounce cans water-packed tuna

(continued)

4 ounces Cheddar cheese, grated
1 teaspoon thyme
1 teaspoon dill weed
Salt and pepper
¼ cup chopped fresh parsley for garnish

In a large stockpot, melt the butter. Sauté the celery, onion, and potato until the potato is done. Add the flour and milk and blend thoroughly. Cook for 5 minutes, stirring, until the mixture thickens. Add the tuna, cheese, thyme, and dill. Season with salt and pepper to taste. Heat over medium-low heat for 5 to 10 minutes. Garnish each serving with chopped fresh parsley.

Hearty Corn Chowder

Serves: 8

4 cups cut-up potatoes (large chunks)
1 large onion, chopped
1 green bell pepper, chopped
2 cups frozen corn kernels
1 cup evaporated milk

In a saucepan, combine the potatoes, onion, and bell pepper with water to cover. Bring to a boil, reduce the heat to low, and simmer for 10 minutes. Add the corn and cook until vegetables are tender, about 10 more minutes. Stir in the milk and bring to serving temperature, stirring well. Ladle into bowls and serve.

Summertime Potato Chowder

Serves: 6

1 can (10¾ ounces) condensed cream of
*   potato soup*
1¼ cups chicken broth
milk, as needed to fill the soup can
1 small onion, cut into chunks
2 scallions, minced

Place the cream of potato soup, chicken broth, and 1 soup can of milk into a blender or food processor and purée for 10 seconds until blended. Add the onion and purée until smooth. Transfer to a serving bowl, cover, and chill overnight. Ladle into chilled bowls and sprinkle with the scallions.

Chapter 8

Hot Salads

A hot salad? Your eyebrows may have gone up when your eyes happened upon the topic of this chapter. Yes, you may have chanced upon a warm potato salad at some point in your life, but here are some other surprisingly tasty choices.

Hot and warm one-pot salads are among the most subtle and original dishes you can serve to family and friends, initially because no one is expecting it. Then, once you conquer them with surprise, you'll stun them again with the flavor and uniqueness of a salad that is a bit different from what they've come to expect.

Hot Salad Dressing

Serves: 6

> 1 tablespoon butter
> 1 teaspoon flour
> $\frac{1}{2}$ cup vinegar
> 2 teaspoons sugar
> $\frac{1}{2}$ teaspoon dry mustard
> $\frac{1}{2}$ teaspoon salt
> $\frac{1}{8}$ teaspoon pepper
> 1 egg yolk, beaten

In a heavy skillet, melt the butter and blend in the flour. Add the vinegar and stir until mixture thickens.

Mix together the sugar, mustard, salt, and pepper and add to the liquid. Cook for 4 minutes. Pour over the beaten egg yolk and mix well. Return to heat and cook 1 minute longer.

Roasted Potato Salad

Serves: 6

> $\frac{1}{4}$ cup olive oil
> 2 pounds red new potatoes, washed and
>   quartered
> 1 teaspoon kosher salt
> $\frac{1}{2}$ cup diced red bell pepper
> $1\frac{1}{2}$ tablespoons minced shallots
> 1 teaspoon fresh thyme leaves
> 1 teaspoon fresh rosemary leaves
> 1 teaspoon freshly ground black pepper
> 1 teaspoon paprika
> $\frac{1}{2}$ teaspoon granulated garlic
> 1 tablespoon fresh lemon juice
> 1 tablespoon chopped fresh parsley

Preheat oven to 400°F.

Heat the olive oil in a cast-iron skillet and add the potatoes and salt. Toss to coat the potatoes well and place in the oven until they are slightly soft (approximately 20 minutes). Add the diced peppers, shallots, thyme,

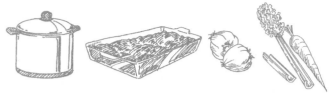

rosemary, black pepper, paprika, and garlic, and toss well again to coat the potatoes evenly. Return the pan to the oven until the potatoes are soft when pierced with a sharp knife (approximately 10 to 15 minutes).

Remove the potatoes from the oven and transfer to a mixing bowl with a slotted spoon; toss well with the lemon juice and parsley. Adjust the salt and black pepper. (For a zestier salad, ½ teaspoon cayenne can be added.) Serve warm or at room temperature the same day. This salad does not save well.

Warm Sweet Potato & Apple Salad

Serves: 12

¾ cup mayonnaise
¾ cup plain low-fat yogurt
1½ tablespoons curry powder
½ teaspoon salt
2½ pounds sweet potatoes (about 7 medium sized), cooked, peeled, cooled, and cut into ¾-inch chunks
2 medium sized Granny Smith apples, cut in ½-inch pieces
1 20-ounce can pineapple chunks, drained
½ cup raisins

In a large saucepan, whisk together the mayonnaise, yogurt, curry powder, and salt over low heat until well blended. While still whisking, add the potatoes, apples, pineapples, and raisins. Toss gently to mix and coat. Cover and continue to cook over low heat for

7 to 10 minutes, until potato is heated through, stirring constantly.

Taco Salad

Serves: 8

2 pounds ground beef
2 2-ounce packages taco seasoning mix
2 large onions, chopped
10 ounces Cheddar cheese, grated
8-ounce bag corn chips, crushed
1 large head lettuce, torn
2 tomatoes, cut into chunks

Prepare taco mix with ground beef according to package directions, adding the onions. In a big serving bowl, combine the cheese, chips, torn lettuce and tomatoes. Just before serving pour taco meat mixture in the bowl and toss with other ingredients. Serve warm.

Beef Tenderloin Salad

Serves: 4

1 tablespoon vegetable oil
1½ pounds 1-inch thick beef tenderloin steaks (roughly equal to 5 to 6 steaks)
Freshly ground pepper
3 cloves garlic, crushed

Salad Dressing:
1¼ cups olive oil
⅓ cup balsamic vinegar
2 tablespoons chopped fresh chives

(continued)

2 tablespoons orange juice
3 tablespoons poppy seeds
Salt and pepper to taste

Salad:

1 cup fresh green beans, washed,
    trimmed, and snapped
1 head Bibb lettuce, torn (not chopped)
    into bite-sized pieces
1 head red lettuce, torn (not chopped)
    into bite-sized pieces
4 small plum tomatoes, chopped into small
    diamond wedges
1 16-ounce can mandarin oranges, drained
1 cup feta cheese, crumbled, about 4
    ounces
¾ cup chopped pecans, walnuts, almonds,
    or cashews
1 small red onion thinly sliced into rings

Heat oil in a heavy large skillet over
medium-high heat. Season the steaks with
fresh ground pepper. Brown crushed garlic in
oil; do not burn. Add meat and cook to
desired doneness. This should be about
5 minutes per side for medium rare. Transfer
steaks to platter. Let stand until they are cool
enough to handle. Cover and refrigerate until
well chilled.

For dressing, whisk all ingredients in a
medium bowl. Season to taste with salt
and pepper.

For salad, cook green beans in a large pot
of boiling salted water until just crisp-tender.

Drain; rinse under cold water. Drain well, and
pat dry. Combine beans with remaining ingredients in a large bowl.

Cut tenderloin diagonally into thin slices.
Add to salad. Add dressing, toss to coat,
and serve.

Beef & Horseradish Salad

Serves: 4

8 ounces fresh green beans
1½ cups baby carrots
12 ounces beef sirloin steak, cut 1-inch
    thick
4 cups torn Boston or Bibb lettuce
1 16-ounce can julienne-cut beets, rinsed
    and drained

Horseradish Dressing:

1½ ounces softened cream cheese
2 tablespoons prepared horseradish sauce
3 to 4 tablespoons milk

Wash green beans; remove ends and
strings. Cut beans in half crosswise. Cook
beans, covered, in boiling water in a medium
saucepan for 5 minutes. Add carrots and
cook for 10 to 15 minutes more or until
vegetables are tender; drain. Cover and chill
vegetables for 4 to 24 hours.

Place steak on the unheated rack of a
broiler pan. Broil 3 inches from the heat for
13 to 15 minutes for medium, turning once.
Thinly slice steak across the grain.

To make the horseradish dressing: Beat together the cream cheese and horseradish sauce in a small bowl. Stir in enough milk to make dressing of drizzling consistency. Chill until serving time. (Makes about ½ cup.)

Divide torn lettuce among 4 plates. Arrange beans, carrots, steak slices, and beets on lettuce. Pass Horseradish Dressing.

Stir-Fried Beef Salad

Serves: 6

1 pound boneless beef round steak
2 tablespoons olive oil
1 clove garlic, minced
8 ounces fresh mushrooms, sliced
1 cucumber, chopped
1 green pepper, cut into strips
1 onion, sliced into rings
1 teaspoon Italian seasoning
1 teaspoon seasoned salt
⅛ teaspoon ground red pepper
1 large tomato, chopped
8 ounces fresh spinach leaves

Partially freeze beef; slice thinly across the grain into bite-size strips. In wok or large skillet cook half the beef in hot oil till browned on all sides. Remove from pan. Repeat with remaining beef and garlic; remove from pan. Add mushrooms, cucumber, green pepper strips, onion rings, Italian seasoning, salt, and red pepper to wok. Stir-fry 3 minutes or till vegetables are crisp-tender.

Return beef to wok; add tomatoes. Cook 1 to 2 minutes or till heated through. Remove meat-vegetable mixture to serving bowl; keep warm. Add spinach leaves to wok; cover and cook for 1 minute or till slightly wilted. To serve, arrange spinach on four bowls or plates; spoon meat mixture atop.

Basil Chicken & Pasta Salad

Serves: 4

¾ cup water
¼ cup Chablis or other dry white wine
¼ teaspoon dried basil
6 black peppercorns
1 bay leaf
1 clove garlic, halved
½ pound chicken breast fillets
2 tablespoons mayonnaise
2 tablespoons plain yogurt
1 tablespoon red wine vinegar
1 tablespoon olive oil
½ teaspoon spicy brown mustard
⅛ teaspoon salt
⅛ teaspoon pepper
1 cup cooked rotini
1 cup cherry tomatoes, halved
¼ cup thinly sliced green onions
Red leaf lettuce leaves

Combine first six ingredients in a large saucepan; bring to a boil. Add chicken; cover, reduce heat, and simmer for 13 minutes or until chicken is done. Remove chicken from

(continued)

saucepan; set aside. Strain cooking liquid, reserving 2 tablespoons liquid. Discard solids.

Chop chicken; set aside. Combine reserved cooking liquid, mayonnaise, and next six ingredients in a large bowl; stir well. Add chicken, pasta, tomatoes, and onions; toss gently to coat. Serve warm on lettuce-lined salad plates.

French Chicken Salad

Serves: 4

3 cups mixed salad greens
1 broiled boneless chicken breast half
½ cup sliced black olives
½ cup minced mushrooms
1 medium avocado, diced
1 medium tomato, diced

Hot Basil Dressing:
¼ cup unsalted butter
¼ cup red wine vinegar
¼ cup olive oil
2½ cloves garlic, minced
1 teaspoon chopped fresh basil
½ teaspoon minced parsley
Salt and pepper to taste
¼ teaspoon capers

Place greens on large plate. Slice chicken in ½-inch strips and place in center of greens. Arrange olives, mushrooms, avocado, and tomato around breast. Serve with hot dressing.

To make dressing: Melt butter in saucepan. Add remainder of ingredients. Heat, but do not boil.

Warm Chinese Chicken Salad

Serves: 4

1 cup Italian salad dressing
2 teaspoons soy sauce
1 teaspoon fresh minced gingerroot
2 skinless, boneless chicken breasts, split
8 cups mixed salad greens, washed and torn
¼ cup chopped fresh cilantro (optional)
¼ cup diagonally sliced green onions
5 fresh California peaches, divided
¼ cup toasted, sliced almonds
2 tablespoons sesame seeds, toasted (optional)

For marinade, in zip-top plastic bag, combine salad dressing, soy sauce, and ginger. Add chicken; close bag securely, turning to coat well. Refrigerate 30 minutes.

For salad, arrange mixed greens on serving plates. Sprinkle with cilantro. Top with green onions. Slice 3 peaches and arrange on lettuce. Remove chicken from marinade, reserving marinade. Grill or broil chicken until browned and cooked through, basting occasionally with marinade.

Halve remaining 2 peaches; baste with marinade and grill about 5 minutes. Slice

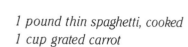

chicken breasts and arrange chicken and grilled peaches on lettuce.

In small saucepan, bring remaining marinade to a boil (this can be done on the grill, if desired). Add almonds and sesame seeds. Pour over salads and serve immediately.

Warm Orzo Salad

Serves: 6

> *2 cups fresh basil leaves, minced*
> *1/2 cup minced fresh parsley*
> *4 cloves garlic, minced*
> *1/2 teaspoon salt*
> *1/4 cup olive oil*
> *1 pound orzo pasta, cooked al dente and drained thoroughly*
> *1 red pepper, chopped*

Combine the basil, parsley, garlic, salt, and oil in a serving bowl. Add the orzo and red pepper and mix well. Toss the salad before serving.

Szechuan Noodle Salad

Serves: 4

> *1/4 cup white wine vinegar*
> *1/4 cup water*
> *2 tablespoons soy sauce*
> *2 tablespoons minced fresh ginger*
> *1 tablespoon sesame oil*
> *2 cloves garlic, minced*
> *1 teaspoon sugar*
> *1 teaspoon Tabasco sauce*

> *1 pound thin spaghetti, cooked*
> *1 cup grated carrot*
> *1 cup frozen peas, thawed*
> *1 red pepper, cut into strips*
> *2 cups bean sprouts*
> *1/4 cup chopped fresh parsley*

In a large bowl, stir together the vinegar, water, soy sauce, ginger, oil, garlic, sugar, and Tabasco. Add the cooked noodles and toss. Add the carrots, peas, red pepper, bean sprouts, and parsley; toss again.

Orzo

Orzo is a kind of pasta that is shaped like a grain of rice. Once rare on these shores, it is readily available today in supermarkets. In Greek cuisine, it is known as kritharaki.

However, it can't stand in for rice in recipes that call for that grain, because it will simply become too mushy. Instead, use it for those pasta dishes where a tiny form of pasta is expected. Because of its size, orzo also has a more delicate taste; the mind is easily tricked.

Parsley and Salad

There are more than twenty varieties of parsley. Two familiar varieties found in just about every supermarket is the flat parsley and the curled parsley. Most salads benefit from at least a couple of sprigs of parsley. The problem is that unless you grow your own parsley and can pick just what you need, the parsley in the supermarket comes in bunches. To keep that bunch of parsley crisp and fresh, store it standing in a glass of ice water in the refrigerator. Change the water every couple of days. The parsley should stay fresh for up to a week.

$^1/_4$ cup honey
$^1/_4$ teaspoon tarragon leaves
$^1/_4$ teaspoon whole basil leaves
$^1/_4$ teaspoon oregano leaves
$^1/_2$ teaspoon parsley leaves
$^1/_2$ clove garlic, crushed
$^1/_2$ teaspoon white pepper
$^1/_2$ teaspoon seasoned salt
1 teaspoon salt
1 tablespoon chopped fresh dill weed

In a bowl, mix the mustard and vinegars. Whisk in the egg yolk. Gradually add the oil, whisking constantly. Stir in the lime juice and honey. Whisk in the remaining ingredients.

Curried Bean and Rice Salad

Serves: 6

1 teaspoon curry powder
1 tablespoon butter or margarine
$^3/_4$ cup vegetable broth
$^1/_3$ cup uncooked white rice
$^1/_4$ cup chopped celery
2 tablespoons chopped green onions
2 tablespoons chopped green bell peppers
1 tablespoon lime juice
1 16-ounce can kidney beans, drained
$^1/_4$ cup plain yogurt
2 tablespoons toasted slivered almonds
$^1/_4$ teaspoon salt
1 dash pepper
1 large tomato, cut in wedges, for garnish
1 sprig fresh parsley for garnish

Lime Dill Vinaigrette

Makes: 3 cups

$^1/_4$ cup Dijon mustard
$^1/_2$ cup red wine vinegar
$^1/_8$ cup white wine vinegar
1 egg yolk
$^3/_4$ cup salad oil
Juice of 1 lime

Sauté curry powder in butter or margarine several seconds. Stir in broth; bring to boil. Add rice; cover and simmer 20 minutes or until all liquid is absorbed. Stir in celery, green onion, green pepper, and lime juice. Chill thoroughly.

Stir beans, yogurt, almonds, and seasonings into rice mixture. Garnish with tomato and parsley.

Oriental Noodle Salad

Serves: 4

2 packages ramen noodles
2 tablespoons peanut oil
$^1/_4$ cup sliced almonds
$^1/_4$ cup sesame seeds
8 green onions, minced
1 head cabbage, minced
$^1/_4$ cup sugar
1 teaspoon salt
1 teaspoon pepper
$^1/_2$ cup peanut oil
6 tablespoons rice vinegar

Break noodles into 1-inch pieces. Heat the oil in a large skillet and sauté almonds and sesame seeds until lightly browned. Add the onions and cabbage and sauté for five minutes, or until translucent. Add noodles. In a cup, mix the sugar, salt, pepper, oil, and vinegar together, and add to noodle vegetable mixture. Toss until heated through.

Black-eyed Pea and Chickpea Salad

Serves: 24

3 tablespoons vinegar
1$^1/_2$ teaspoons salt
$^1/_3$ cup olive oil
$^1/_8$ teaspoon hot pepper sauce
2 cloves garlic, crushed
5 16-ounce cans black-eyed peas, rinsed and drained well
1 16-ounce can chickpeas, rinsed and drained well
$^1/_2$ cup chopped pimientos
$^1/_2$ cup chopped green onions
Lettuce leaves

In a large bowl, beat vinegar and salt until salt is partially dissolved. Add the oil, pepper sauce, and garlic until well blended. Stir in the black-eyed peas, chickpeas, pimientos, and green onions. Toss to coat. Cover, and chill for several hours, stirring occasionally. Serve on top of lettuce-lined bowl or platter.

Warm Cucumber Salad

Serves: 8

$^1/_2$ cup cider vinegar
$^1/_3$ cup sugar
$^1/_2$ cup olive oil
1 teaspoon Worcestershire sauce
6 cucumbers, peeled, seeded, and sliced

(continued)

2 onions, peeled and sliced
1 clove garlic, crushed
¼ teaspoon salt
½ teaspoon ground black pepper

In a large saucepan, mix together the vinegar, sugar, oil, and Worcestershire sauce. Heat over low heat until well blended. Add the cucumbers, onions, and garlic, and stir well. Add salt and pepper. Cover and heat for about 7 to 10 minutes. Serve warm.

Warm After-the-Holidays Salad

Serves: 4

2 cups diced cooked turkey
1 cup pineapple chunks, well drained
1 cup diced celery
½ cup sliced green onions
¼ cup dry roasted peanuts
1 cup chopped seedless green peppers
⅔ cup mayonnaise
2 tablespoons chopped chutney
1 tablespoon lime juice
½ teaspoon curry powder
¼ teaspoon salt
Lettuce leaves, optional

In a large skillet, toss turkey, pineapple, celery, onions, peanuts, and peppers over low heat. Stir in the mayonnaise, chutney, lime juice, curry, and salt until well blended. Serve on lettuce leaves if desired.

Hot Red Cabbage & Apple Salad

Serves: 4

1 small head red cabbage, shredded
1 medium onion, finely sliced
1 apple, peeled and shredded
3 tablespoons apple cider vinegar
¼ cup apple juice
¼ cup water
2 teaspoons sugar, or to taste
Salt and pepper to taste
1 tablespoon chopped fresh parsley for garnish

Put the cabbage, onion, apple, vinegar, juice, water, sugar, salt, and pepper into a large saucepan. Cover and cook on medium-low heat for about 30 minutes, stirring occasionally. Cook until cabbage is soft. Serve with parsley sprinkled on top.

Warm Shrimp-Pear Pasta Salad

Serves: 4

2 teaspoons Dijon mustard
½ teaspoon dill weed
Hot pepper sauce, to taste
8 ounces spiral pasta, cooked and drained
2 fresh Bartlett pears, sliced
½ cup chopped red bell peppers
½ cup chopped green bell peppers
2 green onions, chopped
¼ pound cooked bay shrimp

1 cup plain yogurt
1 head butter lettuce, separated and
*   washed*

Mix dressing by combining yogurt, mustard, dill weed, and hot sauce. Mix all other ingredients, except lettuce leaves, with dressing. Arrange salad on bed of lettuce.

Blackened Shrimp Salad

Serves: 4

16 medium shrimp, peeled, deveined, and
*   split length to tail*
¼ cup Cajun powder
1 tablespoon butter
3 tablespoons olive oil
1 tablespoon balsamic vinegar
Salt and pepper to taste
4 cups mixed salad greens, torn
1 scallion, thinly sliced
1 tomato, cut thin wedges
1 green apple, peeled and sliced

Coat the shrimp with the cajun powder. In a small, cast iron skillet heat the butter on high until it is very hot. Add the shrimp and stir constantly for 3 minutes, or until they are just done. Set them aside and keep them warm.

In a small bowl combine the olive oil, balsamic vinegar, salt, and pepper. Whisk the ingredients together to make a vinaigrette.

In a medium bowl place the salad greens, scallions, tomatoes, and apples. Toss the ingredients with the vinaigrette to coat thoroughly.

In the center of each of 4 individual serving plates place the tossed salad. Place the blackened shrimp, standing up, around the salad.

Pasta in Hot Salads

Hot pasta can be a great addition to hot salads. To save time, cook a batch of pasta in advance. Once cooked, rinse immediately under cold water, drain thoroughly and then pat with paper towels to absorb the remaining moisture. Place in a large lock-top plastic bag and refrigerate. The pasta will keep for up to three days.

To reheat, simply empty all the pasta out of the plastic bag into a pot of boiling water for one minute. Drain well and add to your hot salad.

Chapter 9

Desserts

Ah, yes, now what you've all been waiting for. The flavors and ease of preparation of these scumptious desserts will still gain much attention—from family and friends as well as delight you.

And if they still don't seem suitably impressed, then inform them that you were able to prepare these wonderful desserts and end up with only one pot to clean up. Now *that* should get their attention.

Ginger Peaches

Serves: 4

4 fresh peaches
1 cup sugar
2 cups water
1 cup dry peach wine
¼ cup candied gingerroot, finely chopped

Blanch peaches for one minute. Peel, cut in half, and remove stone. In a large saucepan, combine sugar, water, and wine, and bring to a boil. Reduce heat to simmer. Add peach halves and ginger and simmer until peach halves are tender, about 20 minutes. Serve warm or allow to cool in juice and serve chilled.

Poached Apples in Wine

Serves: 4

5 cups dry white wine
1½ cups sugar
Zest of 1 large lemon, cut into very fine strips
4 Granny Smith apples

Boil wine, sugar, and lemon zest in large saucepan 10 minutes. Meanwhile, pare and core apples, leaving apples whole. Add apples to wine; reduce heat to low. Barely simmer, turning apples frequently, 25 to 30 minutes. Remove apples to serving dish. Boil poaching liquid until syrupy, about 15 minutes. Pour ½ cup syrup over apples; cool to room temperature. Remove lemon zest from remaining syrup with slotted spoon; sprinkle over apples.

Spicy Pumpkin Pie

Serves: 8

⅔ cup granulated sugar
⅛ teaspoon salt
½ teaspoon cinnamon
½ teaspoon ginger
½ teaspoon ground nutmeg
1 pinch ground cloves
1½ cups canned pumpkin
1 teaspoon vanilla extract
1½ cups evaporated skim milk
½ teaspoon orange rind
3 egg whites, slightly beaten
1 9-inch unbaked pie shell

Preheat oven to 450°F.

Combine the sugar, salt, cinnamon, ginger, nutmeg, and cloves. Stir in the pumpkin. Add the vanilla, evaporated skim milk, orange rind, and egg whites. Beat with an electric mixer until smooth. Pour into the unbaked pie shell and bake 10 minutes. Reduce the heat to 325°F and bake until a knife inserted in the filling comes out clean, about 45 minutes.

Strawberries in Butterscotch Sauce

Serves: 4

> *1 cup brown sugar*
> *1 cup corn syrup*
> *¹/₂ cup heavy cream*
> *3 or 4 drops of vanilla*
> *¹/₄ pound fresh strawberries, washed and hulled*

Combine sugar and corn syrup in saucepan. Stir over low heat until sugar dissolves. Cook for 5 minutes. Remove from heat. Stir in cream and vanilla. Beat about 2 minutes until sauce is smooth. Pour warm sauce over strawberries.

Poached Pears

Serves: 4

> *4 firm pears (Bosc)*
> *1¹/₂ cups red wine*
> *Juice of 1 lemon*
> *³/₄ cup brown sugar*
> *Vanilla ice cream*

Plain Vanilla Alternatives

The next time a recipe says vanilla extract, reach for a bottle of different flavored extract instead. In the grocery store, you'll see almond extract as well as lemon, orange, mint, and even coconut. Vanilla is a great old standard, but there's a whole world of untapped flavors out there to help add some zip to your frostings and icings as well as to your cakes and cookies.

Peel, core, and halve pears. Simmer wine, lemon juice, and sugar in heavy pot for about 7 to 8 minutes. Preheat oven to 350°F. Lay pears next to each other in a baking pan that will hold the pears snugly next to each other. Pour liquid over them and cover tightly with aluminum foil. Make slits in foil. Cook pears in oven for about 10 minutes and then turn pears over. Cover again and cook another 10 to 15 minutes until pears are tender and liquid is slightly reduced. Serve warm over vanilla ice cream.

Saving Your Custard

If, despite your best intentions, your custard ends up overcooking and curdling because you had to answer the phone, beat on low speed with a hand-held mixer for a few minutes to remove the lumps and make it presentable again. This technique also works if the custard becomes lumpy after it cools or after it's been in the refrigerator for awhile.

Drain cherries, reserving juice. Add water to make 1 cup liquid. In small saucepan, mix together sugar and cornstarch. Gradually stir in cherry juice until smooth. Bring to a boil over medium heat, stirring constantly. Boil for 1 minute. Add cherries and lemon juice; keep warm. Just before serving, add brandy, if desired, and ignite. After flame dies down, spoon over ice cream or cake a la mode.

Custard Sauce

Serves: 4

3 egg yolks
2 tablespoons white sugar
Pinch of salt
1 cup milk, scalded
¼ teaspoon vanilla

In a double boiler, beat yolks slightly with fork. Add sugar and salt. Add milk gradually, stirring constantly. Cook over hot water until mixture coats spoon, stirring constantly. Chill and add vanilla. Serve with fruit to dip.

Asian Pear-Quince-Apple Sauce

Makes: 5 cups

1 cup sugar
2 cups water
1 cinnamon stick
2 quinces, peeled and cut into two-inch chunks

Cherries Jubilee

Serves: 6

1 16-ounce can pitted sweet cherries
⅓ cup sugar
2 tablespoons cornstarch
Water
1 tablespoon fresh lemon juice
⅓ cup brandy (optional)
Ice cream or cake a la mode

2 Asian pears, peeled and cut into two-
 inch chunks
2 Pippin apples, peeled and cut into two-
 inch chunks
1/2 cup low-fat vanilla yogurt

In a large casserole over medium heat, combine the sugar, water, and cinnamon stick and cook until the sugar is dissolved. Add the quince and bring to a low simmer. Cover and cook for about 40 minutes, stirring occasionally.

Add the pears and apples and continue cooking for about 30 minutes, stirring occasionally, until the apples have softened. Remove the cinnamon stick. Serve warm, at room temperature, or chilled, with a dollop of vanilla yogurt.

Strawberry Sorbet

Serves: 8

1 pint fresh strawberries
3/4 cup orange juice
1/2 cup milk
1/4 cup honey
2 egg whites
1 tablespoon honey

Remove hulls from berries. In a blender container, place berries, orange juice, milk, and honey. Cover; blend 1 minute or till smooth. Pour mixture into 9 x 9 x 2-inch pan. Cover; freeze 2 to 3 hours or till almost firm.

In a mixer bowl beat egg whites with electric mixer on medium speed till soft peaks form. Gradually add honey, beating on high speed till stiff peaks form. Break frozen mixture into chunks; transfer frozen mixture to chilled large mixer bowl. Beat with electric mixer till smooth. Fold in egg whites. Return to pan. Cover; freeze 6 to 8 hours or till firm. To serve, scrape across frozen mixture with spoon and mound in dessert dishes.

Sweetened Condensed Milk

1 cup powdered milk
2/3 cup sugar
1/3 cup boiling water
3 tablespoons melted butter

Mix all in blender. This makes the equivalent of one 14-ounce can.

Pineapple Stuffing

Serves: 6

1/2 cup butter
1 cup sugar
4 eggs
1 28-ounce can crushed pineapple, drained
6 slices bread, cubed or torn
1 teaspoon vanilla

Preheat oven to 350°F.

In a large mixing bowl, cream the butter and sugar; add eggs and vanilla and beat well. Add pineapple and stir in bread cubes. Bake in greased 1 1/2-quart casserole for 1 hour.

Angel Lemon Pudding

Serves: 6

1 tablespoon unflavored gelatin
1 tablespoon cold water
1 cup boiling water
1/2 cup sugar
1/2 cup cold water
1/4 cup lemon juice
1 teaspoon grated lemon rind
1/2 cup nonfat dry milk
1/2 cup ice water
1/4 teaspoon lemon juice

Soften gelatin in 1 tablespoon cold water. Add boiling water to dissolve. Add sugar, 1/2 cup cold water, 1/4 cup lemon juice, and lemon rind. Chill until very thick, about 90 minutes.

Chill a deep mixing bowl and beaters. Add dry milk, ice water, and 1/4 teaspoon lemon juice to bowl. Beat until fluffy, then chill. Break up lemon mixture with fork and add to whipped milk mixture. Beat well with electric mixer until pudding is fluffy but not too soft. Chill until firm.

Sweet Banana Risotto

Serves: 4

1 cup Arborio rice, uncooked
3 ripe bananas, peeled and sliced
1/4 cup brown sugar
3 cups milk
1/4 cup crème de cacao liqueur
1/2 teaspoon cinnamon

Preheat oven to 375°F.

Sprinkle about a third of the rice in the bottom of a 2-quart casserole dish. Then sprinkle on a third of the bananas and a third of the sugar on top of them. Repeat layers in thirds until you're done. Pour on the milk and crème de cacao and sprinkle with cinnamon.

Cover and bake until the liquid has been absorbed and the rice is tender, about 1 hour. Serve warm.

Bread & Raisin Pudding

Serves: 8

>   2 loaves stale white bread, crusts
>   removed, cut into 1½-inch cubes to
>   make about 12 cups
>   1 cup golden raisins
>   1 egg
>   2 egg whites
>   2 tablespoons olive oil
>   2 tablespoons sugar
>   ½ teaspoon freshly grated nutmeg
>   1 teaspoon vanilla extract
>   6 cups low-fat milk

Preheat oven to 325°F. Lightly coat an oval or rectangular 3-quart baking dish with oil. Layer the bottom of the dish with half the bread. Sprinkle the raisins over the bread. Layer the remaining bread over the raisins.

In a large bowl, whisk the egg, egg whites, and olive oil together. Whisk in the sugar, then the nutmeg, vanilla, and milk until blended.

Pour the milk mixture over the bread and press down on the top gently with your hand. The milk mixture should come just to the top of the bread; add more milk if necessary. Cover the dish with aluminum foil, sealing the edges and making a dome to keep the foil from sticking to the bread.

Place the dish in a larger baking pan. Fill the larger pan with hot water to within an inch of the top of the baking dish. Bake for 1 hour and 45 minutes, or until the pudding is very lightly browned and slightly crisped.

Pasta Desserts???

In one short decade, the American pasta lexicon has gone from merely spaghetti and macaroni to such wonderfully trilling words as radiatore, farfalle, and tagliatore. And even dessert. Why not? Cooks have used rice as an integral dessert ingredient for centuries, so why not pasta? Use these recipes as a springboard for your own imagination, as well as the other recipes in the book. Where could you substitute a type of pasta for another ingredient? Let your imagination run wild.

Uncover and let cool in the baking dish. Serve warm.

Rice Pudding

Serves: 6

>   1 quart milk
>   1 quart water
>   ½ stick butter
>   Dash of salt
>   ½ to 1 cup sugar (according to taste)
>   ½ pound long-grain rice

(continued)

Rice Pudding Memories

For me and for many other people, a cold dish of rice pudding conjures up all kinds of good feelings about childhood: it's sweet, it's not much work to eat it, and if your grandmother prepared it in a slightly different way than your mother, you probably liked hers better. Today, you can create new memories for you and your family by giving it your own personal touch. Grated chocolate on top is always nice, but a nip of amaretto stirred into the pudding after cooking, or using citron instead of raisins, are new ways to add spice.

2 eggs, well beaten
Vanilla (optional)
Raisins (optional)

Put the milk and water in a large pot. Add the butter, dash of salt, and sugar, according to taste. Bring these ingredients to a boil and add long-grain rice. Cook about 45 minutes or until thick, stirring often (otherwise, it will stick to the bottom of the pot). Beat the eggs and add enough water to make 1 cup liquid. Remove pudding from heat; add egg mixture and bring back to a boil. Add vanilla and raisins if desired. Pour into a large bowl or pan; sprinkle with cinnamon and let set.

One-Minute Rice Pudding

Serves: 2

½ cup cooked rice
½ cup milk
1 tablespoon wheat germ
2 tablespoons raisins
2 tablespoons sunflower seeds
1 teaspoon honey

Mix together all the ingredients in a saucepan and cook over medium heat. Reduce heat, cover, and cook for 5 minutes.

Hot Zabaglione

Serves: 4

8 egg yolks
½ cup sugar
¾ cup dry Marsala wine, sherry, or port

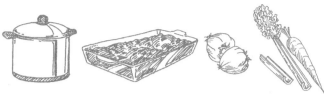

In a large bowl or the top part of a double boiler, beat egg yolks and sugar until pale and thick. Set bowl or top part of double boiler over simmering water; do not let water boil. Add Marsala, sherry, or port slowly, beating constantly. Zabaglione is ready when mixture has tripled in volume and it is soft and fluffy, after 4 to 6 minutes. Spoon into individual glasses. Serve immediately.

Variation: Cold Zabaglione

As soon as Zabaglione swells up into a soft mass, set bowl or top part of double boiler over a bowl of ice water. Continue stirring until cool. Spoon into glasses and refrigerate until ready to serve.

Coffee and Rum Mousse

Serves: 6

> 1 tablespoon powdered gelatin
> 1/4 cup light rum
> 1 cup hot freshly-made strong coffee
> 3 egg yolks
> 6 tablespoons superfine sugar
> 1 cup heavy cream
> 3 egg whites

Sprinkle gelatin over rum and let rest until the powder has absorbed the liquid, about 5 minutes. Add the hot coffee to the rum and gelatin and stir until completely dissolved. Beat the yolks until thick and pale; beat in

the sugar until the mixture has increased in volume and is even paler.

Gradually beat in the hot liquid and let cool. When the mixture has started to thicken, whip the cream until it almost holds its shape; fold in carefully. Whip the egg whites to soft peaks and fold in as well. Pour the mixture into a 5-cup mold, and refrigerate for at least three hours to set.

Canned Versus Fresh Fruit

Fruit and cake-type desserts are one of the few kinds of desserts where canned fruits can be easily substituted for fresh fruits, which can create wonderful surprise desserts during cold weather. Just be sure to drain the fruit thoroughly—if specified—before using it in the recipe, or else you could end up with a mushy mess. You can even mix two different types of fruit in the same recipe with ease.

Index

257

259

263

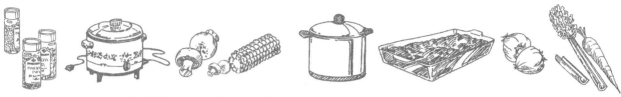

Add your favorite one-pot recipes here:

Recipe Name:

_____

_____

Yields: _____

_____

_____

_____

_____

_____

_____

_____

_____

_____

_____

_____

Recipe Name:

_____

_____

Yields: _____

_____

_____

_____

_____

_____

_____

_____

_____

_____

_____

_____

Recipe Name:

_____

_____

Yields: _____

_____

_____

_____

_____

_____

_____

_____

_____

_____

_____

_____

_____

Recipe Name:

_____

_____

Yields: _____

_____

_____

_____

_____

_____

_____

_____

_____

_____

_____

_____

_____

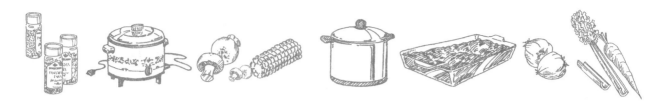

Recipe Name:

_____

_____

Yields: _____

_____

_____

_____

_____

_____

_____

_____

_____

_____

Recipe Name:

_____

_____

Yields: _____

_____

_____

_____

_____

_____

_____

_____

_____

_____

Recipe Name:

_____

_____

Yields: _____

_____

_____

_____

_____

_____

_____

_____

_____

_____

Recipe Name:

_____

_____

Yields: _____

_____

_____

_____

_____

_____

_____

_____

_____

_____

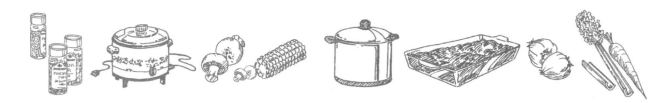

Recipe Name:

_____

_____

Yields: _____

_____

_____

_____

_____

_____

_____

_____

_____

_____

_____

_____

Recipe Name:

_____

_____

Yields: _____

_____

_____

_____

_____

_____

_____

_____

_____

_____

_____

_____

Recipe Name:

_____

_____

Yields: _____

_____

_____

_____

_____

_____

_____

_____

_____

Recipe Name:

_____

_____

Yields: _____

_____

_____

_____

_____

_____

_____

_____

_____

EVERYTHING

The Everything Low-Fat, High-Flavor Cookbook
by Lisa Shaw

Trade paperback, $12.95
1-55850-802-3, 288 pages

Low-fat cooking is no longer a fad: it has become a way of life for millions of us who are either battling the bulge of just trying to eat healthy. But low-fat doesn't have to mean "no taste, no texture" anymore. The fat reducing tricks and techniques used in this book have been so perfected, you won't even miss the artery-clogging ingredients you craved in your favorite entrees, salads, and even desserts. This book features over 300 delicious recipes suitable for every category of entertaining.

The Everything Dessert Cookbook
by Lisa Shaw

Trade paperback, $12.95
1-55850-717-5, 304 pages

Featuring over 300 mouthwatering recipes for all types of desserts, *The Everything Dessert Cookbook* is a wonderful indulgence for anyone with a taste for sweets. Written with easy-to-follow instructions, these delicious recipes can be created with ingredients found in any kitchen. You'll find all kinds of recipes from American "comfort" desserts to classic French fare. These sweet-tooth pleasing recipes are perfect for entertaining large groups of just celebrating with your family. Whether you are a chocolate fiend or have a passion for creme-filled pastries, this cookbook provides recipes for every possible type of dessert.

Available Wherever Books Are Sold

If you cannot find these titles at your favorite retail outlet, you may order them directly from the publisher. BY PHONE: Call 1-800-872-5627. We accept Visa, MasterCard, and American Express. $4.95 will be added to your total order for shipping and handling. BY MAIL: Write out the full titles of the books you'd like to order and send payment, including $4.95 for shipping and handling, to: Adams Media Corporation, 260 Center Street, Holbrook, MA 02343. 30-day money-back guarantee.

We Have

EVERYTHING

I ♥ EVERYTHING

More bestselling Everything titles
available from your local bookseller:

Everything **After College Book**
Everything **Astrology Book**
Everything **Baby Names Book**
Everything® **Bartender's Book**
Everything **Bedtime Story Book**
Everything **Beer Book**
Everything **Bicycle Book**
Everything **Bird Book**
Everything **Casino Gambling Book**
Everything **Cat Book**
Everything® **Christmas Book**
Everything **College Survival Book**
Everything **Crossword and Puzzle Book**
Everything **Dating Book**
Everything **Dessert Book**
Everything **Dog Book**
Everything **Dreams Book**
Everything **Etiquette Book**
Everything **Family Tree Book**
Everything **Fly-Fishing Book**
Everything **Games Book**
Everything **Get-a-Job Book**
Everything **Get Ready For Baby Book**
Everything **Golf Book**

Everything **Guide to Walt Disney World®,**
   Universal Studios®, and Greater Orlando
Everything **Home Buying Book**
Everything **Home Improvement Book**
Everything **Internet Book**
Everything **Investing Book**
Everything **Jewish Wedding Book**
Everything **Low-Fat High-Flavor Cookbook**
Everything **Money Book**
Everything **One-Pot Cookbook**
Everything **Pasta Book**
Everything **Pregnancy Book**
Everything **Sailing Book**
Everything **Study Book**
Everything **Tarot Book**
Everything **Toasts Book**
Everything **Trivia Book**
Everything® **Wedding Book**
Everything® **Wedding Checklist**
Everything® **Wedding Etiquette Book**
Everything® **Wedding Organizer**
Everything® **Wedding Shower Book**
Everything® **Wedding Vows Book**
Everything **Wine Book**